How Nordic are
the Nordic Medival Laws?

Ten Years After

*Cover illustration: Codex Holmiensis C 37, ff. 28v/29r, c. 1276:
Marginal annotations in the oldest manuscript containing
the Law of Jutland dating from 1241 shows a continuous preoccupation
with the textual structure of the law throughout the Middle Ages.
Published with approval by the Royal Library, Copenhagen*

Per Andersen, Kirsi Salonen,
Helle I.M. Sigh & Helle Vogt (eds.)

How Nordic are the Nordic Medival Laws?

Ten Years After

Proceedings of the Tenth
Carlsberg Academy Conference
on Medieval Legal History 2013

DJØF Publishing
Copenhagen 2014

Per Andersen, Kirsi Salonen, Helle I.M. Sigh & Helle Vogt (eds.)
How Nordic are the Nordic Medieval Laws?
Ten Years After
1.edition

© 2014 by DJØF Publishing
Jurist- og Økonomforbundets Forlag

All rights reserved.
No part of this publication may be reproduced,
stored in a retrieval system, or transmitted in any
form or by any means – electronic, mechanical,
photocopying, recording or otherwise – without
the prior written permission of the Publisher.

Cover: Bo Helsted
Print: Toptryk Grafisk, Gråsten

Printed in Denmark 2014
ISBN 978-87-574-3225-1

The publication of this volume is funded by
The Carlsberg Foundation

Sold and distributed in Scandinavia by:
DJØF Publishing Copenhagen, Denmark
Email: forlag@djoef.dk
www.djoef-forlag.dk

Sold and distributed in North America by:
International Specialized Book Services (ISBS)
Email: orders@isbs.com
www.isbs.com

Sold in all other countries by:
The Oxford Publicity Partnership Ltd
Email: djof@oppuk.co.uk
www.oppuk.co.uk

Distributed in all other countries by:
Marston Book Services
Email: trade.orders@marston.co.uk
www.marston.co.uk

Contents

Introduction 1

How Nordic are the Ole Nordic Laws – Ten Years Later?
Ditlev Tamm 3

How Nordic are the Nordic Laws?
Jørn Øyrehagen Sunde 23

Rights, Obligations, Domestic Relations, and '*ius naturale*',
the Right Order of Things: A Strategy for Research
into the Nordic Medieval Laws
Helle I.M. Sigh and Helle Vogt 39

Intestate Inheritance as a Family Matter: *Ius Commune*,
Statutes and Cases from Florence
Thomas Kuehn 59

The Swedish Ecclesiastical Legislation and the Question
of its Nordic Character
Bertil Nilsson 81

How Nordic are the Biblical Social Ideals as Expressed in the
Early Scandinavian Church Laws?
Torstein Jørgensen 113

The Origins of the Swedish Medieval Laws
– a State of the Art, from My Perspective
Stefan Brink 129

Law, Language and Crime in Denmark and England:
A Comparative Approach
Jenny Benham 145

Indigenous or Universal? A Comparative Perspective on
Medieval (Frisian) Compensation Law
Han Nijdam 161

Scandinavians by the Papal Well of Grace and Justice
at the Eve of Reformation
Kirsi Salonen 183

Scandinavia Consults 'Rome', ca.1104-1202:
Contexts and Consequences
Anne J. Duggan 199

Papal Letters Relating to Medieval Scandinavia – A Survey
from the 11th Century to the Beginning of the Western Schism
Peter Ståhl 231

Contributors 247

Introduction

Per Andersen, Kirsi Salonen, Helle I.M. Sigh, and Helle Vogt

The Tenth Carlsberg Academy Conference on Medieval Legal History, which took place in May 2013 at the Carlsberg Academy in Copenhagen, brought together scholars from both Nordic and non-Nordic countries to discuss questions related to 'How Nordic are the Medieval Nordic Laws are'.

Ten years ago this question was raised for the first time at the first conference of what became a series of Carlsberg Academy Conferences on Medieval Legal History. The aim at that time was to question the traditional interpretation of 'the Nordic' being something different from 'the common European' (whatever that is), and ever since the question about how Nordic the Nordic laws actually were has been an underlying subject of all the Carlsberg Conferences, no matter whether the topic of the conference was law and power, law and marriage or law and disputing. Now, ten years later, we return to the original question and try to sum up to what degree the traditional interpretation has changed during these years, thus placing Nordic legal history and research in a European context.

No doubt, in these ten years the interpretation of the Nordic laws has changed from a specific Nordic to a more common European perspective, understanding the Nordic laws as a part of a common European tradition. Thus, the traditional interpretation that the Nordic medieval laws were expressions of an ancient Nordic culture has been under change since the first Carlsberg Conference and this volume sums up the current stage of research and raises new questions.

As usual, the conference culminates in publication of the proceedings, which are gathered in the present book. We have at hand a collection of twelve articles on varying themes illustrating and discussing whether the

Introduction

'Nordic medieval laws' form and are characterized by a specific legal identity and tradition or not. Additionally, the book shows some of the aspects of Scandinavian legal historical research at the moment.

Contributors are Jørn Ø. Sunde (Bergen), Lars Ivar Hansen (Tromsø), Helle Ingrid Møller Sigh (Thorsminde) and Helle Vogt (Copenhagen), Thomas Kuehn (Clemson), Bertil Nilsson (Gothenburg), Torstein Jørgensen (Stavanger), Stefan Brink (Aberdeen), Jenny Benham (Cardiff), Han Nijdam (Leeuwarden), Kirsi Salonen (Turku), Anne J. Duggan (London), Peter Ståhl (Stockholm), and Ditlev Tamm (Copenhagen). We thank all authors for contributing both to a successful conference and thought-provoking publication.

*

The conference and the publication of this volume were made possible through generous funding from The Carlsberg Foundation. As organizers and editors we wish to express our special gratitude, once again, to the Carlsberg Academy for providing us with the spectacular venue that gives the conference series its special ambience, namely the mid-nineteenth century villa of the founder of the Carlsberg Breweries, I.C. Jacobsen. As usual, our thanks also go to the caretaker of the estate, Svend Rasmussen, for his patience and invaluable help in making the event run smoothly.

Also a great thanks to Jytte Mønster and Helle Hjort Christiansen from the Department of Law at Aarhus University for proof reading the manuscript, finding all the errors that the editors did not see.

Aarhus, Thorsminde, Copenhagen and Turku
August 2014

How Nordic are the Old Nordic Laws – Ten Years Later?

Ditlev Tamm

1. Introduction[1]

The 2013 Carlsberg Academy conference celebrates that ten years have gone since the first conference on the theme *How Nordic are the Nordic laws?* took place at the Carlsberg Academy. At that time nobody had imagined and definitely not known for sure that this was the start of a series of conferences which have become somewhat of an institution among historians of medieval law and history. The conferences have all been recorded in well-redacted reports which have been well received and widely known internationally.

In this conference we are turning back on the question then put award of how Nordic are the Nordic laws. Quite some new research has taken place and been published since the first conference, and we have looked forward to hearing what new pieces can be added to the picture of our medieval laws.

My own personal experience with the old Danish medieval laws goes way back to my time as a law student in Copenhagen in the 1960s. The teaching of legal history was concentrated around the old laws. We read them and as you may suspect Roman law was read at a medieval university. One by one we went through the 241 articles of the Law of Scania and then piece for

1. The following reflections are based on the introduction and lecture given at the 2013 Carlsberg Academy conference. The oral style has been kept and references are kept at a minimum as most authors or works are easily found and mentioned in other contributions in this volume.

3

piece the three books of the Law of Jutland. Stig Iuul (1907-1969), then professor of legal history and director of the course and himself a capacity in medieval Danish law, would as a professor in medieval Bologna have the articles read aloud, paraphrase them and make his comments to each of the articles. As students we eagerly wrote down what we understood of his comments as glosses to the text, which was read in a modern Danish edition.[2] We thus got quite a good grasp on the medieval Danish partnership in family law, the power of the householder, what capital lots were, how you compensated for killing or wounds, the position of kinship and the rights and duties of the kin and use of hot iron compurgators in the procedure. We knew about the way in which land was distributed in an ancient village, when you were entitled to hang thieves, how to treat cattle that happened to end up in other persons' fields not to speak of the few contractual relations mentioned. Who could not but admire King Canute and the men behind him who gave words to the pretensions of the King as a legislator in the ordinance of homicide from 1200, not to speak of the anonymous redactors of the prologue of the law of Jutland composed on the basis of quotations from the *Decretum Gratiani* and *Liber Extra* thus spanning in time with its literary references from Isidor of Seville around 600 and until 1234.

Perhaps the Law of Scania is still the more interesting of the two laws, which we read, as it takes us more directly into the laboratory of those who about 1200 tried to formulate written rules of conduct without really having a model to follow, than does the more polished Law of Jutland. The Law of Jutland in its prologue tells us about the law, the power of the King and the Church in a way that is still worth quoting. Its system of procedure based on permanent boards which investigated the cases is definitely more advanced than that of the Law of Scania that still retained the *ad hoc* juries. However, we miss in the Law of Jutland those small discussions on what the law is in particular fields, which we find in its Scanian counterpart and also this feeling of dealing with a text written by pioneers in the writing down of rules. In the following I shall therefore focus on the Law of Scania in its Danish and Latin version.

In the conference with the same title as today held at this place in 2003 we tried to sum up what was then the state of the art as to the research on the medieval Nordic law. The basic idea of this conference ten years later is to reflect on what has happened since then – if something has happened. A basic question in this connection is whether we are really reaching new results or whether we are in some way moving around in a circle that makes the same questions pop up with determined intervals? Sometimes new answers are given to old questions without being based on new factual

2. E. Kroman & S. Iuul (ed.), *Danmarks gamle Love paa Nutidsdansk* 1-3 (Copenhagen: 1945-1948).

knowledge. But even if that is in some way the case, still the level of understanding the laws is becoming higher, we know more about the sources and the questions they pose, we combine them in new ways and we see the Nordic law in the light of a new and still broader and at the same time more detailed knowledge of the law in other European countries not to speak of Canon law.

2. Law and language

After this general introduction to the theme I will turn to my real subject, which will concentrate on the old Danish laws and on the relation between the Nordic laws. My first point will be some reflections on the Nordic language and the way in which the idea of a common Nordic language in the middle ages may enhance our understanding of the relation between the Nordic laws and perhaps also other laws written in the vernacular. It is still to a high degree work in progress. The starting point is the fact that Nordic medieval law as well as old Anglo-Saxon law were written down in the vernacular as opposed to the earlier tribal laws of the Visigoths, the Franks, the Burgunds, the Lombards, the Alemans, the Bavarians etc. As is well known, it was a working thesis put forward by the Germanist school of legal historians in the 19th century[3] that these law were closely related, that they to a high degree could be considered the writing down of an old oral tradition and that you might draw conclusions from them to the existence of a Germanic *Urrecht*. In this respect the *Germania* of Tacitus, which was rediscovered in the 15th century, played an important role with its desscripttion of the pure life of the Germanic tribes and their values such as solidarity and trustworthiness (*Gefolgschaft* and *Treue*). Some of these ideas for obvious reasons became discredited after having been celebrated during the Third Reich. However, some of the ideas of a common base and especially the comparative aspect based on reflections on the institutions and the language of the laws are still valid and should guide us when we try to grasp the essence of Nordic medieval law. With some reason Arnaldo

---

3. As iconic examples shall here be mentioned the inaugural lesson by Karl von Amira, 'Über Zweck and Mittel der germanischen Rechtsgeschichte' (1930) and the translation of the tribal laws organized by the Akademie für deutsches Recht (1933-1945) which under the 'Gruppe Germanenrechte' published texts and translations of the medieval Germanic laws among those a selection of Nordic laws. The Danish Zealand Law of Erik was thus translated by the German scholar Claudius von Schwerin.

Ditlev Tamm

Momigliano in 1954 mentioned '*Germania*' as 'one of the hundred most dangerous books ever written'.[4]

After 2003, a project on translating the Nordic medieval laws into English was started. This project has been going on in a collaboration coordinated by the Centre of Scandinavian Studies in Aberdeen. The old Icelandic law is already accessible in English. Nordic law in this context therefore includes the old Norwegian laws, the laws of the Gulating and the Frostating and the two Church laws of Eidsivating and Borgarting, the Danish laws of Scania, Zealand (laws of Valdemar and Erik) and Jutland[5] and the several laws of the Swedish landscapes. It is a quite ambitious project which hopefully will end in a complete *corpus* of Nordic medieval law in English. This project has led to a new understanding of the laws and also to new horizons of comparison.

Danes, Norwegians and Swedes still do understand each other when each of them speaks her or his own language, however, difficulties are growing in this common understanding, which for centuries has been an important feature in the relation between the countries and which is also important for the understanding of how a Nordic law terminology came into being. In 1529, the Danish Humanist Christian Pedersen in his translation into Danish of The New Testament could send greetings 'to all Danes, Swedes and Norwegians and to all others who understand our tongue'.[6] There definitely were distinct Nordic languages at his time and also in the centuries from about 1100-1300, when the laws were written down, but differences were not such as to impede a common understanding and, as can be read from Christian Pedersen, the Nordic tongue could be conceived as a common language. Words and concepts could cross borders and we must imagine a Nordic area basically without linguistic boundaries. This does not mean that languages were not different or that problems of understanding could not arise, but when it comes to the language written down in the laws many words used would have parallels or might even stem from another Nordic language. The language spoken was known as *dǫnsk tunga*, the Danish tongue, which was a common denomination for Nordic language.[7] In

---

4. See C.B. Krebs: *A most dangerous book: Tacitus Germania from the Roman empire to the Third Reich* (London: 2011).
5. The Danish medieval laws were edited in 1933-1940 as *Danmarks gamle Landskabslove*. The high quality of this critical edition facilitates the translation. German translations can be found of the Zealand Law of Erik (v. Schwerin) and the Law of Jutland (Klaus v. See).
6. C. Pedersen, *Det nye Testamente* (Antwerpen: 1529).
7. What is said in the following on the history of Danish and Nordic languages is to a high degree based on the *magnum opus* by P. Skautrup, *Det danske sprogs historie* 1-4 (Copenhagen: 1944-1968).

Icelandic law we even find a specific protection of those coming from other Nordic countries as opposed to others. In the Grágás, *Staðarhólsbók, Vígslóði*, (art. 97) it is stated that if foreigners are killed, Danes Swedes or Norwegians *(danskir eða svænskir eða norrænir)*, who come from one of the three Kingdoms, where our tongue *(vár tunga)* is spoken, their kin shall be entitled to make a case if they are in Iceland. But of all other tongues than the Danish *(af ǫllum tungum ǫðrum en af danskri tungu)* no other than father, son or brother is entitled to start a case of homicide based on kinship, and then only if they were already known personally in Iceland[8].

The Icelandic historian Snorre about 1230 spoke of *á Norðrlǫndum* and he wrote about *hǫfðingja þá, er ríki hafa haft á Norðrlǫndum ok á danska tungu hafa mælt* (Prologus til *Saga Olafs Konings hins Helga*), those Lords who had their domains in the Northern countries and spoke Danish. After 1200, due to the rise of the Norwegian Kingdom and probably especially the expansive politics of the Norwegian King Haakan Haakonsson, the way the Nordic language is spoken in Norway and Iceland becomes known as *norrænt mál, norræn tunga* or *norræna*, and still reading the legal texts of Iceland and Norway poses questions different to those arising when trying to understand the Danish texts. Such a common understanding may have taken place still in the 13th century and have included Northern Germany. The Uppsala Canon Nils Sigvatsson asked at the beginning of the 1320s the Pope to nominate a specific confessor for Nordic travellers to Rome and his reasons were the distinction of the Nordic languages that could not be understood by other people.[9]

An interesting and intriguing question is the way in which a Nordic legal terminology came into being. It seems that comparing the Nordic laws and from a Danish standpoint reflecting on how knowledge of Icelandic law and Icelandic expressions could have influenced those who were turning Danish words into legal terms may be fruitful for the understanding of the coming into being of a new legal language. This is still a field to be developed but it seems that a study of legal terminology that may include the old Anglo-Saxon laws can throw light on the meaning of the words used in medieval Danish laws. The term 'Nordic' thus in a sense may include not only the Nordic countries but also the other side of the North Sea. It may turn out to be a fruitful field to compare the laws written in the vernacular in an area in which the language was not a barrier. In this way a common understanding of those laws may be achieved and also differences will be seen which

---

8. See A. Dennis, P. Foote & R. Perkins (ed.): *Laws of Early Iceland* I (Reykjavik: 1997), 160.
9. 'idyoma illorum trium regnorum Datie scilicet Swetie et Norwegie adeo sit ab omni alio ydeomate extraneum et distinctum quod nec ab Alamannis possit intelligi etiam in communibus', edited in *Danmarks Riges breve*, 2. Rk, 8:311 (1953).

contrast these tribal laws to those written down earlier and used Latin as their legal language. For a new way of understanding these relations a starting point from the assumption of a community of language may be fruitful. Such a research would not try to discover a Germanic *Urrecht*, but it would try to find similarities and loans based on a study of the common legal language which we find reflected in the laws.

3. How old are the old Danish laws?

In the following I will turn to the medieval Danish laws trying to add some new arguments to the question: How old are the laws and how are they related to each other?[10]

Denmark is traditionally seen as divided into three different legal zones, known as 'provinces' or 'lands'. The first documented laws written down are two so-called 'Church Laws' from the two provinces of Zealand and Scania. The Church Law of Zealand is dated 1171 and a similar law from Scania is about the same time. In these laws, we find articles on e.g. homicide which were included in the later laws, whereas other articles, e.g. on marriage in forbidden degrees, supplement the later laws. They can be attributed to initiatives of Absalon, Bishop of Roskilde, and Eskil, Archbishop of Lund and thus are testimonies of the central role of the Church in the writing down of the law. These laws which present themselves as agreements between the people and the bishop (or in Scania the Archbishop) have often been neglected as the precursors they actually are, when it comes to the redactions of the respective laws of Scania and Zealand. The bishops were granted their part of the tithe paid to the church and compromises were made by the church as to the enforcement of Canon law. It was thus e.g. possible for the husband who accused his wife of adultery to have her forced to carry hot iron to free herself of the suspicion, even if Canon law in such cases would prefer such cases to be handled by the bishop. The Church Law of Scania consists of only thirteen articles on the consecration of churches (art. 1), the nomination of ministers (art. 2), disturbance of the peace (art. 3), cutting in the wood of the church (art. 4), sacrilege and donations to the church (art. 5), marriage within the forbidden degrees (art. 6), violence against parents or siblings and murder and witchcraft (art. 7), the Archbishop's due in case of offenses (art. 8), festivals and accusation of a wife for adultery (art. 9), slaves (art. 10), the jurisdiction of the bishop and summons and excommunication (art. 11), confession and the

---

10. For a general introduction to the Nordic laws reference can be made to the work of D. Strauch, *Mittelalterliches nordisches Recht bis 1500: Eine Quellenkunde* (Berlin & New York: 2011) which gives an updated overview of the literature on the laws.

payment of tithe (art. 12) and date (art. 13). From this Church Law a few passages were included in the later Law of Scania thus the rules of donations to the church (half or whole capital lot), the procedure of murder and adultery and the proof of hot iron in the form of marching on glowing ploughs. The Church laws are instrumental as to the understanding of the role of the bishop in the law-making and the close relation between the Diocese of Lund and Roskilde as to the law. From about 1180, we may date the oldest text of the specific rules for the royal guard (*hird*).

It is worth noting that similar agreements called Church Laws were made in both Zealand and Scania which points to the strong links between the two provinces which can also later be seen when it comes to the redaction of the Law of Scania and the Law of Zealand about and after 1200. As to both Scania and Zealand, the legal province and the diocese geographically covered each other as opposed to Jutland with its six dioceses.

Scania is an area especially rich in legal initiatives about 1200. That very year a well-known Statute on Homicide was issued in Latin which we later find included in a Danish translation in the redaction of a complete Law of Scania. When this redaction of the Law of Scania in Danish was actually completed cannot be determined with exactitude, however, a reflection on the relation between the Danish version of the law and a version of the law in Latin made by the Archbishop Anders Sunesen (sometimes known as the *Liber legis Scaniae*) may bring us closer to an understanding of the crucial importance of the writing down of the Law of Scania (*Skånske Lov*) for the whole project of writing down the Danish Medieval laws. We will later come back to this question. The Law of Scania still mentions the ordeal of hot iron as a current way of proof and thus should be dated to a time before 1215 when this ordeal was repudiated at the Fourth Lateran Council as we reason to think that hot iron was not used after that time. The Latin version of the Law of Scania by Anders Sunesen mentions the Statute on Homicide from 1200 as 'recent', an indication that his version was redacted rather shortly after his access to the Archbishopric in 1201. Anders Sunesen also includes what he mentions as recent legislation by the King Valdemar who ascended to the throne in 1202. We cannot actually determine whether the Danish or the Latin version is the older, however, it might be a good hypothesis that the initiative to have the Law of Scania written down stems from the new Archbishop and that the two projects are not too distant in time from each other and both stem from shortly after 1202 with the Latin version being slightly more up to date as it includes the newest legislation on homicide which in Danish is only known as one of several later *additaments* to the Law of Scania.

Also the writing down of the Law of Zealand was continued and from an early date, which may be before or after 1200, date a redaction of the Zealand law which we know as the 'Book on Succession and Crime'

(*Arvebog og Orbodemaal*) which comprises most of the law of succession, partnership and distribution of the household within the family and crimes as adultery, homicide and wounding and other personal injuries. This law was later supplemented by articles taken from the Law of Scania and still later two chapters on the law on theft and on slaves were added. As such we know this law as the younger redaction of the Zealand Law of Valdemar, which we know from manuscripts dated about 1300. Another tradition of Zealand law is found in the so-called 'Law of Erik'. This version of the Zealand law somewhat follows the pattern of the Law of Valdemar as to law of succession, family law and also as to the inclusion of articles from the Law of Scania. The Law of Erik however is much more specific as to how the assemblies (*ting*) functioned and seems to have been redacted with the advice of someone who was well versed in daily practice of cases brought before the assembly. The laws of Valdemar and Erik are different versions of the law of Zealand and as such considered two different laws, however, it should be noted that they concur in most rules. The Law of Erik especially supplements the Law of Valdemar as to practical procedure law. It is longer and more detailed than the other laws and in general it seems to be written down as a statement of what is actual judicial practice.

Whereas it seems rather obvious that the initiative as to the writing down of the Law of Scania may stem from the Archbishop Anders Sunesen, the situation is less clear in Zealand. The bishop of Roskilde in the period 1191-1214, Peder Sunesen, was the brother of Anders Sunesen, and his successor (and nephew) Peder Jacobsen (bishop 1215-1225) had been a Canon in Lund with his uncle Anders Sunesen, however, we do not have indications as to the role of the bishop of Roskilde in the writing down of the law and no connection can be traced form the various redactions of the law to the diocese in Roskilde. Only it is clear that the Law of Scania was known in Zealand and copied whenever it was useful to supplement the rudimentary redaction of the Law of Zealand. The existence of two versions of the law and the extended history of the redaction of final laws may point to a less centralized process of writing down the law. The Laws of Scania and Zealand were written down without any legitimation of a central power. The Law of Jutland was redacted later. In the prologue included in the manuscripts of the law, the redaction of this law was finalized in March 1241 at a meeting in the town of Vordingborg with the presence of the King and his three sons, the bishops and 'the best men' in his Kingdom. Other sources link the law to the figure of Gunnar, bishop of Viborg 1222-1251, and as such one of six bishops in Jutland. The legal province of Jutland included the island of Funen and comprised after the reorganisation of bishoprics in 1060 six dioceses, Viborg, Ribe (either Viborg or Ribe was the centre of the only diocese of northern Jutland created in 988, the first bishop of Ribe was consecrated in 948), Aarhus and Vendsyssel (separated in 1060 from

Viborg, first at Vestervig, later Børglum), including also Slesvig (originally Hedeby founded in 948), and Odense (founded before 988 and comprising the island of Funen and also the islands of Langeland, Lolland and Falster, Als and Aeroe), thus the size of the province and the number of ecclesiastical centres were less favourable to a centralisation of the law-making procedure in the hand of one leading figure of the church as was the case in Lund or Roskilde. This may explain that the redaction of a law of Jutland was dragged out and was only successfully accomplished in 1241.

The prologue and its dating of the law raise certain questions. It may thus be asked whether the prologue was an original part of the law or whether it is a later addition. This seems indicated by the fact that the prologue mentions the Archbishop of Lund as the 'then' archbishop. Also the prologue in itself which its sentences based on The Canon law collections of *Decretum Gratiani* and *Liber Extra* reflect on the law, the position of the kin and the relation between Church and State may be a later independent collection of *regulae juris* or *brocardica*, which have been included later in manuscripts of the law the earliest of which date from a time after 1241. The redaction of the Law of Jutland also seems to have been based on the Law of Scania and the layout of the law is pretty much the same even if it is divided in three books. The main differences may be seen in the way in which cases of homicide and personal injury, border cases and cases of theft are handled. Such cases were now investigated by permanent 'boards' consisting of eight men nominated by the King to serve at the local assemblies. Also in Scania and Zealand such boards were introduced, but they were chosen ad hoc for each case and the King was not included in the selection procedure. The question has also been raised whether the Law of Jutland which thus gives the King a more central role than the other laws may have been given with the intention of being a law not only for Jutland but for the whole kingdom including the two other provinces. This question has been discussed for centuries and it is still discussed. No decisive arguments, however, have been brought forward which could make such an assumption more than a hypothesis.

4. The language of the Danish laws

The old Danish medieval laws contain from 994 (The Law of Scania) to about 1300 different words (Law of Jutland). The terminology consists of daily words some of which, however, are used in a legal context, which gives them a specific significance.[11] There is no indication that the laws

11. Among the words used we can distinguish a layer of old words as *arf* (succession), *egha* (property), *skothæ* (convey), *tak* (surety). In the village we find *toft* (curtilage)

Ditlev Tamm

have been recorded in an oral version before they were written down. The language of the laws frequently uses fixed expressions e.g. *Akær æth æng* (field and meadow), *gift ællær gulfæst* (married or engaged), tautologies *ia oc wilia* (consent and will) or alliterations as the Law of Scania, ch. 105, which mentions damage by *Horn, hof, hundz tand.* The article, however, may have as its model St. Augustin quoted in *Decretum Gratiani*, C. 23, Q. 5, c. 8. Augustin says that it is no sin for a Christian if his ox, horse or dog kill someone, as in that case *aut ideo non debent Christianorum boves habere cornua, aut equus ungulas, aut dentes canes.* The number of loan words is scarce, mostly found in the Law of Jutland and mostly terms from the Church.

5. A Latin version of the Law of Scania and its European dimension

The question of language becomes especially interesting in the text of the Law of Scania which is attributed to Archbishop Anders Sunesen and known in four manuscripts. The author is a man learned in the law, with knowledge of both Roman law and Canon law and the current practice of the local assemblies, when it came to the actual usage of the Scanian law. His Latin is not a plain and simple legal Latin but the language of someone well versed not only in legal texts but also with solid knowledge of classical Latin literature and a certain tendency to demonstrate his domination of the language by creating poetically sounding metaphors or using hidden quotations. He renders the Law of Scania as it is written down in the old Danish language but he deviates from the order of the Danish law and follows his own system adding explanations and sometimes even rules which are not found in the Danish text. We may call it a treatise on Scanian law with a broader scope than just rendering the text. He seems to be fond of differences of opinion as to the law and explains such dilemmas in detail. His book is concerned with both civil and criminal justice before the local assemblies, which he calls just *jus* or provincial assemblies. A long tradition based on the manuscripts attributes this treatise to Anders Sunesen. We do not know exactly when this treatise was first written down. It does mention legislation from the time of the King Valdemar, who ruled from 1202 to

and within the field of torts and crime we find *wathæ* (unhappy event), *bardaghi* (assault), *drap* (killing), *hærwærki* (gang crime), *ran* and *tiufnæth* (seizure and theft), *hæfnd* (revenge), *deila* (proceed), *skiliæ* (disputeor decide), *manz bot* (wergeld), *thokkæbo*t (fine for contempt), *frithløz* (outlawed). Some of the persons are *bondæ* (householder, farmowner), *bryti* (from: brytja: farm-bailiff), *landbo* and *gardsæti* (tenants), *frælsgifvin* (freed), *threll* (slave) and the more official *umbuthsman*.

1241, which means that it must have been written after Valdemar became king. It also mentions a statute given by his predecessor, King Canute (ruler from 1182-1202), in the year 1200 as 'nova' which indicates that it must have been written down rather shortly thereafter. Anders Sunesen himself became Archbishop after the death of Absalon in 1201, and probably for these reasons we may see the collection and systematization of the Law of Scania as one of his priorities when he took over this position after his great-uncle. Thus we may with some insecurity date the treatise as well as the Danish version of the law to a time not very much later than 1202. A *terminus ante quem* is given by the intensive dedication in the treatise to the use of ordeals in the shape of proof by hot iron. We know that the church on the Fourth Lateran council in 1215 officially distanced itself from the ordeal of hot iron and an undated Danish royal statute which we know in its version for the province of Scania abolishes the use of hot iron and substitutes it with men nominated to investigate those cases that formerly were decided by the proof of hot iron. There is doubt as to both the date of this statute and to its being accepted immediately, however, considering both the strong position of the Archbishop and of the King, in Scania there is reason to believe that Anders Sunesen would not in his text without commenting critically upon it give extensive explanations as to the use proof of hot iron if at that time it was not used any more or used contrary to the decrees of the Church and the King. This means that the treatise must have been written before or about 1215 at the latest. The same term goes for the Danish redaction of the Law of Scania. This law includes a translation of the royal statute in Latin on homicide from the year 1200 and also mentions legislation by King Valdemar, however, a new statute on homicide mentioned by Anders Sunesen apparently had not been issued at the time when the Danish redaction was finished. However, even if the Danish text might be slightly older, the differences as to the substance are few, and there is reason to believe that the Danish version and the Latin one are written down approximately at the same time and perhaps even out of the same endeavour to ascertain what the law of Scania actually was. In this connection it does not seem an all too dared assumption that the Archbishop himself – as already mentioned – was instrumental both as to the initiative of having the law written down in Danish and as to the Latin version. This leaves us with a question to be treated more in detail later, whether the collection of knowledge of law contained in the Danish text was actually established by the Archbishop to be used as material for his Latin treatise, the Danish version being a spin-off, or whether the Latin version is a learned work made later, when a full Danish text was there, and without such direct connection to the redaction work of the Danish law. Or, as a third possibility, the two texts may have been redacted more or less simultaneously with different aims, and such that also the making of a Latin version may have influenced the Danish text. This would explain e.g. why the chapters on contracts in the Law of Scania, which shows influence from Roman law, are brought as the last part of the law and thus could be a later appendix.

Little is known of the life of Anders Sunesen apart from his official career. What we know about his early life stems from the dedication to him in the *Res Gesta Danorum* by the contemporary historian Saxo, who mentions that he had studied and even been a teacher in France, Italy and England. The cousin of his father, Absalon, had studied in Paris as did his brother, later bishop of Roskilde, Peder, and we therefore assume that Anders Sunesen also got his basic education there after having been in school in Denmark, probably the cathedral school of Roskilde. If Anders Sunesen in fact went to Bologna, which we believe,[12] he will even if he concentrated his studies in theology, have met a law school marked by the heritage of prominent lawyers, a history already reaching more than half a century back and a tradition of teaching the law based on a close study and interpretation of the texts and the glosses explaining and systematizing the text. To really dominate the material, both the Roman law texts and the glosses and *summae* and other legal textbooks years of study were needed, and how far Anders Sunesen made it we do not know, but both his style and hidden quotations give the impression of a person acquainted with the way of legal thinking.

During a stay in Bologna a student might apart from Roman law and Canon law and an intense legal atmosphere also get to know the Lombard law, the *Libri Feudorum*, on feudal law and thus to some degree legal texts dating back to the 8th century reflecting a way of thinking the law similar to what was found in the Nordic countries at that time. One of the crucial questions in Nordic legal history is actually whether any influence from Lombard law can be seen in the Nordic medieval law[13]. As a man of the church and probably at an early date picked out by his super rich Zealand family to follow an ecclesiastical career it is obvious that Anders Sunesen during his stays abroad has studied Canon law and also that he must have acquainted himself with at least so much Roman law that was necessary for

---

12. Among the students who he could have met in Paris and later in Bologna was Lotario da Segni, the later Pope Innocent III, to whom, judged from the letters from the pope sent to him as archbishop, Anders Sunesen seems to have had a good contact. During his stay in Paris also the academic foundation must have been laid that enabled him to compose the Hexaemeron, a poem in 8040 hexameters which describes the work of creation.

13. See to this still but cautiously E. Sjöholm, *Gesetze als Quellen mittelalterlicher Geschichte des Nordens* (Stockholm: 1976) and the fruitful discussion between her and Ole Fenger in *(Dansk) Historisk Tidsskrift* (1979-1981). See also Stefan Brink's article in this volume.

the understanding and more profound study of Canon law. It is rather clear from the text that he at least knew Roman law on a basis corresponding to the elementary textbook, the Institutes of Justinian, but most probably he has also studied parts of the Digests containing the texts of the Roman lawyers and Codex being the collection of the imperial legislation.

In England by the end of the 12th century there was an increased interest not only in Canon law and Roman law, but it was also the time when Common law was coming into being by the practice of the king's court at the Exchequer with its own leader and educated judges. The reign of King Henry II from 1154 to 1189 was crucial in this process of creating a new legal system. At that time England could look back on a long history of the law starting with the old Anglo-Saxon laws since the 7th century, the laws of King Alfred for the late 9th century, the laws of Ine and Canute in the 11th century, the tradition of Danelaw since the 9th century, the laws of Edward the confessor and from the early 12th century the work called *Leges Henrici Primi*, which shows influence from Isidore of Seville, the influential French canonist Ivo of Chartres and Frankish law. Above all this, the courts were creating a new common law and first treatise of this law was published most probably between 1187 and 1189 namely the *Treatise on the Laws and Customs of the Realm of England* commonly called 'Glanville'.[14] This work is attributed to Ranulph de Glanville who was a judge and chief justiciar of England in the years 1180-1189. Anders Sunesen may have known this work which appeared at a time in which he was likely to have been in England. The way in which Glanville exposed the English law as it was handled by the royal courts, comes close to what Anders Sunesen did in his treatise on the Law of Scania as it was handled by the local assemblies. There are similarities and it is tempting to assume that Anders Sunesen was inspired by the work of Glanville. In that case we will have to recognize contemporary England as the place where the idea of writing down Danish law was forged. Around 1199 a collection of law known as the *Trés ancient coutumier* appeared in Normandy. The style of this work is different from the work of Anders Sunesen but it demonstrates how the time around 1200 seemed favourable for such collections.

If Anders Sunesen in fact visited England it would have been at a time when the murder of Thomas Becket in 1170 was still in vivid remembrance. He would not have met John of Salisbury who died in 1180, but he may have met Glanville and his successor William Longchamps who also wrote a treatise on the law, known as *Practica legum et decretorum* (1183-1189). Longchamps stemmed from Normandy, he was closely related to Prince Richard and was sent on an embassy to Paris in 1189. In 1190, Longchamps

---

14. I have used the edition with translation by G.D.G. Hall, *The treatise on the laws and customs of the realm of England commonly called Glanvill* (Oxford: 1993).

was appointed bishop of Ely and thus had a career similar to what would be the career of Anders Sunesen as chancellor of the Danish king on his return and later Archbishop. Whether or not they met is pure conjecture, however, it should be noted that in England in the second half of the 12th century a school of Anglo-Norman canonists who wrote treatises and other works on canon law was active. Vacarius had taught Roman law in Oxford and written the so-called *Liber Pauperum* in which both Justinian's *Codex* and *Digests* were quoted. Anders Sunesen may have acquainted himself with some of this scholarship which was made in fragmentary local legal surroundings more similar to those of his homeland Zealand or Scania than the universities of Paris or Bologna. But common to England, Italy, France and also Denmark was the encounter of two different legal approaches, the learned law as it was taught and studied at the universities and the local law as it was practiced by laymen in the local courts and assemblies. Whatever is the true inspiration for Anders Sunesen to write his treatise on the Law of Scania it was only possible because he had the university training as a scholar to systematize and understand the law as he did and exposed it in the treatise. The treatise is the only extant piece of Danish legal scholarship before 1450. It not only gives us invaluable information of how justice was handled at its time but its particular charm is probably due to its mixing knowledge of local law with reflections stemming from a mind formed by university studies and blistering from intelligence and learning.

Anders Sunesen follows the system of the Danish text starting out with the conditions for taking inheritance, the division of households and the right to dispose of the household, all rules that may be seen as crucial in society. The author uses a latinisation of the Danish word *bonde*, the householder to indicate this central figure in the law. The *bondone* is also known as the *pater familias* and Anders Sunesen thus clearly mingles well-known Danish concepts with those from Roman law. Also different categories of landowners as *aldungebønder* or *hotolbønder* are kept in their Danish form. An example of how Anders Sunesen will latinize Danish concepts is also found in the chapters on conveyance of land. For the Danish ceremony the verb *scøthæ* was used, which he in ch. 38 calls *scotare* and he forms also the substantive *scotatio*. At that time there was no clear distinction between Civil law and Criminal law as to procedure or compensation to be paid in case of offenses, however, in his ch. 43 Anders Sunesen marks a transition to another field namely homicide and other crimes by introducing the Devil, the enemy of mankind, as the instigator of homicide. The chapters on homicide and the payment of compensation give information as to the procedure which is not found in the Danish text, e.g. we are told of the oaths to be given by the family of the killer and the family of the victim in order to mitigate the shame by receiving compensation instead of taking revenge and in order to prevent revenge (ch.46). These oaths are given in their

Danish version. Also we find a detailed and instructive description of the procedure to be followed at the assembly when the compensation shall be paid.

A question treated with utmost care is the summoning before the assembly, known in the text simply as *jus*, just as you would expect to find it in a work meant for those who in practice should handle cases or be asked their advice at the assembly. The days to be fixed and the excuses to be made and the proof to take place is explained in detail and repeated for each kind of conflict or offense.

A difference between Anders Sunesen and Glanville is that such crimes that were handled by local courts are not treated in any detail by Glanville who concentrates on the procedure before the royal courts. Such courts did not exist in Denmark at the time. The treatise of Anders Sunesen is therefore exactly directed to those handling cases before the local assemblies, whereas we are ignorant of any procedure before the King. As to what we would conceive as the criminal pleas, Anders Sunesen seems to base his system on on a rather simple division into the protection of respectively life and body, freedom and property. Regarding property there is a basic distinction as to the crime of theft and other kinds of disrespect for ownership as not respecting the fields, other people's woods or their right not to be overflowed or keeping water for their own fishing. The difference between the serious accusation of theft which was heavily punished and normally directed against someone on a social level who had difficulties in defending himself or finding others to do it, and the other more trifling offenses as to someone's property is marked by placing an extensive explanation of the different ways of carrying hot iron between those two parts of the treatise, even if the proof by hot iron can still be an issue in cases of adultery and fire, the treatment of which in the Treatise follow after the protection of the fields, woods and waters. Adultery is clearly seen as an offence committed against either the husband or in case of unmarried women the family, the marriage strategy of which was hampered through rape or illicit intercourse. It should be noted that according to the old Church Law the husband could already force his wife to prove innocence of adultery by the proof of hot iron (ch. 127), whereas a similar right for the wife in case of her husband's adultery did not exist.

The purpose of the Treatise seems clearly to have been didactic. Some end the Treatise with the words ... *composuit ad utilitatem totius terre* (the work was done for the benefit of the whole province). And definitely as has been said the purpose of explaining the law and guiding those who might be in a position to be the leader of an assembly or give advice to parties must have been important as probably also the basic idea that knowing Latin including legal Latin and being good at it was useful. According to a rather dared and not well-founded theory by Michael Gelting the purpose was to provide a papal representative, Gregorius de Crescentia, whose visit to Denmark in 1223 had been announced by the pope with a survey of the law. The Treatise according to the conjectures was built upon a redaction of the Law of Scania made around 1220 by a commission in order to establish the law after the Fourth Lateran Council. The way the Treatise is written not least if compared to the contemporary Treatise of Glanville indicates that the two works both aimed at giving information to those who needed guidance as to the law of how conflicts were to be solved. It could also have been used as teaching material at the school which we assume was attached to the cathedral, but it seems more directed to persons with some practical knowledge or need of such knowledge when consulted about the local law.

Explanations, definitions and the mentioning of different opinions as to what the law is, is a characteristic of Anders Sunesen's style. Ch. 25 mentions how a person who has promised to answer for others can be forced to carry hot iron and that 'he is thus held accountable for the folly of his temerity that he would answer for someone ingrate'. In ch. 37 it is explained that an oath must stand: 'as it is not to be believed, that they (the oath-helpers) must thus be unmindful of their salvation, that they will prefer something of this world for it', and on the term of three years for prescription it is said: 'Not without reason was such brevity of prescription introduced, because it is not advantageous for the ownership of property to be in uncertainty for a long, and a timely decision appears to cut down the root of evils before it happens that harm sprouts from it'. Ch. 143 on hire of land is introduced by a general statement: 'As for some people it is necessary to hire out their land, and for others to rent land that is not their own, it is clearly stated, in order that the tenant is not oppressed by the power of the hirer out nor the hirer out is cheated by the cunningness of the tenant, that one party shall abstain from harming the other'. Also metaphors like crops as 'a gift of God' (ch. 102), or that 'the generosity of human society grants certain things from another person's wood even if the owner does not give his assent' (ch. 115). The most famous of such more poetic figures is, however, what in ch. 127 is said about the rule that a husband could force his wife suspected of adultery to carry iron that 'for some part is it is so that this human law, just as an obedient maid or a female slave$_1$ who follows her mistress's steps, is modified by the pre-eminence of divine law, which dictates that marriages are subject not to the scrutiny and regimen of the assembly but of heaven$_2$, not of a secular court but of the spiritual church, and which does not permit the separation from the marriage bed to be performed by the trial of hot iron'.

In a few cases reference is made to divergences between the King and the local conception of the law. Thus the King will abolish compensation for damage caused by falling into ditches (ch. 101) and also ch. 100 and 125 has such examples.

A total of twelve chapters in the Treatise are without correspondence in our text of the Law of Scania:[15]

Even if Anders Sunesen has chosen to bring some chapters in another order or add his explanations or personal remarks, the text is easily recognizable as that of the written law. However, the specific ecclesiastical background of the author adds new dimensions to the text in his rendering. Whereas the Danish text is a plain writing down of rules, the Latin text moves in different spheres. The popping up in ch. 43 of the Devil gives the text a transcendal dimension which is also found in the ch. 102 in which the fruits of the fields are mentioned as given by God or when in ch. 127 it is stated that marriage is a matter to be judged by the heaven and not by earthly courts. Several references are given to natural equity and thus the law of man is placed in a setting governed by God and norms higher than the written law itself. There is nothing surprising in this. Anders Sunesen was familiar with the *Decretum Gratiani* which in its first part also stresses different divisions in the law between divine and secular law. For Anders Sunesen to stress, even if discreetly the law is man-made and only a contingent phenomenon with the function of helping people to settle their conflicts peacefully and himself to ease this task by writing his Treatise was just a consequence of his Episcopal duties. He sometimes adds reflection on human nature as when the pietas of the mother is mentioned as a reason to grant her custody of small children, or how much more people are inclined to behave badly than does good (ch. 48). It is obvious that apart from the question of marriage, where he apparently had to accept the old law already laid down in the agreement known as the Church Law of Scania, he did not see his task as criticizing the local law but as finding ways to reconcile it with Canon law if any difference could be ascertained. Thus he explains why the person injured should be remedied also in case of accident (ch. 67). That Anders Sunesen did follow the line of the secular law and only casually reveals himself as representing the Church may of course also be seen as a sign that he himself had been instrumental in collecting the law and had had the possibility of influencing the Danish version. Only where he apparently could not get through with his canonical points of view, as in the case of the accusation of adultery, he resigned and suggested in his own Treaty other ways of solution. Noteworthy are also his references to statutes or opinions of the King. The law is not only what the *prudentes* of the assembly in Lund would have as law, the King is a player whose consent adds to the authority of the law, but who can also still be considered a mere player who could not without local consent change the law. The treatise, however, is not a theoretical reflection on the law but apart from the more

---

15. Chs. 23, 36, 38, 43, 44, 47, 61, 64, 80, 81, 84 and 140. Some of them just bring in definitions or explanations whereas seven stands alone.

general remarks a very much down-to-earth description of how to proceed in different cases. A main scope seems to be guiding through the procedure at the assembly when a conflict was raised. This explains the relative importance he gives the rendering of the exact procedure to be followed when someone is summoned.

Also in Glanvilles *Treatise on English Law* the summons are central and a first chapter is dedicated to the explanation of how to proceed. Remarkable parallels can be found in the system explained by Glanville and in Anders Sunesen's Treatise. In both cases like the procedure of ecclesiastical excommunication, which is even mentioned by Anders Sunesen, the basic rule is that a defendant shall be summoned three times (ch. 41, 57, 90, 91). If he then appears, he has the right to excuse himself by alleging that he was not summoned or that the summons were invalid as he was on pilgrimage, in search of his animals or had fallen ill (41, 72, 91, 132 cf. also ch. 88 on terms when a person accused of theft refers to people living afar or separated by the sea). Also in Glanville we find a chapter corresponding to ch. 91 on sending 'essoiners' to prove that the defendant is lawfully excused from coming either because he is sick or because he has been in the neighbourhood or has travelled far away. Another parallel to Glanville is found in Anders Sunesen's treatment of situations in which a free person is claimed to be a slave or a slave is claimed to be free.

In quite some cases Anders Sunesen abstains from translating Danish terms into Latin and renders them in old Danish. The reason for this is not necessarily that no translation can be found, but some terms in Danish may have been so crucial to the procedure that they should be known in the original language by the person who used his Treatise in practice. Thus a specific term of three years called *thrænnæ halmæ* (three years of using land), the way in which the kinsmen's part of a compensation was known, *sal*, specific oaths *jafthnethe ed, trygd, asswerueth*, categories of householders who could swear to questions of land, the *alldungebøndær* or *(h)otelbøndær*, the *(h)ornum* for land ouside the village community, forms of hot iron like *scuz iærn* and *truxiærn*, the weapons carried by gangmen, the *folcvapn*, wounds inflicted by accident *wathasar*, intent *ond viliæ*, outlawry *frithløs* or denial of food *matban*, the specific crime of destroying animals, *gornithingsverk*, a measure *tolfmynning*, specific categories of persons as noblemen *hetwarthe man*, reeves and tenants, *brytæ, landbo* or the contractual obligation of *halzfæ*. In two cases he has made his own Latin words based on Danish words, the *bondones* of *bondæ*, the householder, and *scotacio* from *scøthæ*, conveying land.

As opposed to Glanville the Latin of Anders Sunesen is not plain and simple. It is an elaborate Latin, even if not quite as much as his contemporary Saxo in the *Gesta Danorum*. However, as already mentioned Anders Sunesen likes poetic figures like the 'small' breathing can make envy flame up (ch. 48), and also if possible finds synonyms in order not to repeat words. The Danish text of the Law of Scania operated with a total of 994 words, whereas the Latin text needs many more. A term like *bot,* the compensation to be paid is rendered by *satisfaccio* or *emendacio* or *compensacio* without any visible difference of meaning. The bishop who takes a fine or compensation of three marks in certain cases, when the parties cannot agree, is known as *episcopus, antistes*, *prosul* or *pontifex.* In ch. 109 three different denominations of the bishop are used.[16]

6. Conclusions

For a long time medieval law was the main focus of Danish legal historians. Also in Iceland, Norway and Sweden the medieval laws had an important place in the study of legal history. In later years a new generation of legal historian has added to our knowledge of the laws and opened the dimension from a more dogmatic or nationally concentrated to their position in a European context. It would be ungrateful not to mention the names of Sten Gagnér, Elsa Sjöholm and Ole Fenger as some of those who in the 1960s and 1970s opened new paths for the study of medieval Nordic laws. Much has been disputed and as already suggested, not everything that is new is necessarily to the point.

In many ways the old Nordic medieval laws are still ruling us from their graves. They have been instrumental as to the course of Nordic legal history and parts of them lived on in newer Codes since 1683 in Denmark (in Norway 1687) and they are still posing us new questions when we study them again. Looking back till the 1960s one cannot but wonder how much our knowledge has increased, perhaps less as to the legal understanding of texts themselves but so very much as to the European legal cultural context into which they should be read.

---

16. The terminology of Anders Sunesen is tinged with vocabulary from Roman law. We meet inpubes, minores and tutores, emacipatio, filiifamilias and paterfamilias, citacio, praedium, fundus, possession,translation dominii, res evicta, hereditas, successores, viriles porciones, communitas, emptio and vendicio, locaccio-conduccio, depositum, pignum, lucrum et damnum, prescripcio, iuris peritus, actor, accusatory, reus, dominus, liber, servus, servus fugitivus, mancipio, ancilla, famula, caucio, agnates and cognates, casus fortuitus, lex, constitucio, homicidium, crimen majestatis, noxe dare, causa mortis, jus postliminium, fidejussor, fur, furtum, colonus, equitas, adulterium, consensus, custodia, diligens, officium, exception, precarium etc.

HOW NORDIC ARE THE NORDIC LAWS?

Jørn Øyrehagen Sunde

1. Why ask in 2003, how Nordic are the Nordic medieval laws?

How Nordic are the Nordic medieval laws? The question was posed at the first Carlsberg conference in Copenhagen ten years ago. A mix of historians, legal historians, philologists, archaeologists and theologians of all ages and from all the Nordic countries and a number of other European countries, met to answer this question.[1] I was one of the participants. At the time I had worked for only two years on medieval legal history, and at the Carlsberg Academy I encountered a series of new perspectives. Some of these were thought-provoking, and all of them have influenced my research ever since – not only my research in medieval law, but on the internationalization of law more generally, independent of time period.

The internationalization of law is a label put on the present legal development on the global level, one that is most intense in Europe, and does not necessarily fit well in all historical periods. Not least because the concept of the nation state, a prerequisite for inter*national*ization, did not emerge until the end of the 18th century. But by first defining internationalization of law as the communication of legal material – from substantial law expressed in customs and in statutes, to legal technologies such as legislation and legal methods, and on to legal ideas in the form of concepts of justice and *Rechtsstaat*. And by thereafter defining the communication as across jurisdictional boarders – from ethnic groups to realms, and on to nations and international bodies like the EU and WTO. We can in the end upgrade this rather ahistorical term by allowing for the many different past processes that, at least in spirit, resemble the present day internationalization of law.

---

1. See D. Tamm & H. Vogt (ed.), *How Nordic are the Nordic medieval laws?* (Copenhagen: 2005).

Squeezing past processes into a modern term like internationalization is a dangerous enterprise, because the past is then often shaped to fit the present. On the other hand, to avoid relating the past to the present is also a dangerous enterprise, because it often estranges the past from the present more than is necessary. And it is the very interplay between the past and the present that is the rationale behind the question How Nordic are the Nordic Medieval Laws? when it was posed in 2003 and again in 2013.

On one hand, the question was posed due to an internal historical and legal historical discourse. Not so much related to Elsa Sjøholm's *Sveriges medeltidslagar – europeisk rättstradition i politisk omvandling* from 1988[2] as to the writings of well-established researchers like Ditlev Tamm,[3] Michael Gelting,[4] Tore Iversen,[5] and Lars Ivar Hansen,[6] and at the time PhD students like Per Andersen,[7] Mia Korpiola[8] and Helle Vogt,[9] who all took an interest in Roman, Canon and even Mosaic legal influence on the Nordic medieval laws.[10]

On the other hand, what made it even more pressing to investigate the influence of these sources of law on Nordic medieval laws was the ongoing internationalization of law, outside the internal historical and legal historical discourse. At the turn of the millennium, the internationalization of law took a leading role not only on the Nordic, but also on the European legal stage.

---

2. E. Sjöholm, *Sveriges medeltidslagar – europeisk rättstradition i politisk omvandling* (Stockholm: 1998). The title translates into 'Sweden's medieval laws – an European legal tradition in transition'.
3. D. Tamm, 'Gulatingsloven og de andre gamle nordiske landskabslove', *Tidsskrift for Rettsvitenskap* 115 (2002), 292-309.
4. M. Gelting, 'Odelsrett – lovbydelse – bördsrätt – retrait lignager: Kindred and Land in the Nordic Countries in the Twelfth and Thirteenth Centuries', in L.I. Hansen (ed.), *Family, marriage and property devolution in the Middle Ages* (Tromsø: 2000), 133-65.
5. T. Iversen, *Knechtschaft im mittelalterlichen Norwegen* (Ebelsbach: 2004).
6. L.I. Hansen, 'The Concept of Kinship According to the West Nordic Medieval Laws', in D. Tamm & H. Vogt (ed.), *How Nordic*, 170-201 and see L.I. Hansen, 'Introduction', in L.I. Hansen (ed.), *Family, marriage and property*, 8-10.
7. P. Andersen, *Rex imperator in regno suo – dansk kongemagt og rigslovgivning i 1200-tallets Europa* (Odense: 2005) and P. Andersen, *Lærd ret og verdslig lovgivning – retlig kommunikation og udvikling i middelalderens Danmark* (Copenhagen: 2006).
8. M. Korpiola, *Between betrothal and bedding – marriage formation in Sweden 1200-1600* (Leiden & Boston: 2009).
9. H. Vogt, *The function of kinship in medieval Nordic legislation* (Leiden & Boston: 2010).
10. In this context we should not forget that also before the Carlsberg Conference in 2003 there had been research on this topic, like O. Fenger, *Romerret i Norden* (Copenhagen: 1977).

How Nordic are the Nordic Laws?

Essential events were, first, the transmission of the European Community to the European Union in 1993, with the subsequent transformation of the European Court of Justice to an increasingly EU-oriented court with extended duties to harmonize law. Second, all citizens of the member states of the European Council got an individual right to take complaints regarding violation of the European Charter on Human Rights to the European Court of Human Rights in 1994, with the subsequent restructuring of the Court in 1998. At the end of the 1990s, lawyers in all corners of Europe started to study how the internationalization of law influenced legislation and court proceedings at all levels. This made the internal historical and legal historical discourse on different sources of legal influence on the Nordic medieval laws more pressing.

Due to this dialectic between an internal historical and legal historical discourse and present changes in society, host Professor Ditlev Tamm, already in his opening speech at the conference in 2003, accompanied the question How Nordic are the Nordic Medieval Laws? with the more general question How Nordic are the Nordic laws?[11] I will do the same thing now, a decade later, by taking a detour to present-day internationalization before venturing back to the Middle Ages to shake up our concepts of national law as the natural order of things. I will mainly use my country of origin, Norway, as an Archimedes fulcrum to show the general trends of internationalization in the Nordic countries in the Middle Ages and today.

2. How Nordic are the Nordic laws in 2013?

A certain degree of internationalization of law has in Norway been the order of the day for decades. For instance, the Norwegian Criminal Law Act of 1902 was changed in 1970 due to the UN Convention on Elimination of Racial Discrimination of 1966.[12] In 1979, the Norwegian Supreme Court for the first time ruled in favour of the European human rights when there was a conflict with Norwegian law.[13] And in 1988, the Norwegian Act on Product

---

11. D. Tamm, 'How Nordic are the Nordic Medieval Laws?', in D. Tamm & H. Vogt (ed.), *How Nordic*, 6, also published in D. Tamm, *The History of Danish Law – Selected Articles and Bibliography* (Copenhagen: 2011), 25.
12. § 135a was added to the Criminal Law Act (*Straffeloven*) of 22.5.1902, no. 10 to fulfil Norwegian obligations after signing the UN Convention on the Elimination of All Forms of discrimination of 21.12.1965, signed by Norway 21.11.1966 and in force here from 6.8.1970.
13. Decision by the Norwegian Supreme Court of 22.9.1979, published in *Norsk Rettstidende* (Den norske advokatforening: 1979), 1079-1085 ('Rt. 1979: 1079'). The Human Rights are not even mentioned in the decision, but former Supreme Court

Liability was an adoption of the EU directive on the same issue from 1985.[14] Still, prior to 1 January 1994, when the Agreement on the European Economic Area between Norway and the EU entered into force, almost fully integrating Norway into the EU in terms of law,[15] it is likely that less than one per cent of Norwegian law was based on legal sources produced outside Norwegian jurisdictional borders.

Twenty years later, and a decade after posing the question How Nordic are the Nordic Medieval Laws? at the first Carlsberg conference, a fair estimate is that between 15 and 20 per cent of Norwegian law is based on legal sources produced outside the Norwegian jurisdiction.[16] The most prominent among these sources are EU law, the European Human Rights, UN law and WTO law. There are good reasons to believe that my own home country, Norway, is fairly representative of all the Nordic countries in terms of the present state of internationalization of law. It is thus appropriate to ask How Nordic are the Nordic Laws? because if between 15 and 20 per cent of Nordic law is not Nordic in origin, its very nature of being 'Nordic' is subsequently diminished.

Why is this fact not in the headlines and on everybody's lips: Nordic law is becoming less and less Nordic! The answer is because no one has noticed. This despite the fact that we are talking about a rapid change in a large portion of Nordic law. The fact that this radical change in Nordic law has gone by almost unnoticed is maybe even more surprising than is the change itself. If such an internationalization of law shocks us, despite its coming about almost unnoticed, it is because of the firm mental grip the notion of national law as the natural order of things has on us.

The fruitful conflict between local and universal law is an old one, and not the topic of this article. Here it is sufficient to state that the present notion of national law as the natural order of things can be ascribed to Charles Montesquieu and his *De l'esprit des lois* from 1748. In this much read treatise, Montesquieu represented Frankish feudal law as an oak tree with deep roots, and thereby visualized how law is a product of factors like

---

judge Gunnar Aasland confimed in an interview 14.5.2012 that it was considerations concerning article 6 in the European Convention on Human Rights and the question of access to court that were decisive in the courts deliberations.

14. The (Norwegian) Act on Product Liability of 23.12.1988, no. 104 and Council Directive 85/374/EEC of 25.7.1985 on the approximation of the laws, regulations and administrative provisions of the Member States concerning liability for defective products.
15. The Act on EEA in Norwegian Law (EØS-loven) of 27.11.1992, no. 109.
16. This is an estimate much indebt to the discussion in House of Commons Library, *How much legislation comes from Europe?*, research paper 10/62 13.10.2010, http://www.parliament.uk/briefing-papers/RP10-62.

climate, topography, religion, culture and history.[17] This changed the focus from universal to local and national law, and Friedrich Carl von Savigny, in his pamphlet *Vom Beruf unserer Zeit für Gesetzgebung und Rechtswissenschaft* from 1814, made this change in focus the very foundation for the German Historical School of Law.[18]

Montesquieu's ideas immediately gained popularity in the Nordic countries.[19] The most obvious and important product of Montesquieu's ideas was a Danish legal history published in two volumes by Professor Peder Kofod Ancher in 1769 and 1776 respectively. On the title page, there is a lithograph of a landscape with a large oak tree bearing the inscription: *in radice vita et spiritus* (in the roots are the life and spirit).[20]

Kofod Ancher translated the Law of Jutland into modern Danish and published it in 1783. The medieval Norwegian laws were already translated and published in 1751-52 by Hans Paus. In the preface of the first volume, Paus underlines the high quality of the medieval Norwegian laws, and boasts without modesty that they can be compared to those of antiquity.[21] Paus, a noted intellectual in Copenhagen, was therefore a proponent for the notion that local and national law was good law. Still, it is difficult to determine whether this is due to a reading of the *De l'esprit des lois*, or simply the fact that universally applicable law must have been a strange idea for someone like Paus, born and bred in Finnmark, the northernmost part of Norway, and even of Europe, and about as far away from a Mediterranean antiquity as one can get.

Paus's publication was reviewed by former law professor Isaac Andreas Cold in 1753.[22] Cold, not yet enamoured with the spirit of Montesquieu's work, on the other hand, had no qualms about stressing the similarities between Roman law and the Gulating Compilation for the western part of Norway.[23] For Cold, similarities between Norwegian medieval laws with the universally valid Roman law were a sign of quality. But Cold was on the losing end of things.

---

17. C. Montesquieu, *The Spirit of the Laws*, eds. and trans. A.M. Cohler, B.C. Miller & H.S. Stone (Cambridge: 1990), 9, 619.
18. Tamm, *The History of Danish Law*, 31-32, but also 27-28.
19. L. Björne, *Den nordiske rättsvetenskapens historia*, 1: Patrioter och institutionalister – tiden före år 1815 (Stockholm: 1995), 356.
20. Tamm, *The History of Danish Law*, 7, 31.
21. H. Paus, *Samling af gamle norske Love* 1 (Copenhagen: 1751), preface (unpaginated).
22. I.A. Cold, 'Samling af gamle norske Love ec. Sammlung alter norwegischer Gesetze', *Nachrichten von dem Zustand der Wissenschaften und Künste in den Köngl. Dänischen Reichen und Ländern* 1:3 (Johann Benjamin Akermann: 1753), 185-210.
23. Cold, *Samling af gamle norske Love ec*, e.g. 207-08.

A little less than a hundred years later, the Norwegian medieval laws were published in their original language by Rudolf Keyser and Peter Andreas Munch. The entire enterprise of travelling to Copenhagen and Stockholm solely to study and compare manuscripts, and then to publish them, was financed by the Norwegian Parliament. Norway regained its independence in 1814, and the publication of the medieval laws was a way to prove that Norway was a nation in its own right with a state tradition different from, but comparable to the Roman tradition. And Munch, a lawyer by education, had read Savigny's *Vom Beruf*.[24] In a letter written in 1847 to Jacob Grimm, a student of Savigny, Munch described the first volume of the Norwegian medieval laws as a tribute to Grimm, Savigny and the other aristocrats of learning in Berlin.[25]

The very national approach to history in general, to legal history more specifically, and to medieval law even more specifically, has been debated and criticized. But it has yet to be abandoned. The reason is that the German Historical School of Law not only marked a change in focus from universal to local and national law, but also to a focus on positive law. Since positive law has predominantly been national law in the 19th and 20th centuries, national law has continued to be the natural order of things long after the ideology of this influential school of law declined in popularity.

The European Human Rights and EU law have, on the one hand, universal aspirations – they are intended to be applied in a similar manner across jurisdictional borders and in quite different environments – and, on the other hand, they are positive law found in positive sources such as treaties, directives, court rulings, more than from logic systems.[26] Hence, The European Human Rights and EU law challenge national law without the doctrine of positive law being questioned.

This has not led to an adoration of universal law once again. First we have to keep in mind that in Norway, and probably in the other Nordic countries, between 80 and 85 per cent of the law is still national law. Second, the margin of appreciation in terms of the European Human Rights, and the margin of discretion in EU law, show that the common sense that was formulated as a doctrine by Montesquieu in 1748 still makes sense today – laws might have to be adjusted to fit the environment in which they are designed to work. And third, most importantly, despite the changes in

---

24. D. Michalsen, 'Rettsvitenskapens rettshistorie', *Tidsskrift for Rettsvitenskap* 115 (2002), 328, note 26.
25. Michalsen, 'Rettsvitenskapens rettshistorie', 32, note 20.
26. Both the European human Rights and the EU-law are by the courts in Strasbourg and Luxemburg treated as systems of laws, but they are mostly based on principles of laws in charters and treaties and not like the principles of Roman and natural law that were mostly based on logical deduction in the 18th century.

law, the perception of law has not changed as rapidly. That is why we are shocked by the estimate that between 15 and 20 per cent of all law in the Nordic countries is based on legal sources produced outside their jurisdictional borders.

3. How Nordic was Nordic law in the Middle Ages?

The rapid changes in European law, especially during the past decade, have caused us to ask, more aptly, How Nordic are the Medieval Nordic laws? Still, we hesitate to ask How Nordic are the Nordic laws? When we do so in 2013, however, we are as shocked by the answer as we are to the answer to How Nordic are the Medieval Nordic laws? a decade ago. We are/were shocked in both cases, because Nordic law is at first glance less Nordic than we thought. Still under the spell of Montesquieu and the German Historical School of Law, we find this unnatural. But what lesson can we learn from our own shock? We can learn that in Nordic societies where some 15 to 20 per cent of the law is based on foreign legal sources, without anyone's noticing, local and national law is not important in itself. To couple good law and local and national law is merely a shortcut. Good law is law adapted to the environment it is set to work in; such law causes as little friction as possible. Good local and national law is, at its best, adapted law. But law with universal aspirations might do the job equally well, if properly adjusted.

It is hence the functionality, and not the origin, of law that matters, and this ought to be the objective of our questions. So in quest of an answer to the question How Nordic are the Nordic Medieval laws?, let us not focus as much on their origin as on how they were designed to work in the intended environment, and hence to create as little friction as possible when applied.

Canon law was a source of law with universal aspirations in the Middle Ages, since it applied in all jurisdictions that were part of western Christendom. Hence, it was a major source of law in the part of Europe that we today call the Nordic countries. In relation to Canon law we also find examples of Nordic laws made outside the Nordic countries but for the Nordic countries. This because parts of the Canon law applied in Sweden, Norway and Iceland and referred to as Christian laws were based on Canon law designed specifically for one of the Nordic archbishoprics as a response to a specific need.

For an instance, Pope Alexander III decided that the herring fishery in Nidaros Archbishopric could continue uninterrupted during the Sabbath, except on the most sacred days of the year.[27] This was done due to the importance of herring fishery to the costal population of the archbishopric. In addition, practical necessities other than economic ones could also motivate new legal norms. Probably to adapt to existing perceptions of authority and representation, Pope Innocent II confirmed a practice of donating land that Archbishop Absalon of Lund referred to as *scotatio*: instead of using a testament the donor, in the presence of witnesses, would take a clump of earth wrapped in a cloth and place it at the end of the *pallium*, held out by the bishop or another prelate, or lay it on the altar, while orally bequeathing the land.[28]

Especially interesting in this context is that Pope Alexander III decided that in Iceland and Greenland the seventh degree as the limit for marriage was impossible to uphold since the islands was so sparsely populated, and instead permitted marriage by relatives as close as the fourth degree.[29] At the Fourth Lateran Council in 1215 this was made the rule for all of Christendom.[30] This is an example not only of legal sources specifically designed for the Nordic countries, but also of how specific needs for this part of Europe would trigger new laws as well.

Nevertheless, such examples are few. Instead of involving Rome when facing a need and/or demand to adjust Canon law, changes could be made through direct negotiations between the Thing – the public assembly – and representatives of the Church.

A general indication that Canon law had to be adopted and altered for the different Nordic jurisdictions is the fact that the Christian laws for each provincial assembly do not resemble each other to a large extent. This is the case even within each archbishopric. In mainland Norway, the Christian laws of the four provinces differ from one another more than they resemble one another. When Archbishop Jon the Red in the 1270s decreed a new

---

27. E. Vandvik (ed. & trans.), *Latinske dokument til norsk historie – fram til år 1204* (Oslo: 1959), 71-73, and P. Landau, 'The Importance of Classical Canon Law in Scandinavia in the 12th and 13th Centuries', in D. Tamm & H. Vogt (ed.), *How Nordic*, 35-36.
28. Landau, 'The Importance of Classical Canon Law in Scandinavia', 36-37, and O. Condorelli, 'On the role of the *ius decretalium* in the spreading of the culture of the *ius commune* in Europe – Studies around a decretal by Innocent III addressed to the Archbishop of Lund (*Ex litteris*, X.1.4.2, 1198)', in H. Haugland & J.Ø. Sunde (ed.), *Encounter of Legal Cultures in the Nordic Realms 1100-1400* (forthcoming).
29. Landau, 'The Importance of Classical Canon Law in Scandinavia', 33-34, and A.J. Duggan, 'Eystein and the World of Learned Law. With special reference to the Fragmentum Asloense: Oslo, Riksarkivet, latin fragment 152, 1-2', in T. Iversen (ed.), *Archbishop Eystein as legislator – the European connection* (Trondheim: 2011), 68-69.
30. Vogt, *The Function of Kinship*, 15.

Christian law, harmonizing the Christian laws of the four provinces, a separate one was decreed by Bishop Arne for the Icelandic part of the archbishopric. Even though the Christian laws of Bishop Arne were made according to the advice of the archbishop,[31] there was still no uniformity of law in the archbishopric. The degree to which the Christian laws of Jon the Red was even applied in the Norwegian part of the archbishopric is uncertain,[32] and is a further indication that the Church had limited power to impose law on the population.[33]

A specific indication that Canon law had to be adopted and adjusted in the different Nordic jurisdictions is reported by Göran Nilsson in his recent account of the making of the younger law of Vestgötaland.[34] His claim is that different editions of the law must be seen as different stages of a negotiation process between the Thing and the Church.[35] The younger law of Vestgötaland is not a Christian law, but Nilsson's research still shows the open, negotiable nature of law in the High Middle Ages, even when the Church was involved and their principles of law were challenged.

Local adjustment of the universal Canon law was not an exclusively Nordic phenomenon, but a part of Church politics.[36] A differentiation was made between *jus commune*, which is the law that applied to all, and *jus proprium*, which was the locally adjusted Canon law. When Pope Alexander III gave the inhabitants of the archbishopric of Nidaros the right to fish herring on the Sabbath, this was a decision pertaining to *jus proprium*. Still, we find in the Christian laws also exceptions to what ought to be part of the *jus commune*. For instance, in the Christian law of Borgarting we find that the local congregation and not the bishop is the body that appoints the pastors in their church.[37] We also find in the same Christian law that the ritual of baptism seems to be more in accordance with the ritual we find in the Eastern Church and not the Catholic Church.[38]

31. G. & M. Stefánsson (trans.), *Biskop Arnes saga* (Oslo: 2007), 38.
32. S. Bagge, *From Viking stronghold to Christian kingdom – State formation in Norway, c. 900-1350* (Copenhagen: 2010), 305-06.
33. See M. Korpiola, 'On Ecclesiatical Jurisdcition and the Reception of Canon Law in the Swedish Provincial Laws', in D. Tamm & H. Vogt (ed.), *How Nordic*, 202-31.
34. G.B. Nilsson, *Nytt ljus över Yngre Västgötalagen* (Stockholm: 2012).
35. See the summary in G.B. Nilsson, 'Vad man bör veta om Yngre Vestgötalagen', *Särtryk ur Tidskrift utgiven av Föreningen för Västgötalitteratur* (2013).
36. See the brief discussion in T. Landro, *Kristenrett og kyrkjerett – Borgartingskristenrett i eit komparativt perspektiv* (Bergen: 2010), 219-23 and J.A. Coriden, 'The Canonical Doctrine of Reception', *The Jurist* 50 (1990), 58-63. See M. Korpiola, 'An Act or a Process? Competing Views in Marriage Formation and Legitimacy in Medieval Europe', in L.I. Hansen (ed.), *Family, marriage and property*, 31-54.
37. Landro, *Kristenrett og kyrkjerett*, 211-13.
38. Landro, *Kristenrett og kyrkjerett*, 30-68.

These kinds of variations were possible because Canon law was not a uniform, strictly decided set of rules. Despite the kind of harmonization of Canon law that *Decretum Gratiani* represents, there was a whole set of interpretations of Canon law that did not always match, and a whole set of rules governing human conduct that was not strictly part of the Canon law. All in all, this means that there was a pool of rules which enabled negotiations and local adjustments without abandoning the overarching universal character of Canon law. Canon law was to some extent like a warehouse where parts could be assembled and adjusted to make workable instruments to regulate society. Hence, when answering the question How Nordic are the Nordic Medieval Laws?, we find that the origin of laws was less important than their implementation even in terms of Canon law.

Canon law was a major source of law produced outside the Nordic countries, but applied within them. With respect of the christening ritual, there would be an expectation that Canon law was applied. But there are also examples of laws produced outside the Nordic countries that were applied within, but without any accompanying push to do so.

For instance, in both the Guta Compilaton for the Swedish island of Gotland, and in the Gulating Compilation for the western part of Norway, there is a provision concerning the purchase of slaves who later turn out to be epileptics. In both compilations, the buyer is entitled to receive a full refund if the slave is returned within one month of purchase.[39] According to the late legal historian Knut Robberstad, this provision might have originated in Mesopotamia, and travelled with the merchandise it concerned – the slaves – along the slave route to the Black Sea, up the Volga and into the Baltic Sea to the island of Gotland, where there was a Nordic slave market.[40] More certainly, the rule that was applied in Gotland might have been observed by slave buyers from Gulating, found reasonable and/or useful, and was then adopted in this legal province in Norway.

Whether the provision on the return of epileptic slaves had its origin far from the Nordic countries, or in Gotland itself, the choice to adopt it in Gulating was purely their own. But to formulate the exact rule that they desired, it was adjusted and amended. In the Gulating Compilation, the provision reads that a slave can be returned if 1) it is epileptic, 2) pregnant, 3) did not carry out the chamber pot in the morning, 4) did not keep its clothes clean, 5) sucked milk from cows, and 6) had serious diseases and/or illnesses. Not only was there a desire to adopt the provision locally, but the way it was altered and changed through adaptation was also a local process.

39. K. Robberstad (ed. & trans.), *Gulatingslovi* (Oslo: 1937), IV-1, and Å. Holmbäck & E. Wessén (ed. & trans.), *Svenska Landskapslagar* 4: *Skånelagen och Gutalagen* (Stockholm: 1943), chap. 32.
40. K. Robberstad, *Rettssoga I* (Oslo: 1990), 11.

The provision was hence a raw material that was reworked, and the ambition was not to copy, but rather to design a provision that caused as little friction as possible when applied.

The functionality of law as more important than the origin of law is also seen in the fate of rules on ordeal – on trial by God. It is usually argued that ordeal was promoted by the Church to replace less desirable ways of resolving conflicts, like for an example combat. In the Norwegian medieval laws prior to the Code of the Realm of 1274, issued by King Magnus the Law Mender, we find provisions on ordeal in both of the preserved compilations of law for Gulating and Frostating, and for the Christian laws for these two legal provinces, and for Eidsivating and Borgarting. Already Pope Alexander III criticized the extensive use of ordeal in Norway.[41] At the Fourth Lateran Council in 1215 clerical participation in ordeals was forbidden.[42] And during a stay in Norway in 1247, Cardinal Wilhelm of Sabina stressed that ordeal should no longer be practiced in Norway.[43] No one in government in Norway, especially in the Church, ought to be unaware of ordeal as an undesirable practice in the eyes of the central institutions of the Church. Still, this piece of foreign law was not abandoned. In the Gulating Compilation, ordeal is prescribed as an instrument of proof in four different cases, two of them part of the Christian laws.[44] In two of the cases it is even explicitly expressed that ordeal takes priority over oath as an instrument of proof. In the Frostating Compilation, applied in the very same legal province where the archbishop of Nidaros was located, ordeal is prescribed in thirteen cases, four of them part of the Christian laws.[45] For example, if three men would row out in a boat, and if only two returned and both blamed the death of the third man on each other, the ordeal was a handy tool to decide which one was the culprit.[46] Functionality, and not the origin of this legal instrument, was what mattered.

When the ordeal finally gave way to another instrument of proof, this was also a piece of foreign law – the jury and jury-like tribunals.[47] The problem was that the ordeal, like other instruments of proof such as witnesses, provided fairly good grounds for deciding a case, but one could still not be absolutely certain. And, as is repeated again and again in the *Konungs*

---

41. *Latinske dokument til norsk historie*, 76-77.
42. F. McAuley, 'Canon Law and the End of the Ordeal', *Oxford Journal of Legal Studies* 26 (2006), 473-74.
43. A. Holtsmark (ed. & trans.), *Håkon Håkonssons saga* (Oslo: 1964), 233.
44. Robberstad (ed. & trans.), *Gulatingslovi*, I-24, I-32, X-9 and XIII-20.
45. J.R. Hagland & J. Sandnes (ed. & trans.), *Frostatingsloven* (Oslo: 1994), II-1 and 45, III-15 and 18, IV-5, 6, 14, 23, 35 and 62, V-29, VIII-16 and IX-10.
46. Hagland & Sandnes (ed. & trans.), *Frostatingsloven*, IV-6.
47. McAuley, *Canon Law*, 474, and Vogt, *The Function of Kinship*, 115.

skuggsià – *The King's Mirror* – from about 1260, the judges have to answer to God for misjudgements due to insufficient investigation of the case.[48] In the Frostating Compilation of Law we find both the problem that the truth became a battle on the numer of witnesses, and an interesting solution to the problem: If two men both can muster witnesses to support their claim, but one has two more witnesses than the other, 12 men shall be appointed to decide the case according to what they find most truthful in the face of God.[49] This provision even has more details on different what-ifs, but it is unnecessary in this context to discuss them. Suffice it to conclude that a jury arrangement, which we find applied in almost one-third of all provisions in the Code of 1274, had the qualities needed to replace the ordeal as a way to settle difficult cases. The jury was partly based on existing legal traditions, and partly on the English jury system.[50] But again, origin was not an issue – it was the qualities of the legal instrument that gave it such a prominent place in Norwegian law from 1274.

But is it really this simple? The preamble of a statute issued in 1302 by King Håkon V, son of King Magnus the Law Mender, states that:

> Sumt man fylgia lagum kirkunnar oc keisarens, en uera skildi rikinu til mykils hafka, oc allu folkenu til mykilla unada er þat byggia. Nu saker þess at uer iattadom gudi i vigslu vara, at uer skuldum þau logh halda oc haldazt leta sem hin helgi Olafr konongr hof oc hans retter eftir komandar hafa sidan til sett og samtyct.[51]

The Norwegian king between 1299 and 1319 hence claimed in the preamble that Roman and Canon law had been harmful for the realm, and the laws to be observed by the inhabitants were those made by St. Olaf and his descendants to the throne. It can hardly be stated more clearly that foreign law is not good law. It is even stated in Old Norse and not Latin, and in an age when Latin was the legal language this was a statement in itself.

---

48. A.W. Brøgger (ed. & trans.), *Kongsspeilet* (Oslo: 2000), e.g. 48-49, 189, 227, 229.
49. Hagland & Sandnes (ed. & trans.), *Frostatingsloven*, XIII-24. The references to God and his role when lawsuits are decided are the same as we find in the *King's Mirror* and in the Code of 1274, and is hence probably from the same time period.
50. J.Ø. Sunde, 'Daughters of God and Counsellors of the Judges of Men – A Study in Changes in the Legal Culture in the Norwegian Realm in the High Middle Ages', in S. Brink & L. Collinson (ed.), *New Approaches to Early Law in Scandinavia* (Turnhout: 2014), 143-161.
51. R. Keyser & P.A. Munch (ed.), *Norges gamle Love indtil 1387* 3: *Lovgivningen efter Kong Magnus Haakonssøns Død 1280 indtil 1387* (Christiania: 1849), 45.

At the same time, this statement is made by a king who ruled the country by a code that is definitely influenced by Roman and Canon law,[52] with the aid of counsellors who had studied Roman and Canon law abroad.[53] Was the king unaware of this? Probably not. The statement has to be read as a warning against accepting law without adjusting it to make it workable. The statement is hence merely a formulation of the old pick-and-choose mentality in Norwegian law.

One could claim that any king would adopt an ideology of adjustment of universal law, because it would serve as a legitimation for bending the law to suit to his personal needs, and not those of society. But King Håkon V himself, both as duke of the eastern part of Norway and the western islands from 1280 till 1299, later king from 1299 till 1319, granted his subjects the right to adjust law.

The Norwegian realm was not a topographically and culturally united territory. Up until the Code of the Realm of 1274, mainland Norway was divided into four legal provinces, partly topographically and culturally different. Even more, Iceland became a part of the Norwegian realm in 1264/65, with a topography and culture quite different from mainland Norway. The same can be said of the other western parts of the realm: Greenland, the Faroe Islands, the Shetlands and the Orkneys. Still, with the advent of the Code of the Realm in 1274, the law of most of the realm was unified. The topographical and cultural differences, of course, remained and were addressed through amendments to the Code for the different parts of the realm. The two first were for mainland Norway, where two of the regions in the eastern, interior part of Norway were granted amendments to the Code in 1293 and 1297 by Duke Håkon.[54]

Iceland was supposed to have its law unified with the law of Frostating in 1271. But the Icelanders refused to adopt more than a tiny fraction of their new compilation of law due to the large portion of foreign law.[55] They finally adopted the *Jarnsiða*, as this compilation of law was later called, in 1273 on the promise that they would soon get a new law. This was issued in

---

52. See K. Robberstad, 'Magnus Lagabøters lovbok', *Medlemsblad for Den norske dommerforening* no. 3 (1974), e.g. 52, 55.
53. K. Helle, *Konge og gode menn i norsk riksstyring ca. 1150-1319* (Bergen: 1972), e.g. 577, 591, 599-600.
54. Keyser & Munch (ed.), *Lovgivningen efter Kong Magnus Haakonssøns Død*, 19-23, 27-30.
55. M.M. Lárusson, 'Járnsiða', *Kulturhistoriskt lexikon för nordisk medeltid* 7 (Viborg: 1962), 566-68.

1281. Again the Icelanders protested, and in 1294, 1305 and 1314 they were granted extensive amendments to the Code by the Norwegian king.[56]

It seems that the Faroe Islands, the Shetlands and the Orkneys were incorporated in the Gulating province in 1267. In 1271 the king had to remind the Faroese that they had been permitted to retain a part of their old laws, but that otherwise they would have to apply the new compilation of law.[57] With the Code of the Realm of 1274 the Faroese once again had their law changed. In 1298 Duke Håkon granted them what is later referred to as the Sheep Letter, which is an amendment to the Code intended for the Faroe Islands.[58]

Summing up, we see that an ideology of adjusting law was not just to protect royal influence on adapted universal law, but an ideology of functionality as the most important feature of law in the High Middle Ages. Thus, even though the origin of law has been underscored as a factor of major importance in the 19th and 20th centuries, we see that origin is of significance only if it does not get in the way of the functionality of law.

What is seen as well functioning law is not the same at all times, in all places and by all people. Instead, it depends on what standard law is measured by. In the High Middle Ages in Norway, the standard for measuring the functionality of law also changed.

The internationalization of law is characterized by individual nations joining a supranational world order. In Europe, the Peace of Westphalia in 1648 can be regarded as the foundation of this supranational world order, since it marks the beginning of public international law, from which for example the European Human Rights, EU law, UN law and WTO law have developed. Still, public international law had existed for a long time, not least during the heyday of the nation state, before a supranational world order emerged following the Second World War. The aftermath of the Second World War, economic growth, the fall of the Berlin Wall and the technological revolution have made a supranational world order a fact of everyday life, rather than a mere political vision, for the citizens of Europe and the world. The internationalization of law is hence a response to an internationalization of society. If we hardly notice the degree to which law today is based on sources produced outside the jurisdictional borders of the nation state, it is because law and society reflect the same kind of social reality, and hence law is found to cause little friction.

Before the Peace of Westphalia in 1648 Christianity constituted the world order in Europe and was made an operational factor in society in the western and middle part of the continent by the supranational Catholic

---

56. G. Storm (ed.), *Norges gamle Love indtil 1387* 4: *indeholdende Supplementer til de tre foregaaende Bind samt Haandskriftbeskrivelse med Facsimiler* (1888), 341-53.
57. Storm (ed.), *Supplementer til de tre foregaaende Bind*, 353-54.
58. Keyser & Munch (ed.), *Lovgivningen efter Kong Magnus Haakonssøns Død*, 33-39.

Church. When they were eventually incorporated into this Christian world order, all the Nordic countries would change their view of when law would cause friction in society.

From a Norwegian perspective, individual and subjective responsibility would have been known before the 13th century, when it became a part of law in the different legal provinces. This is so because the notion of individual and subjective responsibility was developed within Irish law from the 8th century and onward.[59] In Ireland, kings would act as judges, and Norwegian chieftains and kings would hence become acquainted with Irish law in their strongholds of Dublin, Wexford, Waterford, Cork and Limerick, where they reigned as local kings. Still, it was first a couple of centuries after the Christianization of Norway that the notion of individual and subjective responsibility became a part of Norwegian law. It was not until Christianity was developed as a system of law, particularly beginning in the mid-12th century, after it had changed not only people's habits but even values, after the torments of the civil wars between 1130 and 1223, and after Christianity had made operational effective lines of communication between Norway and the intellectual and political centres at the continent, that Norwegian law changed in terms of the idea of individual and subjective responsibility. This change in law occurred only after other changes had taken place, and what would have created friction in society was a smoothening factor instead.

This can be exemplified by looking at the provisions concerning repayment of debt in the Gulating Compilation and the Code of the Realm of 1274, where the provision in the latter is based on the provision in the first. According to the Gulating Compilation, debt must be paid, and if the debtor cannot fulfil his obligations, he becomes a debt slave – he has to work for the creditor until the debt is paid and can be forced to work with accompanying beatings to both the upper and lower parts of the body.[60] According to the Code of the Realm of 1274, debt must be paid. The exception is if the debtor is subject to an accident that deprives him of the ability to fulfil his obligations. In such cases, the debtor does not have to pay until he is able to do so. But if the debtor is able, but unwilling to fulfil his obligations, he becomes a debt slave also according to the Code of 1274. And if the debtor escapes his enslavement, he is to be punished. The exception is if the debtor escapes in order to fulfil obligations having higher priority than repaying his debt;[61] this would include, for example, providing for his family. While any unfortunate person could become a debt slave according to the Gulating Compilation, only a lazy person with no one to

---

59. F. Kelly, *A guide to early Irish law* (Dublin: 2001), 149-57.
60. Robberstad (ed. & trans.), *Gulatingslovi*, IV-15
61. A. Taranger (ed. & trans.), *Magnus Lagabøters landslov* (Kristiania: 1915), VIII-5.

provide for could become a debt slave according to the Code of 1274. The change in terms of debt repayment is due to the Christianization of Norwegian society and all the already mentioned factors of a change in world view.

So when we ask How Nordic are the Nordic Medieval Laws?, we have to keep in mind that law is not only a question of local and national circumstances, but also of the world order overarching them. When this world order changes, the view on how law functions in society also changes. And law that is in accordance with the world order will not seem foreign, whatever its origins.

4. Conclusions

Nordic medieval legal history changed in 2003 with the First Carlsberg Conference on Medieval Legal History. From this point on, the idea of an internationalization of law in the Middle Ages has no longer been an enigma. However, ten years later we still need to further investigate the phenomenon. My contribution is to begin with the internationalization of law today to enable us to overcome the prejudice of the 19th and 20th centuries that good law is local and national law, by asking the question How Nordic are Nordic Laws? Proceeding from this, I have directed the focus from the origin of law to the functionality of law. Such a change in focus is the next step which, according to my observations, is emerging within the research tradition that has dominated Nordic medieval legal history since the conference in 2003. This research is important not only to understand the law of the Middle Ages, but also to understand the law of the present.

RIGHTS, OBLIGATIONS, DOMESTIC RELATIONS, AND *'IUS NATURALE'*, THE RIGHT ORDER OF THINGS: A STRATEGY FOR RESEARCH INTO THE NORDIC MEDIEVAL LAWS

Helle I.M. Sigh and Helle Vogt

1. Introduction

The purpose of this article is to present a preliminary research strategy for investigating domestic relations laws within the body of medieval Nordic provincial and national laws, formulated in a close dialogue with old customs and learned law in the dynamic and transformative political era of the 12th and 13th centuries; and thus to continue the last ten years of research into the medieval Nordic laws and the influence of learned law on the Nordic realms.[1] The approach will be exemplified by analyzing examples from the Nordic laws to illustrate how this strategy could be taken further. This article is thus intended more as an approach to studying the Nordic laws than as an exhaustive comparative analysis of the laws themselves.

It is an anthropologic assertion that every society establishes formal and informal rules to regulate conduct, or what might be defined as 'social ordering' between individuals and/or groups. In this context Clifford Geertz has argued that analyzing a legal system/regulations (oral or written) of a

---

1. For the last few decades legal historians have emphasized the importance of learned law in their studies of the medieval Nordic Laws. This influence was also the focus of the first Carlsberg Conference in 2003. See P. Andersen, D. Tamm & H. Vogt (eds.), *How Nordic are the Nordic laws?* (Copenhagen: 2011 – 2nd edn).

society provides a way of understanding its value systems and normative orders and of exploring the relationship between law and culture, viewing law as constitutive of cultural practices and itself defined by culture.[2] Hence, particular legal phenomena, especially in legal contexts, relate to such matters as ideology, social class, and gender. In this context some legal phenomena may be understood to refer to a kind of universal logic – such as the correlative categories 'right' and 'duty' which will be the focus of this article – which is imbued with different cultural meanings depending on time and place.

When reading through the Nordic laws it is evident that the reciprocal categories of 'right' and 'duty' appear as important structuring elements, regulating mechanisms in relation to human interactions which give the laws an internal cohesion and extend transversely across different legal areas. In this article we will investigate the logic behind the interrelated legal categories by deconstructing the language of the laws. Following Geertz's reasoning, it is our hypothesis that the construction of domestic relations laws within the body of medieval Nordic laws was influenced by and to some extent constructed as a response to *ius naturale*, that is the canonistic categories of thought as expressed in the juristic vocabulary of natural right and obligations in the 12th and 13th centuries.[3] This normative order was founded on the following theological reasoning: In creating man and woman, God instituted the human family and endowed it with its fundamental constitution. Its members were persons equal in dignity, and the natural relationship of the family led to certain expectations and responsibilities on the part of all concerned, reflecting a coherent system of interlocking rights and duties that thus arose from natural obligations between marital partners, their children, and also their families of origin. The natural relationship of the family was articulated as existing for the common good of its members and of society.[4]

---

2. C. Geertz, *Local Knowledge: further essays in interpretive anthropology* (New York: 1983); see also L. Rosen, *The anthropology of justice: law as culture in Islamic society* (Cambridge: 1989).
3. The law of nature in relation to the Roman concept of *ius gentium* was not formulated before the 16th and 17th centuries, but the law of nature implies the conceptualization of medieval categories of thought about the right order of things as a foundation for, e.g., human rights.
4. For a discussion of *ius naturale* and the reasoning behind conceptions of 'rights', 'duties' and 'obligations' between parents and children in the canonical texts and to some extent theological ones, see Ch.J. Reid Jr., *Power over the Body, Equality in the Family: Rights and Domestic Relations in Medieval Canon Law*, (Grand Rapids: 2004), 1-25, 170.

Rights, Obligations, Domestic Relations

The present article will advance our hypothesis and exemplify our approach by investigating three legal areas related to the relationship between parent and child: paternal governance, inheritance rights in relation to legitimate children, and house-leading.

2. Previous research into domestic relations laws

In the last twenty years medieval legal historians have investigated the legal cultures of the Nordic realms from an international perspective, focusing on such topics as the impact of canon law on the Nordic laws. In the course of research into law and domestic relations, several theses have been proposed as to the legal impact of the canonistic principles of *libertas matrimonii* (the right and freedom of the individual to choose a spouse) upon the formation of marriage, and *depitum conjugale* (the reciprocal rights and duties between the marital partners with respect to coitus, *depitum carnale*, and the living out of marital life in general) upon domestic relations, in connection with such issues as authority, property rights, and inheritance rights.[5]

Some studies have focused on the development of individual rights, conjugal rights, and the rights of the family of origin or kin and the limitation of these legal rights in relation to, for example, the right to contract marriage even in the face of familial opposition. Looking at the emancipating potential of *libertas matrimonii*, legal historians have argued that the Nordic laws show a tension between the individual and the kin groups on both sides. Secular law showed the acceptance of the freedom to contract marriage, but still recognized the traditional authority of the father/guardian of the woman. A legal marriage was based upon the woman's guardian's consent as well as the consent of the couple. A clandestine marriage without parental consent was valid, but not legal. Thus legal and social control (most often, of the daughter) was commonly established through property or

---

5. Nordic legal historians build their scholarly work on a long tradition. Since the 1970s the formation of marriage in canon law and its impact on secular law in different regions has been the subject of great scholarly interest. See for example M.M. Sheehan, *Marriage, Family, and Law in Medieval Europe: Collected Studies* (Toronto: 1996); J. Goody, *The Development of Family and Marriage in Europe* (Cambridge: 1983); J.A. Brundage, *Law, Sex, and Christian Society in Medieval Europe* (Chicago: 1987); R.H. Helmholz, *Marriage Litigation in Medieval England* (Cambridge: 1974); Ph.L. Reynolds & J. Witte Jr. (ed.), *To Have and to Hold. Marrying and Its Documentation in Western Christendom, 400-1600* (Cambridge: 2007).

inheritance rights that secured some rights to the guardian.[6] Other legal historians have examined familial authority in connection with the way property rights were allocated in the community of property between husband and wife and the family of origin/kin, and the tension between the authority of the father/husband and the concept of pre-emption to land ('*odelsrett*'/'*lovbydelse*') that arose from the impact from canon law on the kinship-based society characteristic of the Nordic realms.[7]

Another school has, on the other hand, looked at 'duties'. Helle Vogt's comparative study on the Nordic laws focuses on the impact on different legal areas of what Vogt calls a 'canonical kinship ideology', which originated from a theological understanding that all Christians had a natural 'duty' or 'obligation' to love blood relatives. Vogt's arguments follow the results found in both Lars Ivar Hansen and Michael H. Gelting's discussions of new modes of thinking and relating to kinship in the Nordic laws.[8]

6. M. Korpiola, *Between Betrothal and Bedding: Marriage Formation in Sweden 1200-1600* (Leiden & Boston: 2009), chap. 3; A.S. Arnórsdóttir, *Property and Virginity: The Christianization of Marriage in Medieval Iceland 1200-1600* (Århus: 2010), chap. 3.2; H.I.M. Sigh, *Samtykke og samfund. Kristningen af ægteskabet i Danmark ca. 1200-1600* (Unpublished Dissertation, Århus: 2011), 92-96. This practice was accepted by some canonists in the beginning of the 13th century as for example by Johannes Teutonicus in *Glossa Ordinariae* (1215). Brundage, *Law, Sex, and Christian Society*, 397 (*Glos. Ord.* to C. 36 q. 1 c. 3 v. *excusata* and C. 36 q. 2 c. 4 v. *nullatenus*). But the legal sanction became much debated during the 13th and 14th centuries, because it was seen as obstructing the principle of *libertas matrimonii*. Already in a papal decretal included in the *Liber extravagantium decretalium* from 1234 it was stated that penalty clauses attached to the engagements of minors were contrary to the right and freedom to contract marriage (X.4.1.29). R.H. Helmholz, *The Spirit of Classical Canon Law* (Athens (GA) & London: 1996), 238; Korpiola, *Between Betrothal and Bedding*, 173. The same point was made later by Johannes Andreae in the 14th century. T. Dean, 'Fathers and Daughters: Marriage Laws and Marriage Disputes in Bologna and Italy, 1200-1500', in K.J.P. Lowe & T. Dean (ed.), *Marriage in Italy 1300-1650* (Cambridge: 2002), 93.

7. See L.I. Hansen, 'Slekskap, eiendom og sosiale strategier i nordisk middelalder', *Collegium Medievale* 7:2 (Oslo: 1995), 103-54; M.H. Gelting, 'Odelsrett – lovbydelse – bördsrätt – retrait lignager: Kindred and Land in the Nordic Countries in the Twelfth and Thirteenth Centuries', in L.I. Hansen (ed.), *Family, Marriage and Property Devolution in the Middle Ages* (Tromsø: 2000), 133-65.

8. H. Vogt, *The Function of Kinship in Medieval Nordic Legislation* (Leiden & Boston: 2010). Vogt has shown the impact of canonical kinship ideology on the structuring of Nordic laws, which provided different rights, obligations, and responsibilities to the members of the household and the wider kin group. The ideology is, for example, visible in relation to the concept *wergeld,* which obligated the closest kin to pay a part of the fine imposed for homicide. See L.I. Hansen, 'The Concept of Kinship According to the West Nordic Medieval Laws', in Andersen, Tamm & Vogt (ed.),

To summarize, previous scholarship has stressed that the canonistic notions of natural right and natural law entailed new ways of thinking about domestic relations laws, but by the same token these notions gave rise to internal tension between 1) patriarchalisation and individual freedom 2) hierarchy and equality 3) the family of origin (kin) and the marital partners. This tension was also embedded in the canonistic categories of thought.[9] From these assumptions, scholars have drawn two overriding conclusions. It has been argued, firstly, that the Nordic laws reflect a development towards greater emphasis on human freedom and individual rights which, in relation to domestic relations, is seen by these scholars as the influence of the theologians seeking to explicate the demands of a sacramental teaching which thus had an impact on law; and secondly, that there was to some extent an incipient movement towards a prioritizing of the nuclear family.[10] But it must be stressed that this development was far from linear and unambiguous, as shown by both Gelting and Hansen in their studies of the logic of and strategies for transferring property in relation to the concepts of *odelsrett/lovbydelse*.[11]

> *How Nordic*, 177-206; M.H. Gelting, 'Odelsrett – lovbydelse – bördsrätt – retrait lignager', 149; M.H. Gelting, 'Marriage, Peace and the Canonical Incest Prohibition: Making Sense of Absurdity?', in M. Korpiola (ed.), *Nordic Perspectives on Medieval Canon Law* (Saarijärvi: 1999), 98-118.

9. An example is the discussions of the validity of marriage without parental consent. Parents had the right and duty to give their daughters away in marriage, but a sacramental marriage was constituted solely by the consent of the couple, even though it was considered an illicit act. Man and woman had the right to marry, but also the duty to follow their parents' guidance. *Decretum* C.32.q.2 d.p.c. 12: 'Cum dicitur: paterno arbitrio feminae iunctae uiris, datur intelligi, quod paternus consensus desideratur in nuptiis, nec sine eo legitimae nuptiae habeantur, iuxta illud Euaristi Papae: Aliter non fit legitimum coniugium, nisi a parentibus tradatur'. *Corpus Iuris Canonici*, in Lipsiensis secunda post Aemilii Ludovici Richteri curas, ad librorum manu scriptorium et editionis Romanae fidem recognovit et adnotatione critica instruxit Aaemilius Friedberg (Leipzig: 1879-1881). For a discussion of this passage, see Brundage, *Law, Sex, and Christian Society*, 238; M.M. Sheehan, 'Choice of Marriage Partner in the Middle Ages: Development and Theory of Marriage', in Sheehan, *Marriage, Family, and Law*, 87, 97.
10. In 1995 the Danish historian Helge Paludan argued that two cultural systems in relation to family-structure were visible in the Danish source material, but by around 1200 the laws reflected a linear development from prioritizing the *familia* towards a focus on a new family-model: the nuclear family. H. Paludan, *Familia til familie. To europæiske kulturelementers møde i højmiddelalderens Danmark* (Århus: 1995).
11. Paludan has been criticized for ignoring the complexity of the laws in his cultural analysis of the Danish source material. See e.g. M.H. Gelting, 'Det komparative perspektiv i dansk højmiddelalderforskning: Om familia og familie, lid, leding og landeværn', *Historisk Tidsskrift* (Denmark) (1999), 146-88.

Our endeavor is thus to combine these two 'schools' by looking at the articulated reciprocal system of rights and corresponding duties. And it is our contention that investigating these two categories and their function in the laws will generate new perspectives and new ways to comprehend domestic relations laws.

3. A legal conceptualizing of the natural order of things: *ius naturale*

In theorizing about the nature of the *ius naturale*, the canonists of the 12th and 13th centuries explored in profound and sophisticated ways the demands placed on marital partners and their children and the claims that they could make by virtue of the 'right order of things'.[12]

The legal historian Charles J. Reid, building on Brian Tierney's extensive work on the development of a juristic language of rights, has shown that in the 12th and 13th centuries the concept of *ius naturale* was re-formulated as a synthesis between individual rights, reflecting a new theological and legal preoccupation with human freedom, and individual obligation in contemporary canon law.[13] As shown by Tierney, the meaning of the word *ius* changed during this period. In the writings of Roman jurists and in early medieval ecclesiastic writing, the semantic meaning of *ius* was 'law' or 'right order'. But in the *Decretum Gratiani* and later canonistic writing, the word was used to signify the claim of individuals as well.[14]

The canonists thus created the concept of possession and free exercise of rights within a legal framework and thereby under legal protection. But the notion of right articulated in the canonistic texts, as will be shown, reflected the proper exercise of human freedom within the constraints of *ius naturale* (which also entailed duties) and within the context of Christian society, thus seeing natural rights and community life as compatible phenomena.[15]

The juristic language in the canonistic texts was, however, constructed in intertextuality. The canonists inherited a substantial body of teaching and

---

12. Beginning with *Decretum* C.VII, 'Quid sit ius naturale'. For a thorough investigation of the canonists and their elaboration on the right order of things, see Reid Jr., *Power over the Body*, passim.
13. Reid Jr., *Power over the Body*, 18-19.
14. B. Tierney, *Idea of Natural Rights: Studies on Natural Rights, Natural Laws, and Church Law, 1150-1625* (Atlanta GA: 1997), 56-58; Reid Jr., *Power over the Body*, 19. But it is evident that the 13th century decretalists used the word as a synonym for inherently subjective terms such as *potestas* (power), *facultas* (faculty), *libertas* (liberty) and *immunitas* (immunity).
15. U. Mosiek, *Kirchliches Eherecht* (Freiburg: 1976), 44.

Rights, Obligations, Domestic Relations

law from late antiquity. For example, the rights language in Roman classical law was to some extent used by the canonists to describe domestic relations in relation to paternal governance, conceptualized as *patria potestas*, which in Roman law meant the authority the head of the household, typically the father, asserted over its members.[16] The influence of patristic fathers such as Augustine is also evident and is referred to in the canonists' discussions.

4. The natural relationship of the family: Paternal governance

The family was in God's plan. Marriage was seen as a part of a special or rational natural law, and the family was composed of a man and a woman united in marriage, together with their offspring. The conjugal community was established upon the consent of the spouses, and building on the patristic tradition, marriage existed for the good of the spouses and for the procreation and upbringing of children.[17]

The natural relationship of the family defined expectations and responsebilities for both parents and children. The reciprocal conjugal rights and duties arose from a natural obligation that was founded on a communityminded sacramental notion of marriage (*depitum conjugale*), which was defined first and foremost in terms of the exchange of rights to the body (*depitum carnale*), but which also embraced the wider concept of the reciprocal rights and duties within an intimate community of life. This perception echoed an old concept drawn from Roman law: the idea that marriage itself was a *consortium omnis vitae* a 'companionship of one's entire life'.[18] In this context the canonists took both the physical and spiritual needs of the marital partners into account. Despite a new interest in individual rights, marital life was thus primarily about community formation. The couple should not pursue personal interests, but should be engaged in meeting one another's needs. Thus, marriage was the organizational

16. Mosiek, *Kirchliches Eherecht*, 69.
17. *Decretum* C. VII: 'Ius naturale est commune omnium nationum, eo quod ubique instinctu naturae, non constitutione aliqua habetur, ut uiri et feminae coniunctio, liberorum successio et educatio, communis omnium possessio et omnium una libertas, acquisitio eorum, quae celo, terra marique capiuntur; item depositae rei uel commendatae pecuniae restitutio, uiolentiae per uim repulsio'. This line of naturalistic reasoning can be seen in Augustine's texts, e.g. Augustine, 'De Bono Coniugali', 1.1, 2-3 and 17.19, 36-37, in P.G. Walsh ed. and trans. (Oxford: 2001). This quotation also echoed Roman law as it was reproduced through the text of Isodore of Seville (Isidor.eod.c.4). See also Reid Jr., *Power over the Body*, 77.
18. Digest 23.2.1. 'Nuptiae sunt coniunctio maris et feminae et consortium omnis vitae, divini et humani iuris communicatio'. *Corpus Iuris Civilis* I-III, ed by Th. Mommsen, P. Krueger, R. Schoeel & G. Kroll (Berlin: 1963-1966).

frame for earthly life based on a spiritual, social, and legal interdependence between husband and wife, which existed for the continuation of mankind and Christianity.[19]

The canonists' family constellation took substantial notice of the children's needs. Parents had a natural duty and obligation to procreate and afterwards to provide for the nurture of their offspring, not only providing them with protection, food, drink, and proper clothing, but also attending to their moral education and spiritual formation.[20] These duties were considered by the canonists as important for creating conjugal harmony – a concept that later developed into one of marital love (an emotional category) – and were primordial and inalienable obligations; a line of reasoning which was founded on the Scriptures. On the other hand, children were expected to reciprocate by honouring their parents, demonstrating respect (filial *pietas*) toward them by true docility and obedience.[21] Furthermore, as the influential canonist of the 13th century Bernard of Parma († 1263) argued, parents and offspring were obligated to see to each other's welfare in time of need, thus obligating children to provide for their parents' welfare in old age.[22] In the summa of Hostiensis (1200-1271) the reasoning became encapsulated in the concept of *pietas* founded on an idea of a transcendent familial 'duty', which referred not only to the maintenance of proper deference and respect in earthly domestic relationships, but might also connote the respect and obeisance owed to God.[23]

---

19. Sigh, *Samtykke og samfund*, 40-44.
20. Ph. Aries, *Centuries of Childhood: A Social History of Family Life*, trans. R. Baldick, (New York: 1962), 353.
21. The fourth commandment is addressed expressly to children and their relationship to their father and mother, and can be characterized as the order of charity. God had willed that after him, children should honor their parents, to whom they owed life and who had handed on to them the knowledge of God. They were obligated to honor and respect all those whom God, for the good of mankind, had vested with his authority. In a theological reading of this commandment, it could be argued that it likewise concerns the ties of kinship between members of the 'extended family', requiring honor, affection, and gratitude toward elders and ancestors, and perhaps illuminates other relationships in society as well. Thus the fourth commandment can be read as a social doctrine for the right order of society.
22. Reid, Jr., *Power over the Body*, 84.
23. The idea of the transcendent familial system of correlative rights and duties – the natural reciprocity based on the right order God made for his creation, had a place in a wider juristic vocabulary. The influential canonist of the13th century Hostiensis transferred the notion onto the relationship between patron and freeman (*obsequiem*): *Hostiensis*, Summa, bk. III, sec. 11, Henricus de Segusio, Hostiensis, Summa (Apud Ivntas: 1962). For a discussion of the development of the notion of *pietas*, see Reid, Jr., *Power over the Body*, 172.

In this context, as other scholars have noted, the canonists employed a rights-vocabulary in which male dominion represented the natural order of things, thus enhancing the power of the husband and father in relation to the governance of the household.[24] This power could, however, be rescinded in cases of maltreatment. On the occasions when the canonists discussed paternal power, they emphasized that this right was not to be used abusively, but was to be employed for the building up of Christian familial love, thereby synthesizing the demands of Christian charity with a canonical view of familial welfare, as argued by Charles Reid. In the *Summa Parisiensis* on the *Decretum Gratiani* it was indicated that paternal power used capriciously could affect the father or husband's spiritual condition, because by his violation of God's will, he committed a sin.[25] But Reid has argued that the canonists conceptualized a framework in which the right to paternal power might be lost through fault, through emancipation, or through operation of law.[26] Thus, paternal power or governance (consisting of both rights and duties and founded on natural obligations) was not easily lost, but not constructed as absolute.

The Nordic laws include language that addresses the right of paternal power. It was the householder (Sweden, Norway, Denmark: *husbonde/bonde*, Finland: *isäntä, isä* (father), Iceland: *húsbóndi, -búandi, bóndi, búandi*) who had the right to govern the family. As with the Roman concept of *patria potestas*, this extended to a right to govern the entire household. The authority that the head of the household asserted over its members was typically exercised by the husband/father.[27] Stig Iuul has argued in a Danish context that before the laws were written down, the father's position may have been even more patriarchal in relation to such matters as children's inheritance rights; an argument which, because of the lack of source material, can be made only speculatively.[28]

In the Nordic laws we have examples of how the father's rights to govern were restricted by his duties, which were based on his obligations toward the household. The nexus of rights and duties between father, mother, and children can be seen very clearly in a chapter in the Law of Jutland, one of the three Danish provincial laws, which covered Jutland and Funen and was

---

24. *Decretum* C. 33, q. 5, c 11: 'Manifestum est, ita voluisse legem feminam sub viro esse [...]'; C. 33, q. 5, c. 12: 'Est ordo naturalis [...] ut feminae serviant viris, et filii parentibus, quia in illis hec iusticia est, ut maiori serviat minor'.
25. *Summa Parisiensis* C. 33, q. 5, c. 11, v. *manifestum est*, ed. by T.P. McLaughlin (Toronto: 1952), 254.
26. Reid, Jr., *Power over the Body*, 94-97.
27. S. Iuul, 'Husbonde', in *Kulturhistorisk Leksikon for nordisk middelalder fra vikingetid til reformationstid* VII (København: 1962), 96-103.
28. Iuul, 'Husbonde', 100.

written down in 1241. Because the chapter concerns sacrilege, it is only to be expected that it would bear some relationship to the canonistic juristic vocabulary of natural right, but the fact that sacrilege is integrated into secular law indicates that the law makers had the intention of incorporating the natural relationship between parents and offspring into the law and thus into medieval society. The chapter states:

> It is not possible for a man to commit sacrilege against his wife or his children, as long as they are in his household, unless he gives his wife and children wounds with the point or the edge of a blade, or breaks their bones, because he shall only discipline them with a stick or with water, if they violate the rules/behave badly, and not with weapons. The same rules apply to his rights in relation to servants in the household. But it is possible for the wife to commit sacrilege against her husband. It is possible for children to commit sacrilege against their parents at any time [...][29]

The father had a right to discipline his wife and children, his (extended) family, but at the same time he was under the obligation to discipline in the right manner. In this context, the paternal right to govern the children contained within itself not only the freedom to judge how to raise one's children and the authority to act upon one's judgment, but the obligation that this be done adequately and appropriately. Paternal power was a right, but it also entailed a duty to see to the proper 'education' of the children. If the father did not act upon a crime of sacrilege the king's representative could raise the case at the local assembly.[30]

Looking from a gendered perspective, previous research has emphasized the strong patriarchal elements in the Nordic medieval laws in relation to authority in the household. And, true, this structure of patriarchal dominance can most certainly be localized. But despite the power inherent in the patriarchal structure, a double role of the father and husband as both commanding (rights) and protecting (duties, based on obligations) within the household is evident – in this context, protecting the child against sin by disciplining or 'educating' him or her. Furthermore the law can be read in relation to the right to discipline, which the children were expected to reciprocate by honouring their parents and through that, God. Here the

29. Man ma a siin hwsfrø oc sinæ børn thær I fællagh æræ mæth hanum æi hælæct a brytæ. Vtæn han wæthær thæm saar mæth od æth æg. Æth slaær limmæ syndær. For thy at han scal ræfsæ thæm of the brytæ mæth staf æth mæth wand. Oc æi mæth wapnæ. Swo ær thæt oc vm leghæ hioon. Æn a hwsbond ma hwsfro wal hælæct brytæ a. Børn a theræ for ældær mughæ allæ timæ ars hælæct brytæ [...] *Danmarks gamle Landskabslove* (hereafter: *DGL*) II, *Jyske Lov*, ed. by P. Skautrup (Copenhagen: 1933), book II, chap. 81, 286-88.
30. *DGL* II, *Jyske Lov,* book II, chap. 81, 288.

Rights, Obligations, Domestic Relations

crime of sacrilege is read as blasphemous behaviour; the act of depriving something of its sacred character – that is, a violation of the fourth commandment of the Decalogue to 'Honour thy father and thy mother'.

In the Nordic laws there are additional examples of the father's obligation to see to his children's need for sustenance and support. He had the natural guardianship and the legal obligation to protect his children, and protection of a person can be read among other things as a matter of care. But the logic behind the letter of the law must be explored further and in more detail. By looking at both 'right' and 'duty', the traditional interpretation of the authority of the householder/father – paternal governance – might be revisited and understood in a more nuanced way. Furthermore, it is important to take into consideration what is *not* articulated in the language of the law.

It must be mentioned that it did matter in relation to paternal governance if the father was the natural father. A stepfather had very limited legal rights in the Nordic laws. In general, when the biological father died the obligation to defend and protect the child was handed over to the closest relative.[31]

5. The natural relationship of the family: The natural rights of legitimate children

Canon law asserted that legitimate children (*naturales*) had a claim to a part of their parents' property by virtue of natural law: a claim to the 'legitimate portion' (*legitima portio*) which was owed to them by nature (*naturae debitum*) and was theirs by right.[32]

A synthesis of legitimacy and inheritance rights was established in the canonistic texts. In this context scholars have shown that the relationship between the parents affected the legal status of the child with respect to the right of inheritance.[33] The canonists clearly affirmed that all illegitimate children were entitled to adequate maintenance and support from their mother and from their father to some extent, if his identity was known or could be proved.[34] Only a child from an illicit sexual relationship, that is, a

---

31. In one of the Danish provincial laws, the Danish Law of Jutland, the guardianship of the stepfather depended on the acceptance of the closest of relatives. *DGL* II, *Jyske Lov,* book I, chap. 30, 75-79.
32. For a splendid discussion of the synthesis of legitimacy and inheritance rights in the canonistic texts see Reid Jr., *Power over the Body*, 152-210.
33. L. Mayali, 'Note on the Legitimization per Subsequent Marriage from Alexander III to Innocent III', in L. Mayali & S.A. Tibbetts (ed.), *The Two Laws: Studies in Medieval Legal History Dedicated to Stephen Kuttner* (Washington D.C.: 1990), 63.
34. R.H. Helmholz, *The Oxford History of the Laws of England: The Canon Law and Ecclesiastical Jurisdiction from 597 to the 1640s* (Oxford: 2004), 560.

child from a relationship which never could become a marriage, could be excluded from inheritance, on the grounds that he or she fell outside the scope of natural law.[35] Thus, the boundaries of the child's claim were set by the nature of the relationship that the parents had with one another. A natural right was the outcome of birth within a marital union, not the result of simply being born into the world.

The system that gradually prevailed in Scandinavia for succession to an inheritance was that the inheritance went directly to all legitimate children in a linear fashion, within the restricted conjugal family.[36] Inheritance did, however, privilege the male sex, giving daughters only half of the portion given to sons.[37] This was the system in all the Danish laws, and it has been convincingly suggested that it was introduced around 1170, when strict laws of succession in relation to inheritance replaced an earlier practice whereby the testator had much more freedom to dispose his property.[38] In Norway and in the Götalands from at least the 12th century men and patrilaterally related relatives (agnates) took precedence in inheritance over women and the matrilineal kin group (enates).[39] This was changed in Sweden around 1260, according to the legend retold in the *Chronicle of Duke Erik* from the 1320s in connection with the marriage between Sophia, daughter of the Danish king Erik IV, and Valdemar of Sweden. Valdemar's father, earl Birger, the de facto ruler of Sweden, promulgated a law establishing that a

---

35. H. Sigh, 'Creating Legal Identities: Children's Property Rights in Danish Medieval Law and the Meaning of Paternity', in P. Andersen (ed.), *Arverettens Handlingsrom. Strategier, relasjoner og historisk utvikling, 1100-2000* (Tromsø: 2011), 19-21; Korpiola, *Between Betrothal and Bedding*, 237.
36. Mia Korpiola and Helle Sigh have argued, with respect to the influence of canon law on the medieval Nordic laws in relation to inheritance rights, that the Danish and Swedish laws reflect a partial acceptance of the three categories of legal identities in canon law, *legitimus*, *naturalis* and *spurius*. See Korpiola, *Between Betrothal and Bedding*, 239. Sigh, *Samtykke og samfund*, 162-64.
37. With respect to later generations in a Danish context, the laws of Scania and Zealand operated on the principle of *gangarv*, meaning that great-grandchildren, irrespective of gender, were treated equally (*divisio in capita*). See Sigh, 'Creating Legal Identities', 17. As for the treatment of later generations in the Norwegian national law, a man's sons took precedence over their paternal grandfather, the man's father. The legal rights of daughters' children were improved as well, but they came after their paternal grandfather. S. Iuul, 'Arveret', in *Kulturhistorisk Leksikon for Nordisk Middelalder fra vikingetid til reformationstid* 1 (København: 1956), 258-66, at 265.
38. See B. & P. Sawyer, *Medieval Scandinavia: From Conversion to Reformation, circa 800-1500* (Minneapolis: 1993), 169.
39. On paternal dominance see Hansen, 'The Concept of Kinship', 182; T.A. Vestergaard, 'The System of Kinship in Early Norwegian Law', *Medieval Scandinavia* 12 (1988), 175.

Rights, Obligations, Domestic Relations

daughter took half as much as a son.[40] This principle was also reflected in subsequent Swedish laws. In Norway, where there was also a clear royal interest in giving daughters the right to take inheritance together with sons, the same principle was introduced in the National Law of 1274.[41] Later the same rules were introduced in Iceland.[42] By at the end of the 13th century, the 'Danish' inheritance principle had prevailed in all the Nordic kingdoms.

The rules of succession in relation to inheritance confirmed that all legitimate children had a natural claim to inheritance; a principle that must be seen as being in agreement with the canonists and their juristic vocabulary. Even 'the privilege of sex', which the Danish archbishop Anders Sunesen identified as 'natural' in his learned explanation of the Law of Scania in the early 13th century, can be seen in this light.[43] Arguably, because the man was supposed to be the head of the household and support his family, for him to receive a larger portion of the inheritance could be said to be fair and most of all, natural. Thus, inheritance or property was in this discourse vested in both males and females in a manner linked to the perception of the sexual division of labour that was founded on the right order of things.

Table 1. Legitimate children's rights to inherit a parent's separate/inherited property

Sweden/-Finland *Urban*	Daughters and sons take equal shares after 1350.
Sweden/-Finland *Rural*	Daughters take a half share, sons a whole share.
Denmark	Daughters take a half share, sons a whole share from the 1170s on.
Norway	Daughters take a half share, sons a whole share after 1274.
Iceland	Daughters take a half share, sons a whole share after 1281.

To summarize, the Nordic inheritance rules with respect to legitimate children can be read as mirroring the natural relationship of the family, or

40. Iuul, 'Arveret', 261-63. In the oldest version of the Law of Västergötland daughters' legal right to inheritance was contingent on the absence of legitimate sons.
41. But there was still a much stronger patrilineal element than in the Danish laws and Swedish laws. Iuul 'Arveret', 264-66.
42. A.G. Magnúsdóttir, 'Islänningarna och arvsrätten 1264-1281', in *Arverettens Handlingsrom. Strategier, relasjoner og historisk utvikling, 1100-2000*, 35.
43. *DGL* I:2, *Anders Sunesens Parafrase*, ed. by S. Aakjær & E. Kroman (Copenhagen: 1933), chap. 14, 480.

the ideology of *ius naturale*, by giving legitimate children a natural right to inheritance, even though inheritance rights varied in relation to gender.

This right was, however, restricted in some of the Nordic laws in different ways. For example, a daughter who married without the consent of her father or guardian lost her right to her part of inheritance, because she was disobedient. In the Laws of Jutland the right was only lost for the woman's lifetime; after her death her part went to her legitimate children.[44] This type of sanction was recommended by some of the canonists. In *Glossae Ordinariae* (1215) Teutonicus suggested a possible legal sanction of this type against a daughter who was under twenty-five years of age and still *filiafamilias* – a clear inspiration from Roman law – and who married without permission from her family.[45] The underlying rationale was natural law. This kind of sanction became much debated in the following centuries, however, because it was seen as contrary to the main principle of *libertas matrimonium*.[46] In the Norwegian law of the realm a woman who had lost her honour was not allowed to inherit together with her brother.[47]

Finally, it must be noted that the natural 'duties' of the children are not elaborated upon very explicitly in the Nordic laws. Nevertheless, what we have shown by looking at the inheritance rights of daughters and the limitations to those rights is that behind the material need to control the transmission of property – which is the main object of the regulation of property rights – there existed a moral obligation or duty for a child (in this case the daughter, but it can be seen in relation to sons as well) to be obedient toward the head of the household or the father, who had the natural authority in the household.

6. House-leading: A legal conceptualization of the natural relationship between parent and child?

Classical notions of *ius naturale* included the belief that kinship, and especially parenthood – relations between children and parents – entailed

---

44. *DGL* II, *Jyske Lov*, book I, chap. 33, 82-84. It was a woman's right to choose a husband, and the solemnization of a marriage was a sacrament only if the marriage was freely entered into by both parties. Without parental consent, however, the marriage was considered clandestine and therefore illicit in legal terms.
45. Brundage, *Law, Sex, and Christian Society*, 397.
46. The *Liber Extra* includes a papal decretal to the effect that secular punishment for clandestine marriage was against the principle of freedom to contract marriage: X.4.1.29. See also Helmholz, *The Spirit of Classical Canon Law*, 238. Korpiola, *Between Betrothal and Bedding*, 173.
47. Iuul, 'Arveret', 265.

obligations that went beyond mere materialistic considerations, as for instance the duty of mothers (and sometimes fathers) to bring up their children,[48] and the children's reciprocal obligation to take care of their parents when they became old and helpless. In a Christian context this understanding of *ius naturale* was strengthened by the theological concept that Christians should love all their blood kin, what Vogt in another connection has called 'canonical kinship'.[49] Taking this into consideration, one would expect that obligations between children and parents would play an important role in determining the rules regarding persons who had become so old, ill, or helpless that they could not support themselves. But the picture is much more ambiguous, especially in the Danish laws.

The Nordic laws presupposed that situations might arise in which a person would need support and maintenance from his or her relatives. According to the Danish provincial laws, a person who could not take care of and support him- or herself because of old age, illness, or some other reason had the option of becoming a 'house-led' (*fletføring*, derived from *flæt*, house or household and *føre*, to lead).[50] The house-led was, in other words, a person who was led into another household for care and sustenance. To be a house-led, the person had to pre-empt himself[51] at the assembly, thereby yielding his autonomy to his closest heirs. If the heirs chose to, they could take turns caring for the house-led, or he could divide his estate between the heirs, keeping one share (his 'capital lot')[52] for himself and then giving it to one of the heirs in return for board and lodging. According to the laws, the person wishing to be a house-led could not force the heirs to receive him, and if the heirs refused to take him in after he had pre-empted himself – or in reality, pre-empted his land[53] – to them at the assembly, he

---

48. '*Jus naturale* is that which nature has taught to all animals; for it is not a law specific to mankind but it is common to all animals. ... Out of this comes the union of man and woman which we call marriage, and the procreation of children, and their rearing'. Ulpian, *Institutiones,* book 1, (D. 1,1,3), in *The Digest of Justinian* 1, trans. & ed. by A. Watson (Philadelphia: 1985).
49. Vogt, *The Function of Kinship*; and see above, the text associated with n. 8.
50. About house-leading in general see H. Vogt, '*Fledføring* – Elder Care and the Protection of the Interest of the Heirs in Danish Medieval Laws', *The Legal History Review* 76 (2008), 273-81.
51. Although for simplicity's sake only masculine pronouns are used in this discussion, it is important to note that a house-led could be either a man or a woman.
52. The amount of property a person could dispose freely was defined by the size of his capital lot, which functioned as a scale for distribution. When an estate was divided, the capital lot was estimated on the basis of the number of heirs and their gender.
53. If someone wanted to sell land that he had inherited, he was obligated to pre-empt it to all his kinsmen, meaning that if any of his kinsmen wanted to buy the land, they were allowed to buy it for a price to be set by a group of prudent men from the area and not

had the right to go to whoever would receive him as house-led with his capital lot.[54]

Entering an agreement of house-leading at the assembly was not only irrevocable; it meant being a part of another's household. Once the house-led had given up all his personal rights and had been put under guardianship, the guardian was obligated to pay and receive fines for acts committed by or done to the house-led,[55] and the house-led would be expected to obey the guardian. In the Law of Jutland the status of a house-led is even compared with a slave's,[56] but with the important difference that violent deeds done against or by a house-led were fined as with other free men, and the guardian did not have a right to ill-treat him. Thus, though one might argue that because it was irrevocable the practice of house-leading created a kind of un-free status, it must also be taken into consideration that a house-led entered the relationship with his guardian voluntarily. That the old person lost some legal rights is not surprising. If he or she had formerly been the householder or mistress before coming into another household headed by someone else, it had to be very clearly laid out what the relationship should be between the parties. There could only be one head of the household, as the laws also emphasize clearly.

It can be difficult to see in the statutes about house-leading the influence of the ideology of *ius naturale* or the natural obligation to take care of the welfare of kinsmen in time of need. The prospective house-led had to pre-empt himself at the assembly in exactly the same way as one would pre-empt land. In addition, when put under extended guardianship his freedom was much more restricted than that of a woman who had a guardian.[57] Finally, he had no right to maintenance from his kinsmen if they refused to receive him: if the property he would bring with him was not worth the effort of taking responsibility for him, they were not legally (but only, one suspects, morally) obligated to take him in. The laws' concern was to keep

---

the market price. If the owner alienated the land without the pre-emption, either he was fined three marks (Law of Scania) or the transfer was invalid.
54. The provisions on house-leading are found in *DGL* I:1, *Law of Scania*, ed. by J. Brøndum-Nielsen (Copenhagen: 1933), chap. 41-44; *DGL* V, *Erik's Law of Zealand*, ed. by P. Skautrup (Copenhagen: 1937), book I, chap. 38-41, 51-57; *DGL* VIII, *Valdemar's Law of Zealand*, ed. by E. Kroman (Copenhagen: 1941), chap. 42-44.
55. *DGL* II, *Jyske Lov*, book I, chap. 32, where it states that the guardian should pay a fine to the king for the breaking of the peace if the house-led wounded the guardian.
56. *DGL* II, *Jyske Lov*, book I, chap. 31.
57. If a woman was violated or assaulted, she had the right to receive the compensation from her guardian, who, since women were legally incapable persons, would raise a claim on her behalf. Women could also be held legally responsible for their crimes and were subject to the same punishments as men.

Rights, Obligations, Domestic Relations

the land within the family, and to make sure that when a person had divided his land with his heirs, the division could not be revoked.

Thus, when looking at the Danish provisions about house-leading one is hard-pressed to detect a sense of obligation toward old and weak kinsmen. What one sees is merely a measure to protect land for younger generations and an elaboration of the rules on inheritance and donations. However, it could be argued that the mere mention in the laws of special rules regarding maintenance for the old and weak shows that the law makers anticipated the need to regulate domestic relations between individuals, parents, children, and the family of origin with respect to maintenance and property. The laws do not explicitly mention any rights or natural claims for the old and helpless to be maintained. No duties or obligations to care for the weak or old were imposed on their children or on other relatives, and there were no sanctions for those who refused to admit a house-led into their household. But it should be noted that the Law of Jutland mentions that a man could not be house-led unless his wife joined him, or unless they were so old that the bishop allowed them to live separately. This shows an influence from canon law and the spouses' right and duty to maintain the community of marital life.[58]

Provisions on house-leading are also found in the Swedish laws.[59] As they generally postdate the Danish laws, it is very likely that the provisions came into Swedish law as a loan or were at least inspired by the Danish laws. Yet even though there are many similarities between them are there also substantial differences, both between Denmark and Sweden and within the Swedish provinces.

The Swedish provisions about how to become a house-led are by and large the same as the Danish: the old person must offer himself publicly to the heirs, and there is a close connection between land/property, inheritance, and the reason why the old person had to become a house-led in order to get maintenance. For example, the appendix to the Newer Westgötalaw says, 'If anyone wants to be house-led, then he shall legally offer himself to his heirs

---

58. *DGL* II, *Jyske Lov*, book I, chap. 32, 80-82.
59. They are found in *Samling af Sweriges gamla Lagar*, ed. by D.H.S. Collin & D.C.J. Schlyter (Stockholm: 1827-1844): I: Older Wästgöta Law, Iordþær Balken, chap. 3, 43; II: Östgöta Law, Ærfþa Balken, chap. 12, 124-25; III: Uppland Law, Jorþæ Balken, chap. 21, 200-01; IV: Västman Law, Jorþa Balken, chap. 17, 183-84; Söderman Law, Jorþa Balken, chap. 17, 82-83; V: Dala Law, Gipninga Balken, chap. 16, 52-53; VI: Hälsinge Law, Jorþæ Balken, chap. 15, 66; *Magnus Erikssons Landslag i nusvensk tolkning*, ed. and trans. by Å. Holmbäck & E. Wessén (Lund: 1962), Jordabalken, chap. 34, 82; *Svenska landskapslagar* V: Wästgöta Law newer edition, ed. & trans. by Å. Holmbäck & E. Wessén (Uppsala: 1946), Jordabalken, chap. 5, 331. Additamenta, 11 § 10, 388.

at the assembly ... as it before is said about inherited land'.[60] And the Svea-laws, the laws from the eastern and northern part of Sweden, state that the heirs should maintain the house-led according to their share of the inheritance, specifying how much land a year's maintenance is worth.[61]

In two very important aspects the Swedish rules differ from the Danish: the personal status of the house-led, and the fact that different rules applied to the childless and to those with children. There is no mention in the Swedish provisions that the house-led should lose all his personal legal rights and obligations and be placed under the power of a guardian. This is not to say that being a house-led – having to give up one's own household and entering another's – did not mean the loss of personal status. Why else emphasize that no-one should be forced to become a house-led?[62] However, since the Swedish rules most likely are inspired by the Danish laws, it is reasonable to think that the Danish references to loss of personal status were deliberately omitted.

In the Svea-laws, the Östgötalaw, and the National Law both the childless and people with children were required to offer their property to their heirs in return for maintenance, if they were unable to take care of themselves. However, if the parents were too poor to pay for their support, the children were nevertheless obligated to take the parents in and support them. If a child refused, he or she was fined three marks per year, the same sum that had to be paid to the king for minor crimes. The childless were also mentioned in the laws, which state that it was the heirs' responsibility to take care of them. However, as no sanctions for noncompliance were mentioned, this appears to have been a moral obligation rather than a legal one.

In the Danish laws is it clearly the interest of the heirs – the next generation – that is being protected and not that of the old person, who can become a house-led only through a process that requires him to surrender his personal autonomy and dispose his property. Moreover, since the laws do not deal with moral obligation, it is very difficult when reading the letter of the law, as it regulates such secular matters as division of property and property rights, to see any influence from *ius naturale*.

60. Ibid.
61. The Hälsingelaw differs a bit. Here, if a person wishing to be a house-led publicly offered himself to his kinsmen and was refused by them, he was entitled to sell enough land for three years' maintenance. When the three years had elapsed, he was to offer himself as house-led again. If at that point the kinsmen still would not receive him or allow him to sell his land, he could go with his land to whoever would receive him: *Samling af Sweriges gamla Lagar* VI: Hälsinge Law, JorÞæ Balken, chap. 15, 66.
62. *Samling af Sweriges gamla Lagar* I: Older Wästgöta Law, Iordþær Balken, chap. 3, 43; *Svenska landskapslagar* V: Wästgöta Law newer edition, Jordabalken, chap. 5, 331.

Rights, Obligations, Domestic Relations

The purpose of the Swedish provisions was also to secure the land for subsequent generations, but in return the children were legally and other kinsmen were morally obligated to tend to the needs of their parents and other old relatives who could not take care of themselves, whether they could pay for it or not. This could be posited that the Danish rules were adjusted to be in accordance with it. Why this difference between the Danish and Swedish provisions for eldercare? There is of course the time dimension, in that the Danish rules were almost a century older than the Swedish,[63] and very possibly the ideology of the 'right order of things' had become more known and accepted by the time the Swedish laws were written down. Another factor could be that because Danish society in the late 12th century was one in which status was linked to the ability to take care of and protect oneself and one's household, old and weak people were regarded with less respect.[64] The house-leading that we find in the laws could have been constructed on the basis of an older institution, going back to a time when the value of a man depended on his capacity to act as a man was expected to act. This would have meant that with respect to the old and weak, the natural relationship between family members articulated in the language of *ius naturale* would have been in opposition to established norms. But that can of course merely be a guess.

7. Conclusion

In the canonists' texts of the 12th and 13th centuries the concept of the right order of things gave an internal cohesion to the articulation of domestic relations laws, binding family members to each other through interlocking rights and duties. In the same period the Nordic laws were being written down. The question to ask is, did this ideology of social ordering influence the structuring of the Nordic laws? The natural relationships within the family were to some extent present in the Nordic laws, and the articulation

---

63. The exception to the rule is the paragraphs in the Older Wästgöta Law, which differ from what is found in the later Swedish laws.
64. In the provincial laws a man was considered to be ill if he could not ride to the assembly to raise a case or could not defend himself against claims raised by others. That a man who lacked the power to defend his honour was regarded a lesser man can also been seen in the paragraphs about adultery. If a man found his wife in the act, the expected response was to kill the lover. Yet the laws have an 'exception clause' for those who were so feeble that they could not take revenge: 'because we say thus, that an adulterer would otherwise be too unfettered in relation to a man who does not have sufficient power to take revenge'. *DGL* VIII, *Valdemar's Law of Zealand, newer edition*, chap. 52.

of interlocking rights and duties, founded on the Scriptures, had an impact on the establishing of domestic relations laws in the Nordic realms, especially with respect to inheritance. But on the other hand, the picture in relation to house-leading as a legal conceptualization of the natural relationship between parent and child was very blurred. The language of the Danish laws includes no formulation of children's obligation to tend to their parent's welfare in time of need. This was, however, institutionalized in the later Svea-laws, where the children's duties towards their parents were strongly emphasized.

It has been our endeavour to synthesize previous approaches to what we have chosen to conceptualize as 'domestic relations laws' by looking at the existing correlative concepts of 'rights' and 'duties'. Looking from a gendered perspective, our analysis of the authority structure in the laws in connection with paternal governance gives a more nuanced picture than presented before. It is, however, important to stress that an investigation of the legal categories of 'rights' and 'duties' in a medieval Nordic context must include more than just the relationships between marital partners and their children and extend to the wider kin group, if scholars are to explore fully the logic/s or the ideology/ies embedded in the legal language. Although such a study lies outside the scope of this article, we believe that the strategy formulated and demonstrated here can be extended to other research in the future.

INTESTATE INHERITANCE AS A FAMILY MATTER: *IUS COMMUNE*, STATUTES AND CASES FROM FLORENCE

Thomas Kuehn

1. Introduction

Intestate inheritance rules are a default system. They define, in the absence of particular settlements through testaments or other devices, an order of succession in terms of degrees of relationship, gender and legal capacity. As such, intestate inheritance laws can yield a normative sense of kinship and family for a given society. The intestacy rules allow us to see persons and property in relationships deemed legally relevant and socially vital.

In the context of a volume on Nordic law, my role is to raise a point of comparison by examining intestate inheritance in late medieval Italy, more specifically in Florence, which was not untypical of Italian cities, at least for our purposes.[1] Florence, like so many other cities of northern and central Italy, exercised the political and legal power to enact statutes. Specifically with regard to intestacy, in Florence and elsewhere statutory rules were intended to supplement or preclude the exercise of the rules of *ius commune*, which resided largely in the Roman law texts of the *Corpus iuris civilis* of Justinian. The vision of family that prevailed in the late medieval Italian commune was clearly no longer that of the late antique empire.[2]

---

1. On Florentine exceptionalism in relation to women and intestacy, see I. Chabot, *La dette des familles: Femmes, lignage et patrimoine à Florence aux xive et xve siècles* (Rome: 2011), 29-41.
2. On these statutes, see F. Niccolai, *La formazione del diritto successorio negli statuti comunali del territorio lombardo-tosco* (Milan: 1940), 170-207; A. Romano, *Famiglia, successioni e patrimonio familiare nell'Italia medievale e moderna* (Turin:

The Roman sense of kinship was broadly cognatic and non-unilinear. That is, blood (as the substance that set filiation and identity) was transmitted by both parents, and equally so to each of their mutual children. Inheritance, though tilted generally to agnatic succession traced through male ties of *patria potestas*, took cognatic ties into account. Male *and* female descendants inherited equally the property (not necessarily the social and political identity) of the *paterfamilias* or other ascendants within the *agnatio*, or lacking *agnati*, within the *gens*.[3] There was a period in Roman history when women were disadvantaged in intestacy to agnatic relatives, for discussion of which Roman jurists had invented the term *consanguinitas*, but Justinian had abolished that distinction, reinstating women to full equality in intestate succession.[4]

Justinian's *Corpus* had barely been promulgated in Italy when the Lombards invaded and any unity of Romano-Byzantine rule was forever disrupted, so its influence on legal practices in the early Middle Ages is hard to track. Its later influence, of course, became preponderant when it served as the basis of the jurisprudential revival that led as well to the establishment of the first Italian university in Bologna, to be followed subsequently by Padua, Perugia and others.[5]

The Roman intestate system, as defined by Justinian and his jurists, was a powerful body of rules and certainly could not be ignored once it resurfaced as an intellectual and institutional force; but it was also peculiar, most so in the context of what came after it. With regard to inheritance, it was notably individualistic in many regards. Ownership rested in the hands of a person (even as a share of ownership with others). It passed by intestacy, or by the *voluntas* of its dying owner, to one or more other persons.[6] While shares were allocated *per capita* among all those, male and female, related in the same degree of relationship to the *de cuius*, they were bound to no collective

      1994), 11-17; F. Leverotti, *Famiglia e istituzioni nel Medioevo italiano* (Rome: 2005), 21-37; Chabot, *La dette des familles*, 11-24.
3. Cf. P. Moreau, 'The Bilineal Transmission of Blood in Ancient Rome', in C.H. Johnson et al. (ed.), *Blood and Kinship: Matter for Metaphor from Ancient Rome to the Present* (New York & Oxford: 2013), 40-60, at 41-44.
4. Moraeu, 'The Bilineal Transmission', passim; see also F. Roumy, 'La naissance de la notion canonique de *consanguinitas* et sa réception dans le droit civil', in M. van der Lugt & C. de Miramon (ed.), *L'hérédité entre Moyen Âge et Époque moderne: Perspectives historiques* (Florence: 2008), 41-66; O.F. Robinson, 'The Historical Background', in S. McLean & N. Burrows (ed.), *The Legal Relevance of Gender: Some Aspects of Sex-Based Discrimination* (Atlantic Highlands: 1988), 40-60; J. Gardiner, *Women in Roman Law and Society* (London: 1986), 5-29.
5. A well-known story, on which see M. Bellomo, *Saggio sull'università nell'età del diritto comune* (Catania: 1979).
6. On property law, see P. Grossi, *Il dominio e le cose* (Milan: 1992).

set of rights or mutual obligations, as a rule. This situation would be greatly complicated by the developments of the Middle Ages when, as one example, the influence of the Church would assert the unity of married couples, as one flesh (*caro*), against the more fluid bilateral transmission of blood.[7] An unavoidable tension between an individualistic bilateral sense of kinship and a more unilineal sense, tending to disadvantage women and their rights and the rights of others through them, became entrenched in late medieval Italy.

The Lombard law carried a distinction between male and female property. It privileged intestacy, rarely admitting wills until the Church was able to exert more influence on practices. Lombard intestacy precipitated a system of quasi-liens, of easements and entitlements of multiple interests on a single item of property. For our purposes it is important to note that a woman's marriage portion took the form of a lien on one quarter of her husband's property (analogous to the practice of dower in Anglo-Saxon law).[8] Canon law and the institutional interests of the Church waded into this situation with questionable effects. On the one hand, the Church clearly disadvantaged women, notably by excluding them from the priesthood, yet it also extended them some capacities not available to them in Roman law, notably by not only allowing them to act as guardians for their minor children but even by promoting them as better suited for the role by virtue of their natural maternal affection.[9] The Church also defended and promoted the use of the testament as its favoured means of devising succession, which also thus permitted pious legacies, suitable burials and measures for the soul of the deceased.[10]

2. The major shift in the 14th century

In the course of the 12th and 13th centuries, Italian cities moved away from Germanic marriage portions and back to Roman dowry, a portion provided

---

7. A. Guerreau-Jalabert, 'Flesh and Blood in Medieval Language about Kinship', in Johnson et al. (ed.), *Blood and Kinship*, 61-82, at 71.
8. Cf. M. Bellomo, *Ricerche sui rapporti patrimoniali tra coniugi: Contributo alla storia della famiglia medievale* (Milan: 1961), 21-25; D. Owen Hughes, 'From Brideprice to Dowry in Mediterranean Europe', *Journal of Family History* 3 (1978), 262-95.
9. M. Gigliola di Renzo Villata, *La tutela: Indagini sulla scuola dei glossatori* (Milan: 1975), 137-59; G. Calvi, *Il contratto morale: Madri e figli nella Toscana moderna* (Bari: 1994).
10. But not as J. Goody, *The European Family* (Oxford: 2000), has it. See D. Herlihy, 'Making Sense of Incest', in D. Herlihy (ed.), *Women, Family and Society in Medieval Europe: Historical Essays 1978-1991* (Oxford: 1995), 96-109.

to the groom generally by the bride's father but certainly from her family and kin. This was a major shift in the conception of family and kinship. It coincided with the ecclesiastical sacramental definition of marriage, which, paradoxically, removed parental discretion and control in favour of the willing consent of the spouses. It coincided as well with the revival of Roman law and with what Manlio Bellomo characterized as the *odium quartae* – a disdain of the terms of Lombard law and the liens it placed on a man's property (also complicating its passage in succession) in the name of his wife.[11]

With the entrenching of dowry in marriages and marital property arrangements, there also came widespread changes in intestacy rules. As Roman intestacy was essentially bilateral and egalitarian in gender terms, it was not the format most cities or their ruling elites foresaw as most useful and equitable for them. There was a fundamental asymmetry in dowry as the daughter took property from the household in the predominantly virilocal situation in Italian cities.[12] This asymmetry needed correction. Cities' means to affect general normative changes was civic statutes. These came to employ clauses embodying what jurists in the schools would come to interpret as *favor agnationis* or *favor masculinitatis* and *exclusio propter dotem*. They would in general limit the intestate share of dowered women to what they had received as dowry, excluding them from anything further on intestacy in favour of their brothers, fathers, nephews, uncles and so forth. The exact shape of the field of male relations excluding dowered women varied from commune to commune, as did the very wording employed. But such measures indeed became so common across Italy that jurists were compelled to recognize the fact and, as we will see, take it into account.[13] As the focus of comparison here will be Florence, it is time to look at her statutes in this regard as one example.

Florence redacted statutes at three points: 1322-1325, 1355 and 1415, although there were continuous processes of legislation that occasionally

---

11. Bellomo, *Ricerche*, 1-25; L. Mayali, *Droit savant et coutumes: L'exclusion des filles dotées, xiieme-xveme siècles* (Frankfurt: 1987); B.M. Kreutz, 'The Twilight of Morgengabe', in S.K. Cohn, Jr. & S.A. Epstein (ed.), *Portraits of Medieval and Renaissance Living: Essays in Honor of David Herlihy* (Ann Arbor: 1996), 131-47.
12. M. Botticini & A. Siow, 'Why Dowries?', *American Economic Review* 93 (2003), 1385-98.
13. See Th. Kuehn, 'Person and Gender in the Laws', in J.C. Brown & R.C. Davis (ed.), *Gender and Society in Renaissance Italy* (London & New York: 1998), 87-106. Such statutes were so common that an entire legal treatise was devoted to them: L. Palazzi da Fano, *Tractatus super statuto communiter per Italiam vigente, quod extantibus masculis foeminae non succedunt*, in *Tractatus universi iuris* 29 vols. (Venice: 1584), vol. 2, f. 279ra-83rb. Romano, *Famiglia, successioni e patrimonio*, 42-49.

touched on intestacy or related issues.[14] The *exclusio propter dotem* figured in from the first under the rubric *De modo successionis mulierum ab intestato* (later changed to *Qualiter mulier ab intestato succedat*).[15] Women's intestate succession was laid out in terms of relationships. First mothers: Mothers could not succeed their children if there were any legitimate children (grandchildren to her), grandchildren, or great grandchildren, or the child's father, paternal grandfather, paternal uncle, brother, sister, or nephew (brother's son). Were there no such survivors, she could claim one quarter of the estate, not to exceed 500 *lire* in value, and not to include houses and buildings (*domus* and *casamenta*). The rest would go to any agnates within eight degrees of consanguinity. There was a progressive exclusion of the female line in the subsequent versions of the statute. In 1325 only the mother's mother was expressly excluded (since an enactment of 1295). In 1355, following on the demographic devastation of the great plague, which left many estates to distantly related heirs, the entire maternal line was excluded. This clause was carried over to the 1415 version.

The mother (and all related through her) was not agnatically related to her children, and the maternal exclusion seems entirely based on agnation, as it was allowed that her own daughter, agnatically related to all her children, excluded her from succeeding to her children. This exclusion was conceptually enabled by the devising of the *arbor consanguinitatis*, which would become a feature of manuscripts of canon law, which replaced the language of flesh, which 'tended to highlight sex and marriage', back to a Roman-inspired language of blood, which, as Simon Teuscher notes, can be 'adjusted to conceptions of kinship that attached greater importance to lineage and descent, the constitution of kin-relationships around a patrimony'.[16] The bodily substance of blood linked one to a paternal substance and gave one privileges in regard to it.

Exclusion of sisters and daughters differed from that of mothers, as they were agnatically related to their brothers and fathers. Still, for sisters there was a lateral exclusion from their brothers in favour of children or grandchildren, other brothers or their sons, or paternal uncles. Daughters were excluded from their intestate fathers, paternal grandfathers, or great grandfathers by the same range of male agnates. In parallel, uterine brothers were

---

14. As in laws passed in 1476-1478, as per Th. Kuehn, *Heirs, Kin, and Creditors in Renaissance Florence* (Cambridge: 2008), 74-77.
15. See Th. Kuehn, *Law, Family, and Women: Toward a Legal Anthropology of Renaissance Italy* (Chicago: 1991), 238-57.
16. S. Teuscher, 'Flesh and Blood in the Treatises of the *Arbor Consanguinitatis* (Thirteenth to Sixteenth Centuries)', in Johnson et al. (ed.), *Blood and Kinship*, 83-104, at 99-100.

excluded in favour of agnatic males, though for them the exclusion had nothing to do with gender.

These exclusions of sisters and daughters were predicated on their being dowered. What if they were not? The flip side of statutes such as this one from Florence was a firm guarantee of a dowry, as it was the material justification of the exclusion on intestacy. In addition, prior to marriage women were assured by statute of alimentary support. In conjunction, widows were assured a right to return to their natal families. In Florence these women were accorded usufruct on the estate, which gave them a lien-like right capable of judicial enforcement, though this usufruct was reduced to a mere *alimenta competentia et decentia* in 1415.

Finally, it should be noted that all three versions of the intestacy statute also addressed testamentary succession by those women who could succeed *iure romano*. They were told to remain content with whatever had been left them; they could not contest the will. In 1415 it was conceded that undowered women left nothing in a testament had a right to a share equal to what they would have received on intestacy, but leaving the will otherwise intact in all its other provisions.

The statutory changes, animated as they may have been by political and economic events, nonetheless showed that intestacy and women's intestate rights were not fixed – however subtle some of the changes were. Part of the dynamic behind such changes was the continuing and creative tension between statutory provisions and those of the learned law. Conceptual conundrums arose in practice with stunning frequency in all communities with such laws. Within a civil law context it fell to academically trained jurists to reconcile the resulting tensions and make the statutes work in an overall context of law. Their interventions took various forms. In Florence the redactions of 1355 and 1415 were in fact entrusted to jurists – Tommaso da Gubbio in the first instance, Bartolomeo Vulpi da Soncino (ca. 1359-1435) and Paolo di Castro (ca. 1360-1441) in the second.[17] Also, specific requests for guidance on thorny problems were at times directed to jurists for interpretive clarification, as that elicited from the renowned Bartolo da Sassoferrato (1313-1357) in June 1351, which resulted in the exclusion of the entire maternal line from intestate inheritance in Florence.[18] There was also a tradition of statute commentary that would spring up in Florence around the redaction of 1415 and that would produce some notable

---

17. On the redaction process, see L. Tanzini, *Statuti e legislazione a Firenze dal 1355 al 1415* (Florence: 2004) and G. Biscione, *Statuti del Comune di Firenze nell'Archivio di Stato: Tradizione archivistica e ordinament* (Rome: 2009).
18. On this, Kuehn, *Law, Family, and Women*, 243-44.

examples whose influence would last even for centuries.[19] The statute *Qualiter mulier* and the subsequent one on inheritance of a woman's dowry would come in for repeated commentary for all the difficult issues they continually raised.

But the main mode of intervention of jurists in the legal elaboration and understanding of intestate inheritance, among so many other things, was undoubtedly the case-related *consilium*. Jurists would render their learned, textually elaborated and justified, opinions on matters of law on the invitation of a judge and/or the parties to a suit.[20] Wedded to the *ius commune* ideologically and methodologically, yet also bound to respect the laws as well as the social, economic and political interests of the communities in which they lived and worked, jurists carefully trod a sometimes treacherous path. For norms and practices that ran counter to *ius commune*, as the intestate statutes so evidently did, they had to find a way to restrict the range of such norms as unsuited to the standards of earthly justice embedded in the Roman law, or they had to find ideological constructs by which they could justify the sweep and effect of such rules.[21] The interpretive strategy of a restrictive reading of a statute that was *contra ius commune* was employed on intestacy statutes. It could be claimed, for example, that categories of kin not included explicitly in the statute 'remain in the disposition of the common law'.[22] This tactic will appear in the cases we will look at. Yet the main interpretive move of the jurists and the true jurisprudential innovation of the 14th century in this regard were the elaboration and insertion of the justifying figure of the *familia* into these discussions.[23]

First it must be noted that the Florentine statute nowhere offers a justifycation for its provisions, nor does it employ the term *familia* or its cognates. It is again not unusual in this respect. Intestacy statutes for other cities similarly shied away from justifications. That of Milan of 1396, for example, found it expedient simply to lay out the terms of exclusion of women and those descended through them and provide guarantees for

---

19. D. Edigati & L. Tanzini, *Ad statutum florentinum: Esegesi statutaria e cultura giuridica nella Toscana medievale e moderna* (Pisa: 2009).
20. Cf. The essays of M. Ascheri and J. Kirshner in M. Ascheri, I. Baumgärtner & J. Kirshner (ed.), *Legal Consulting in the Civil Law Tradition* (Berkeley: 1999).
21. On jurisprudential interpretation, see M. Sbriccoli, *L'interpretazione dello statuto: Contributo allo studio della funzione dei giuristi nell'età comunale* (Milan: 1969).
22. As in a Florentine statute commentary of Alessandro Bencivenni (1385-1423), mentioned in Kuehn, *Law, Family, and Women*, 245 and 248.
23. The timing coincides with that Jalabert found for recourse to blood to express the substance of kinship (Jalabert, 73).

dowry. With minor variations it is just like that of Florence.[24] Express justification of intestacy rules on the grounds of family came only in later statutes, like those of Ferrara.[25] Such justifications, in other words, came to be contained in statutes only long after jurists had introduced them in their commentaries and cases. Earlier statutes aimed to place property in male hands, agnatic male hands to be precise, but they did not indicate why that mattered. And they did not privilege one male over the others in the same class of heirs. There was, in other words, no form of primogeniture in such statutes, as there was in feudal law, which also operated in the territories of some Italian cities.[26]

Such explanations of intestacy rules in terms of family may have been lacking in 13th and 14th century statutes because such families were lacking. In the immediate context in which intestacy statutes were first drawn up, to follow on a position suggested by Andrea Romano, the maintenance of social progression and wealth rested on associations among men, usually but not always or necessarily related. These were the *consorteria*, to use a term current in Florence. They expressed *un forte impulso verso le aggregazioni familiari strutturate in famiglie estese orizzontalmente*.[27] Documents of the 13th century use 'family' to indicate those living together in common, as a *consorzio, che spesso si configurava come la societas di più 'famiglie' appartenenti alla medesima 'parentela' che si riuscivano in consortium, mettendo in comune i loro patrimoni*.[28] This definition was fed by and fed into a tendency to voluntary agglomerations of people, related by blood and property no less than the then-forming guilds united those of the same craft or occupation. Different forms of property persisted, each with their own type of ownership and order of succession – notably dowries and various *peculia*. A number of devices would serve to hold such agglomerations together. One sees contracts of *fraterna*, contracts not to alienate property beyond the *familia*, and other modes, including renunciations by dowered women to seek anything more than their dowry, as they exited to take their

---

24. Biblioteca Trivulziana B 1 (Statutes of 1396), fols. 154r-56r. On Milanese law, see Th. Kuehn, 'Gender and Law in Milan', in A. Gamberini (ed.), *Renaissance and Early Modern Milan* (Leiden: 2015); M.C. Zorzoli, 'Una incursione nella pratica giurisprudenziale milanese del Seicento e qualche riflessione sui temi che riguardano la famiglia', in *Ius mediolani: Studi di storia del diritto milanese offerti dagli allievi a Giulio Vismara* (Milan: 1996), 617-57.
25. *Statuta urbis Ferrariae nuper reformata anno domini MDLXVII* (Ferrara: 1567), f. 115v. See Niccolai, *La formazione del diritto*, 104-05; Kuehn, 'Person and Gender', 101.
26. On feudal law, see Romano, *Famiglia, successioni e patrimonio*, 68-72.
27. Romano, *Famiglia, successioni e patrimonio*, 33.
28. Romano, *Famiglia, successioni e patrimonio*, 34.

Intestate Inheritance as a Family Matter

place in other households. One could argue that intestacy statutes simply replaced the need for individual renunciations with a general norm. It may be analogized to the right of *ritratto* – the right of kin to buy back any property alienated to an outsider.[29] The group was a matter of those living together, sharing bread and wine (to use a familiar metaphor of the time for such kinship), inhabiting some vital piece(s) of property, like a defensible tower, in the turbulence of the 13th century communes.[30] Descent and inheritance helped peg one's right to be part of a group but it did not yet, or not everywhere, yield a sense of the group as also extended in time as well as in a neighbourhood or domestic space; it did not yet become inalterably linked to a *patrimonium*.

3. The contribution of the jurists

There is an important degree to which jurists contributed the conceptual linkage between family and patrimony and provided a coherence to the group as a substantive and thus, to a degree, corporative entity, as something other than and over and beyond the individuals with their rights over discrete properties or shares, and as something enduring in time on a natural and not simply contractual basis. I make no claim that jurists were solely responsible for such theorizing and certainly not that they were in any way free or even merely aloof from the social, economic and political events of their day. Certainly cultural developments, such as last names and coats of arms, whether or not originating among feudal nobility, propelled a sense of family as a durable entity, whose patrimony included such devices, which in general were rooted in and stood for the very honour of the family (itself inheritable).[31]

One of the first to theorize about statutes, including intestacy rules, was Alberico da Rosciate (ca. 1290-1354), a Bergamasco who served in various capacities for the Visconti. His *Opus statutorum* addressed the practical problems raised by statutes in relation to *ius commune*, following a short tradition of statute commentary back to Alberto Gandino (d. post 1310) at the end of the 13th century.[32] Gandino's main concern had been criminal

---

29. Romano, *Famiglia, successioni e patrimonio*, 41.
30. On the metaphor *ad unum panem et vinum* and the households of the Florentine catasto of 1427, see C. Klapisch-Zuber, "A une pane et uno vino': The Rural Tuscan Family at the Beginning of the Fifteenth Century', in C. Klapisch-Zuper, *Women, Family, and Ritual in Renaissance Italy*, trans. L.G. Cochrane (Chicago: 1985), 36-67.
31. On honour and family, see Kuehn, *Law, Family, and Women*, 129-42.
32. S.v. I. Prosdocimi, 'Alberico da Rosate', in *Dizionario biografico degli Italiani* 1 (1960): www.trecani.it/enciclopedia/alberico-da (Accessed 18.3.2013). The first

procedure, and procedure was another enormously important area of statutory law, as it was the cities and other jurisdictions that actually established and operated courts of law.[33] Alberico, however, was concerned more widely with all statutes. He saw the rationale for intestacy statutes to lie in a form of public utility *ut familiarum dignitas et memoria conservetur, quae conservatur per divitias et per inopiam minuitur.*[34] The family perpetuated itself *per prolem masculinam*. Here then was an ideologically transparent justification. Family was a matter of *dignitas* (reputation and standing, including its honour), which rested on wealth passed in the male line. The exclusion of dowered women, who upon marriage contributed to the wealth and the *proles* of a different male line, then seemed sensible. It was the preservation of the *memoria* over time that was posed as integral to the group and to the utility of its city.

It was perhaps even more so Alberico's most illustrious contemporary, Bartolo da Sassoferrato, who solidified this construct of *familia* in jurisprudence. It was precisely in commenting on the Roman rules of intestacy, without overt reference to the statutes of Italian cities, that Bartolo concluded that *familia accipitur in iure pro substantia*. That *substantia* passed logically and seamlessly from father to son (not to daughter).[35] *Substantia* that could endure over time, houses and lands, but also blood and memory, it seems, gave family an essence beyond the people who composed it at any one time. If it is the case, as Margaret Jane Radin has famously theorized for modern Anglo-American law, that full personhood requires some control over external resources, over property, in other words, then it might also be the case (though for a rather different law) that personhood for the family comes in the form of intergenerational control of property (if only for men).[36] That does not mean that we can overlook issues of power embedded in such a formulation or ignore the contested areas of property and

---

quarter of the 14th century is singled out as the crucial moment by M. van der Lugt & C. de Miramon, 'Penser l'hérédité au Moyen Âge: une introduction', in van der Lugt & de Miramon (ed.), *L'hérédité*, 3-37, at 13.

33. The best account on this score is M. Vallerani, *Medieval Public Justice*, trans. S. Rubin Blanshei (Washington, D.C.: 2012).

34. Cited in M. Sbriccoli, 'Politique et interprétation juridique dans les villes italiennes du Moyen Âge', *Archives de philosophie du droit* 17 (1972), 99-113, at 109; Romano, *Famiglia, successioni e patrimonio*, 2; Th. Kuehn, '*Memoria* and Family in Law', in G. Ciappelli & P. Lee Rubin (ed.), *Art, Memory, and Family in Renaissance Florence* (Cambridge: 2000), 262-74. Alberico's treatise is in *Tractatus universi iuris*, vol. 2, fols. 2r ff.

35. On which, see Th. Kuehn, 'Bartolus's Definition of Family: An Aspect of Juridical Thought at Petrarch's Time', in F. Piovan (ed.), *Petrarca e il diritto* (Rome: forthcoming).

36. M.J. Radin, 'Property and Personhood', *Stanford Law Review* 34 (1981-82), 957-1015.

personhood, especially for women.[37] These statutes gave men legal personhood as owners and transmitters of meaningful pieces of property and the bulk of the patrimony, while eliding the vital contribution of women to the patrimony, patriline and household, to the *onera matrimonii* their dowries nominally sustained, and to the very *proles masculina* that truly could not be perpetuated without them.

The statements of Alberico and Bartolo were offered in an academic rather than forensic context, for all that they clearly had practical origin, if not intent. It is tempting to see conceptualizations of family in terms of linear inheritance as a shift of focus from the large *consorzi* that lay behind so much urban political upheaval in cities such as Florence in the late 13th and early 14th centuries. Portions of such *consorzi*, once politically disenfranchised, were later able to rehabilitate themselves as distinct lineages with new names and coats of arms.[38] A different stage was reached, however, when such linear agnatic notions came into play in actual cases, as they did before the end of the 14th century. There is no way to tell where, when and how that first was. Nor is there liable to be much sense in a potentially hopeless and endless quest to determine temporal priority. It seems to make sense, rather, to pick up the thread at different chronological points and see how intestacy was handled at those points. We can certainly do that for Florence.

A good place to begin is with a Florentine case that involved two of the most prominent jurists, Perugian by provenance, to practice and teach in Florence, namely the brothers Baldo (1327-1400) and Angelo degli Ubaldi (1325-1400). Angelo taught in Florence after 1388 and Baldo was there from 1385 to 1390. So these two *consilia* may hail from the two years they were both in Florence.[39] The version consulted is that of a 16th century printed edition of Angelo's *consilia*, so the case facts are sketchy. A man named Martino di Giovanni of Florence had died intestate, leaving his wife (Nente) and an infant daughter, who soon died. The problem for Baldo was determining if the wife inherited from her daughter or if the girl's estate went to a paternal aunt named Sanora. This was a case then in which there was no possibility of inheritance by men and thus seemingly no issue of

---

37. Note the direction of one critique, S.J. Schnably, 'Property and Pragmatism: A Critique of Radin's Theory of Property and Personhood', *Stanford Law Review* 45 (1992-93), 347-407; also J.D. Jones, 'Property and Personhood Revisited', *Wake Forest Journal of Law and Policy* 1 (2011), 93-136.
38. C. Klapisch-Zuber, *Retour à la cité: Le magnats de Florence, 1340-1440* (Paris: 2006).
39. See L. Martines, *Lawyers and Statecraft in Renaissance Florence* (Princeton: 1968), 499; s.v. G. Ermini, 'Baldo', in *Enciclopedia italiana* (1930): www.trecani.it/enciclopedia/baldo (Accessed 29.3.2013).

preserving a male line and family wealth. The mother claimed the entirety of the estate through her daughter, but the aunt argued (rather, it was argued for her by a representative) that the mother, by terms of the intestacy statute, could inherit only a quarter, and that not to exceed 500 *lire*.

Baldo first addressed the issue whether the statute left all to the mother. The 'infallible' rule of statute interpretation, he alleged, was to determine the *ratio* or *mens* behind the law and apply it.[40] However, where the rationale of the statute was not apparent but a matter of conjecture, then the *generalitas legis* had to be restricted, lest someone be unduly harmed or prevented from realizing some gain (*lucrum*). So he decided.

> In the terms proposed, a restriction can and must be placed on the second part of the statute, and it is understood that the mother is not excluded by agnates in whole or in part from the lucrative succession to her child, because it is not understood to be the intent of the statute, although the quality of this statement must be restricted to its reason and cause rationally conjectured, according to which it is not extended to the female sex in said second response, as far as persons excluding a mother.[41]

A mother did not deserve to be left out of such an inheritance; that would be 'absurd'. The aunt did not exclude her as the intent of the statute was to *providere agnatis masculini sexus excepta sorore*.

Then Baldo raised the *ratio statuti*. According to him, the statute responded to a certain *consuetudo moderna* that had animated the legislators. In part that custom was that surviving agnates 'succeed to the duties of the dead', and thus it was only just that they also gain the positive values of succession. But it was also a political good:

> by reason of a certain public utility, which demands their faculties be conserved for individual agnates, so that the dignity and honour of families might be safe, which are not conserved without wealth ... and because honours and public utilities or burdens are to be extended to the more powerful and honest people

---

40. A. degli Ubaldi, *Consilia* (Lyons, 1551), *cons.* 281, fols. 154r–55rb, at 154rb: 'Et ideo ubicunque potest de ratione legi constare per eandem legem vel aliam possumus et debemus absolute verba legis astringere ad id tantum ad quod ratio se extendit et hoc est infallibile'.
41. A. degli Ubaldi, *Consilia* (Lyons, 1551), *cons.* 281, fol. 154va: 'sic in propositis igitur terminis, potest et debet consequenter dari restrictio in secundo statuto dicti statuti: et per agnatos mater excludi non intelligatur in totum vel in partem a luctuosa sui filii successione, quia non intelligitur esse de mente dicti statuti, quamvis debet huius sermonis qualitas restringi ad eius rationem et causam rationabiliter coniecturatam: secundum quam non porrigitur ad sexum muliebrem in d. secundo responso quo ad personas excludentes matrem'.

> ... because it is in the interest of the *res publica* to be ruled by the more worthy and wealthy and not by paupers and abject persons.[42]

And he went on,

> this was the reason, it is conjectured, moving the modern legislators, and even more so because it happens through agnates of the male sex, according to what is commonly known, that the memory of agnation and of the agnates is perpetuated and preserved, which everyone wishes to be done naturally, and this is done by the persons of agnates of the male sex and not by women, because in them is not the aptitude to preserve memory of agnation but to end it.[43]

This was, in short, the rationale for such statutes that Alberico had offered: men preserved the family's dignity, which now we see, thanks to Baldo, was also a matter of public utility, more so as the juristic maxim had it that a woman did not perpetuate her family, she ended it.

Baldo roamed across various textual bits of the statute solidifying this conjectural reading of its intent. One of the more interesting devices was his reading of the clause that not only limited a mother's share to a quarter, no more than 500 *lire*, but that also expressly precluded houses and such from coming to a woman. This too showed him that the legislator was thinking of agnates and the *proles masculorum*:

> It is considered most grave and injurious to see the house of one's progenitors, their fount and the site in which the renown of agnation has long been embedded and they have been accustomed to retain the name of the agnation, devolve outside to strangers, and one can see the images of one's ancestors, their *fama* and *signa* removed.[44]

42. A. degli Ubaldi, *Consilia* (Lyons, 1551), *cons*. 281, fol. 154va: 'Secundo, ratione cuiusdam publice utilitatis, quae exposcit facultates suas singulis agnatibus conservare, ut familiarum salva sit dignitas et honestas, que absque divitiis non conservatur ... quia honores et commoda publica, sive munera, potioribus et honestioribus inducenda sunt ... quia interest rei publicae per digniores et ditiores regi, et non per pauperes et abiectos'.
43. A. degli Ubaldi, *Consilia* (Lyons, 1551), *cons*. 281, fol. 154va: 'Et haec fuit ratio movens coniecturative modernos iurislatores, et insuper quia per agnatos virilis sexus contingit, secundum communiter accidentia perpetuari et conservari memoria agnationis et agnatorum. Quod optat quisque naturaliter in se fieri, et hec fit per personas agnatorum virilis sexus, et non vir [sic] feminas, quia in eis non est apta perpetuari memoria agnationis sed finiri'.
44. A. degli Ubaldi, *Consilia* (Lyons, 1551), *cons*. 281, fol. 154vb: 'gravissimum et iniuriosissimum esse dignoscitur domum progenitorum fonte suorum et situs in quibus antiquata est fonte agnationis fama et retinere consueverunt agnationis nomen, ultra ad

Still, though he had carefully constructed a plausible rationale for the statute, Baldo had to concede that the portion of the statute dealing with mothers was 'obscure' as to the persons who reduced her share to a *minusculum*. It was agnates, indiscriminately, that the legislator had privileged over the mother. The sister, however, seemed to have no greater right. To make her more worthy of inheritance would be to work an inequity. And it would hardly be rational to let her sex serve to exclude the mother. She just did not meet the statute's intent. The lack of male agnate simply meant that the *dispositio* of the statute was at an end, and that of *ius commune* took over, by which the mother was due the entire inheritance of her daughter *debita iure naturali*.

Angelo began his follow-up *consilium* noting how *subtiliter et diffuse* his brother had proceeded. But his problem situation was different. Instead of the possibility of succession by an aunt in preference to a mother, seemingly precluded by his brother's opinion, Angelo posed the possibility of a fifth-degree agnate (named Lamberto) succeeding, and there was also now the existence of a uterine brother to the deceased infant daughter to take account of. By the terms of the rationale Baldo had teased from the statute, with which Angelo ostensibly agreed, it would seem that Lamberto should exclude the mother. There were even within the civil law's older texts, *iure vetustissimo*, such as the *SC Orficianum* and *Tertullianum*, ones that sanctioned such exclusionary rules. But Angelo took the contrary view, notably not invoking any generalized intent of social policy and public utility behind the statute, but claiming that the statute allowed exclusion of the mother only by fourth degree agnates at most.[45] The uterine brother did not exclude her either. The statute said nothing about uterine children being preferred to the mother. The statute, according to Angelo, seemed only to want to hold to the *gradus prerogativa* as set forth in *ius commune*.

Both Baldo and Angelo had come down on the side of maternal inheritance, though in different fact situations. It is interesting that both saw the same rationale in the statute, developed, it is true, much more fully by Baldo. But in the face of potential male heirs, that rationale could not serve Angelo's purpose and he did not invoke it. He did not attempt to argue that a fifth degree agnate fell outside any meaning of *familia*, and he did not develop that argument or even dwell on the uterine brother's lack of agnation in considering his claims.

    extraneos devolutas: et imagines maiorum suorum potest fama sua et signa videre repulsa'.
45. A. degli Ubaldi, *Consilia* (Lyons, 1551), *cons.* 282, fols. 155ra-rb: 'Excluditur igitur agnatum quinti gradus de quo statutentium non loquiter inclusive sed exclusive ex regula'.

Intestate Inheritance as a Family Matter

There is a certain level of jurisprudential gamesmanship in the brothers' *consilia*. If they were not entirely making up the case facts, they had certainly separated them to create distinct problems. Their opinions may have served more to supplement academic positions. What of an undoubtedly real case? Let us look at one handled by a bevy of Florentine lawyers contemporary to the Ubaldi. The issue in this case ran closely parallel to Angelo's. Did an agnate beyond the fourth degree exclude a uterine brother?

The deceased whose estate was in question, an Antonio, had left a fifth degree agnate, Bartolomeo, who was his cousin's son; and he had a half-brother named Francesco. Francesco argued for the estate on the grounds of being closer in degree of relationship and not excluded by the statute.[46] The only effect the fifth degree agnate had was to keep the brother's share to the same size as a mother's, who was the link to his half-brother. The statutory clauses mentioning uterine kin in fact excluded them from inheriting from each other in the presence of fourth degree agnates of the father.[47]

Five Florentine jurists weighed in on the case. Two of them, Francesco Cambioni da Prato (fl. 1380s) and Lodovico di messer Francesco Albergotti (d. 1398), did little more than add their corroborative signatures to the collective effort. The first real opinion was offered by Giovanni de' Ricci (ca. 1342-1402), who was from an old Florentine family.[48] His opinion is entirely, to use the proper term, 'unmotivated'. That is, there are no citations to authoritative texts of *ius commune* to support his argument (more likely in an opinion rendered for a court than in a partisan opinion for one party).[49] Ricci's opinion is based solely on a reading of the statute, concluding that Francesco, the uterine brother, got only a quarter, beyond real estate, up to 500 *lire*, with the rest to Bartolomeo. In essence Francesco's claim lay through his mother, so he was held to what she would have received. Rosello de' Roselli (fl. 1380s) in his brief opinion made one reference to the commentary of Bartolo da Sassoferrato to support the claim that the statute's prohibition on uterine inheritance worked in favour of agnates. The intellectual substance, such as there is, in this *consilium* lies in the contribution of Onofrio de' Bartolini, a Perugian (ca. 1350-1413). He examined a

---

46. BNF, Panciatichiano 138, fols. 165r-66r: 'nec magis favetur quam mater quia lex sic scripta est servanda et magis repulsio matris debet limitari'.
47. ASF, Statuti 16 (Podestà, 1355), fols. 97v-98v: 'Fratres vero uterini vel alii nati ex linea feminina non possint succedere alicui vel aliquibus eorum fratribus uterinis defunctis existentibus ex latere patris vel aliquibus coniunctis ex latere patris, saltem usque in quartum gradum inclusive'.
48. On him and the others, see L. Martines, *Lawyers and Statecraft in Renaissance Florence* (Princeton: 1968), 482, 498.
49. F. Mancuso, *Exprimere causam in sententia: ricerche sul principio di motivazione della sentenza nell'età del diritto comune classico* (Milan: 1999).

counter argument in favour of uterine succession to the effect that the general exclusion of the *linea feminina* in the initial clause of the statute did not override the special treatment of uterines in the second clause. An interpretive maxim that a *statutum odiosum* (as this was to the female line) should be restrictively construed militated in this direction, as otherwise 'these persons who are excluded by the statute are said to be effectively disinherited'.[50] But he sided with all the others that in the presence of a fifth degree agnate the uterine brother received merely a maternal share. While the statute might seem odious to the uterine, it was clearly favourable to agnates 'for the sake of preserving the dignities of families' (*gratia conservande dignitates familiarum*). Bartolini's then was the only opinion that rose to the level of stating a statutory rationale, but it effectively invoked it as an argument that sealed the judgment.

These two sets of opinions (those of the Ubaldi and of the five Florentines), both heralding, it seems, from the late 14th century, give witness to the willingness of jurists to intrude the ideological image of family into statute interpretation of intestacy rules. That willingness would become more general in the wake of further social and legal changes. If we return for a moment to Romano's tracing of family changes, we find that exclusion of dowered women was only the first step in the direction of holding family patrimony intact and transmitting it through the generations. Recourse to fideicommissary substitutions, generally added to testaments, coupled with prohibitions against alienation of pivotal properties (urban residences and rural estates) 'outside the family' (*extra familiam*) became the favoured tools of family preservation, even as these measures limited the discretion of heirs and gave a greater reality to the sense of family as a temporally perduring entity.[51] One jurist who played a pivotal role in theorizing and justifying the use of the *fideicommissum* in that manner was the Sienese Bartolomeo Sozzini (1436-1506), who taught in Pisa for periods, which was subject to Florence and brought him into contact with a number of Florentine cases. His treatment of an intestacy case provides us with an excellent final example of how entrenched the notion of family preservation had become by the end of the 15th century, when recourse to *fideicommissa* (much the legal opposite of intestacy) became widespread.[52]

---

50. BNF, Panciatichiano 138, fol. 166r: 'Iste enim persone que per statuta excluduntur quodammodo dicuntur exheredari'.
51. Romano, *Famiglia, successioni e patrimonio*, 60-68.
52. On the *fideicommissum*, see M. Piccialuti, *L'immortalità dei beni: Fedecommessi e primogeniture a Roma nei secoli xvii e xviii* (Rome: 1999) and S. Calonaci, *Dietro Lo scudo incantato: I fedecommessi di famiglia e il trionfo della borghesia fiorentina (1400 ca. - 1750)* (Florence: 2005). On Sozzini, see R. Bargagli, *Bartolomeo Sozzini: giurista e politico (1436-1506)* (Milan: 2000).

Intestate Inheritance as a Family Matter

Sozzini's case probably dates from the 1490s. It is typical of so many of his opinions which, while prolix, did not try to be exhaustive of all opinions and approaches. His aim was to be practical.[53] The case's facts are minimal. No names, dates, or specific situations. Just the assertion that at issue was whether paternal cousins (*fratres patrueles*) excluded a sister from her brother's estate. This was very similar to the earlier case of the five Florentines, except that here there was a sister, an agnate who excluded a mother from inheriting according to the statute, as opposed to a uterine brother.

Sozzini began by saying that a simple reading of the Florentine statute's words could allow one to say that sisters were not excluded, because *fratres patrueles* were not simply *fratres* and thus were not expressly listed as an excluding presence. He claimed several locations in Baldo's commentaries in support, as well as a host of other authorities (his was most definitely a 'motivated' presentation), and he said it was absurd to part company from so many concurrent opinions.[54] Then he took into account the ideological argument. While it was the case that the *ratio statuti* was *agnationes et familia conservaretur* (citing Baldo), that *ratio*, which was not expressed, should not be extended to other persons, 'and especially because as I said the *ratio* is not expressed so from that which could be or not be it does not seem licit to argue exhaustively, as Bartolo wanted in our matter'.[55] A look at the wording of the statute showed that it excluded sisters first in favour of their brothers, then of the brother's son, and only thirdly for the uncles; and thus it did not seem to privilege uncles' sons. Further, the sister excluded her mother by the first clause of the statute and the cousins there did not keep the mother from claiming her fourth. The legislators had more esteem for the sister than her cousins.

Sozzini then pivoted to the opposite position and spent the rest of the opinion (more than 80 % of its eight folia) refuting the initial arguments in favour of the sister. It all hinged on the ideological reading of the statute in terms of family preservation. The *mens statuentium* was to favour the paternal line to the maternal, which seemed not at all iniquitous to Sozzini. A veritable thunderstorm of ideological references to family followed. In the course of the next five pages, one runs across six references to con-

---

53. Bargagli, *Bartolomeo Sozzini*, 225. She places his most productive period in the years 1488-93.
54. BNF, Magliabechiano xxix 193, fols. 249r-56v, at fol. 249v: 'Unde cum hec opy. Videatur fore ab omnibus approbata absurdum videtur et in consulendo et in iudicando ab ea recedere'.
55. BNF, Magliabechiano xxix 193, fol. 249v: 'et maxime quia ut dixi ratio non est expressa, unde ab illa que potuit esse vel non esse non videtur licite extensive arguere ut voluit Bar<tolus> in materia nostra'.

serving the *dignitas familiarum* (or *familiaritatis*) and a couple more to preserving agnation. To Sozzini's mind the statute's intent was to preserve family through circulation of wealth in the hands of agnates and, within agnates, to favour men over women.[56] In the course of these pages Sozzini referenced the very same *consilia* of Angelo and Baldo that we have seen, even unashamedly using Baldo's very words regarding the agnatic association and meaning of the family house.[57] Males were preferred to females, agnates to cognates. There could be no jurisprudential doubt on this score, even though Baldo's *consilium* had in the end licensed inheritance by a mother against an agnate woman. Sozzini's wrap up of this line of argument is worth repeating:

> From which I conclude that although Baldo and some others hold that it cannot be said that such is the sole *ratio statuti*, yet commonly jurists say the contrary, from which common opinion one should not depart, and especially in our statute in which quite apparently is gathered the *mens et ratio statuentium* from all the principal clauses and dispositions in said statute, especially in our statute we have Bartolo, Baldo and Angelo advising as otherwise I have advised in our statute and learned men have advised. Therefore it is concluded that the sole intent and *ratio* of the legislators was to conserve wealth in agnation through which family dignity is conserved.[58]

So the very same *consilium* of Baldo that we have seen and that helped Sozzini set up his argument was thus also bracketed aside because it seemed to allow more than one rationale to the statute. Baldo, after all, had cited that family rationale only to be able to use it to put part of an estate in the hands of the mother, as the situation of an inheritance dispute between

56. BNF, Magliabechiano xxix 193, fol. 250v: 'Ex quibus patet indubitanter statutum in hac parte movetur ea ratione et mente ut familiaritatis dignitas conservetur. Secundo loco intentio statuentium fuit inter agnatos masculos feminis preferre'.
57. BNF, Magliabechiano xxix 193, fol. 250v: 'que exceptio in prole masculorum consistens quibus gravissimum et iniuriosissimum etiam domum progenitorum fonte suorum et situs in qua fonte antiquata est agnationis fama et retinere consueverunt agnationis nomen, videtur ad extraneos devolutas et imagines maiorum suorum hoc est arma et signa videntur revulsas'.
58. BNF, Magliabechiano xxix 193, fol. 251r: 'Ex quibus concludo quod licet Baldus et quidam alii teneant quod non possit dici quod illa sit ratio unica statuti, tamen communiter doctores contrarium dicunt, a qua communi opinione non est recedendum, et maxime in statuto nostro in quo apertissime colligitur talis mens et ratio statuentium ex principalibus immo omnibus capitulis et dispositis in dicto statuto in specie in statuto nostro habemus Bartolum, Baldum, et Angelum consulentes ita alias in statuto nostro consului et consuluerunt doctissimi viri. Concluditur ergo quod unica intentio et ratio statuentium fuit conservare divitas in agnatione per quas familiaris dignitas conservatur'.

Intestate Inheritance as a Family Matter

women meant the rationale did not apply. As one of those women had in fact been agnate, one wonders if Sozzini was not subtly signalling his disagreement with the conclusion Baldo had reached. It is certain that he was intent on using the principle of agnatic succession as his pole star to guide the way to his conclusion. That rationale worked with a cousin, as Baldo himself opined, according to Sozzini, in a Sienese case that had involved some of Sozzini's own *consanguinei*. He too noted that the statute, while *odiosum* in excluding a sister, was *favorabile* in including paternal cousins. The exclusion and inclusion were simply opposite sides of the effect of the statute aimed for. Uterine brothers were excluded because, as Angelo had said in the *consilium* above, the *ratio conservande agnationis* was not served by them.

Slicing ever finer hairs, or so it seems, Sozzini proceeded through his ten arguments, following from his ideological starting point, that *fratres patrueles* excluded the sister. Along the way he mentioned the *ratio conservande agnationis* three times, not that it was ever far below the surface of his sometimes tedious disquisitions. In the seventh argument he found opportunity to state that if one wanted to point out that some women, like a sister, were agnate, 'I can respond that although a woman is agnate, she is in the female line, because she is the head of the female line, she should be excluded'.[59] The fact that there was a singular *ratio* to the statute licensed an extensive reading. It was, after all, the sole explanation for everything in it.[60] So Sozzini could conclude that any sort of agnate male was always preferred to cognates and even agnate women.

The end of his opinion returned to the problem that the statute did not expressly give its rationale, leaving it to be conjectured, but he brushed that aside with an intriguing metaphor:

> So we may say in our case that by the intent [of the statute] a cousin, because he is an agnate male on account of whom the dignity of families is preserved, is preferred to an agnate sister, a woman who transits to other families. To which conclusion one may arrive because something one establishes from the intent is taken as if expressed, but such intent can be gathered from the words ... from which I can conclude that although in regarding the words it cannot be denied this question contains no little difficulty, yet if we inspect the intent with the eyes of a lynx, I think any erudite and prudent judge will follow this decision.[61]

59. BNF, Magliabechiano xxix 193, fol. 254r: 'possum respondere quod femina licet agnata est in linea feminina quia est caput linee feminine excluderetur'.
60. BNF, Magliabechiano xxix 193, fol. 255r.
61. BNF, Magliabechiano xxix 193, fol. 256v: 'Ita dicemus in casu nostro ut ex mente patruelis quia agnatus masculus propter quem familiarum dignitas conservatur prefertur sorori agnate femine que in alienas transit familias. Ad que accedat quoniam aliquid constat ex mente habetur pro expresso, sed talis mens ex verbis colligi potest. .

The eye of the lynx, seemingly able to detect what others cannot, including perhaps what lay beneath the surface, interestingly also evokes the later academy founded in 1603 that came to include Galileo among its members. Sozzini may not have understood it this way, but he had established the family – its wealth and dignity – not without help from others, to be sure, as the scientific principle, unexpressed but truly lying behind intestate inheritance.

4. Concluding remarks

So after this brief trip through jurisprudence, legislation and forensic reasoning about intestacy, where are we? I think we have seen that learned jurists, beginning around 1350 and more so thereafter, coinciding with the period of the great commentators of the law, were able to supply a rationale for statutory intestacy rules that again and again excluded dowered daughters and other women from inheriting any more than the dowry paid or owed to them. This rationale spoke to the public utility of preserving the wealth and dignity of families, which was the function of agnatic descent and inheritance. This principle, moreover, became the basis to extend the agnatic and masculine bias enshrined in these statutes to categories of descent or degrees not overtly mentioned in the texts of the statutes (as Sozzini extended it to *fratres patrueles*). In the absence of invoking the principle of family, one might be held to, or opt for, a more restrictive and literal reading of the statute (as Angelo degli Ubaldi was) that would result in the exclusion of agnates not otherwise expressly mentioned.

Recourse to the image of family and to the social and political desirability of helping it, in its wealth and dignity, last across generations was a device that also countered the individualistic sense of rights and property ownership that was embedded in *ius commune*. The later widely diffuse habit of use of *fideicommissa* in testaments would insert the image of family – at least for the elites who were their most frequent users – most powerfully into the consciousness and lived reality of agnate descendants. These devices took the place of the contracts and dowry renunciations that had held the earlier *consorzi* together, now stitching people and property in a generational death grip. Name and blood linked the patrilineal kin. Use of patronymics spread along with coats of arms and other family insignia. Urban palaces and rural estates became part of the identity of Italian elites. Debates over the nature of true nobility, as an essence transmitted in the

> . . Ex quibus concludo quod licet inherendo verbis non possit negari hanc questionem difficultatem non parvam, tamen se mentem lynceis oculis inspiciamus arbitror quemlibet iudicem eruditum et prudentem hanc decisionem sequeretur'.

Intestate Inheritance as a Family Matter

blood or a virtue that arose in consequence of service to city or prince (*politica et civilis nobilitas*) were definitively settled in favour of the former, aided in part by the legal positions developed by jurists such as Bartolo.[62] As David Warren Sabean has remarked, 'in baroque culture there was a palpability, substantiality and corporality to the lineage. And the family was perceived on a vertical axis in terms of legitimate descent and succession, all emphasizing agnatic ties, the flow of vital substance through male lines and an extreme egoism of familial descent'.[63] Certainly the family Sozzini talked about was such a vertical axis directing a downward flow of property (as something that more than belongs to a family but is its essence) without regard to marriages to other lines and without, it seems, in any way recognizing the experience of household as a factor in transmission.

How does this compare to intestate practices elsewhere – for our purposes, mainly the Nordic countries? According to one judgment, Germanic inheritance systems were 'a flexible legal system that was more favourable for women and children than the neo-Roman legal systems of southern Europe'.[64] This judgment rests on a seeming lack of priority to males in Germanic laws, except with regard to fiefs. It is claimed as well that Danish rules, while limiting a girl to half as much as her brother, still placed her before uncles and grandfathers. There was also an optative measure allowing return of one's portion into the whole to be then shared among all heirs.[65]

Nordic inheritance rules, like those found in Denmark, were not gender blind, as Helle Vogt has shown.[66] Above all, what strikes me in her account is that 'dowries were considered advancements' whose value was counted into a daughter's inheritance portion. Daughters could inherit with their brothers, even if a smaller share, and in that option of sharing there seems some recognition of the household and lived experience as part of the

---

62. Cf. G. Delille, 'The Shed Blood of Christ: From Blood as Metaphor to Blood as Bearer of Identity', in Johnson et al. (ed.), *Blood and Kinship*, 125-43; G. Castelnuovo, 'Revisiter une classique: noblesse, hérédité et vertu d'Aristotle à Dante et à Bartole (Italie communale, début xiiie-milieu xive siècle)', in van der Lugt & de Miramon (ed.), *L'hérédité*, 105-55.

63. D.W. Sabean, 'Descent and Alliance: Cultural Meanings of Blood in the Baroque', in Johnson et al. (ed.), *Blood and Kinship*, 144-74, at 163. He places the crucial period for this as beginning in 1400, when our first cases took place.

64. D. Nicholas, *The Northern Lands: Germanic Europe, c. 1270-c. 1500* (Chichester: 2009), 259.

65. Nicholas, *The Northern Lands*, 259, 267-68; B. Sawyer & P. Sawyer, *Medieval Scandinavia: From Conversion to Reformation, 800-1500* (Minneapolis: 1993), 180-81.

66. H. Vogt, *The Function of Kinship in Medieval Nordic Legislation* (Leiden: 2010), 155-83, esp. 170-75.

identity of heirs, who each take something from that to their own households, in turn – and that more horizontal experience presents some contrast to the verticality of the Italian juristically conceived *familia*. In Italy dowry was indeed that female inheritance portion, even as it was conceded that it was not the portion due a daughter in *ius commune* (termed the *legitima*).[67] That was the result of intestacy statutes, not of the *ius commune*. I might suggest that the Danish-Scandinavian system that relatively disadvantaged women may have drawn inspiration not from Justinian's *Institutes*, which contained an account of the laws that he overturned in favour of gender equality, but from knowledge of practices and the first rules being formulated in centres like Bologna to deal with dowry and inheritance.[68] No proof of the point. Just a suggestion.

---

67. Th. Kuehn, 'Dos Non Teneat Locum Legittime: Dowry as a Woman's Inheritance in Early Quattrocento Florence', in P. Andersen et al. (ed.), *Law and Marriage in Medieval and Early Modern Times* (Copenhagen: 2012), 231-48.
68. On the possible influence of the *Institutes*, see Vogt, *The Function of Kinship*, 180-81.

THE SWEDISH ECCLESIASTICAL LEGISLATION AND THE QUESTION OF ITS NORDIC CHARACTER

Bertil Nilsson

1. Introduction

When asking the question *how* Nordic are the medieval Nordic laws, it implies that they are Nordic in some way. Hardly anyone would deny that this is true. However, the ecclesiastical legislation should be regarded as fundamentally specific, the reason being that it is directly connected with the Christianization and establishment of the Church in the Scandinavian realms. With regard to the Swedish realm this process went on especially during the 11th century and the first half of the 12th century.

In an early phase of the ecclesiastical establishment in Sweden, the Church's 'law' was not Nordic. Instead it was a matter of international West European church law. Yet this is not entirely true, because formally there was no collected, generally decreed church law until after 1234, when Pope Gregory IX promulgated his own and other popes' decretals in the so-called *Liber Extra*.

The most appropriate way to put it is probably that there was ecclesiastical legislation in the early phase as well as later on during the Middle Ages which was applicable to the Western Church, but there were local variations between and within different church provinces. Partly the variations concerned such things that were not dictated to the Church as a whole, partly things that led to compromises between the international legal ideal and the regional conditions and requirements. Some phenomena were self-evident and existed everywhere, namely the ones that constituted the fundamentals of the Church, such as the clergy, church buildings, and different types of services. How such phenomena were regularized juridically in detail differed depending on the decisions, agreements and arrangements that were made locally. In Sweden, the local juridical authorities consisted of the different provinces' decision-making bodies, the so-called *landsting* (county assemblies). So, regarding to Sweden and what was designated by the term law, the different provinces constituted the basis. At this type of assemblies decisions were made that overall were called 'sections of church law' (*kyrkobalkar*) being parts of the different provincial laws. They reflect the legal interaction between the representatives of the Church and the ones of the local community. Thus, the aim of this article is mainly to determine what ecclesiastical legislation there was in Sweden and its character regarding the question of Swedish/Nordic contra international.

2. Church law in Sweden before the time of the provincial laws

Papal decrees in the form of letters addressed to different instances in Sweden are known since the year 1080. On 4 October 1080, Pope Gregory VII (1073-1085) asked the Swedish king to send a bishop or a suitable cleric to Rome in order to inform him about the demands emanating from the Apostolic See, and that he should consequently inform about them at home.[1] At about the same time another letter arrived, which cannot be dated exactly, addressed to the kings Inge and Hallsten, in which the pope summarized his instructions for the on-going organization of the Church in Sweden.[2]

Two letters from Pope Anastasius IV (1153-1154), one of them addressed to the Swedish king and the secular dignitaries of the realm, the other one to the Swedish bishops, give the impression that cardinal legate Nicolaus Breakspear, when visiting Sweden in 1153, promulgated statutes (*statuta / constitutiones*) concerning the freedom of the Church, marriage, prohibition against wearing of weapons, *privilegium canonis*, 'and other things that had the salvation of the people in view'.[3] Whether his promulgations resulted in a written document is not known; no record has been preserved. As far as I have been able to establish, the statutes have not been referred to later on in

---

1. *Diplomatarium Suecanum* 1- (Stockholm: 1829-), (hereafter: DS) DS #24; Also in *Svenskt diplomatariums huvudkartotek över medeltidsbreven*, (hereafter: SDHK), in www.nad.riksarkivet.se SDHK #170.
2. DS #25 = SDHK #169.
3. DS #38 = SDHK #186; DS #820 = SDHK #187. — On the cardinal legate's visit to Scandinavia, see A. Bergquist, 'The papal legate: Nicholas Breakspear's Scandinavian mission', in B. Bolton & A. Duggan (ed.), *Adrian IV the English pope (1154-1159). Studies and texts* (Burlington: 2003), 41-48.

the Swedish church province, which might indicate that they have never existed in the written form.

Not least during the pontificate of Pope Alexander III (1159-1181), the Swedish church province, which was instituted in the year 1164 under the leadership of the archbishop of Uppsala, was provided with a number of letters. They all aimed at putting the church province under the protection of Saint Peter in order to implement the ideals of Canon law also in Sweden.[4] For instance, Pope Alexander during the latter part of the 1160s (the letter cannot be exactly dated) claimed that *privilegium fori* ought to be put into practice in Uppsala.[5] Somewhat later he made the same requirement with regard to *privilegium canonis*.[6] And in the most comprehensive letter the pope tried to make the Swedes implement Canon law regarding marriages and last wills. There he also made instructions concerning the paying of tithes as well as prescriptions about sacrilege with regard to church buildings and ecclesiastical property.[7]

Concerning the 12th century it should be noticed that no equivalent to the document called *Canones Nidrosienses*, in force in the Norwegian church, seems to have existed in Sweden.[8] Furthermore, during this century was no recorded domestic law containing ecclesiastical legislation has been preserved to our day in contrast to Denmark and Norway.

To what extent the papal decrees from the late 11th and 12th centuries, were spread in Sweden, we do not know, neither whether they had any palpable consequences for the peasantry before the time of the first appearance of fragments of provincial laws. The earliest preserved examples of Swedish attitudes towards Canon law date back to the beginning of the 13th century and consist of royal privileges. For instance, King Sverker (Karlsson r. 1196-1208) confirmed the papal requirement for *privilegium fori* and made exemptions with regard to charges to the king from ecclesiastical property.[9]

It still remains to be investigated whether the context, or parts of it, of the law collections older than the *Liber Extra*, such as Burchard of Worms' *Decretum* from 1012-1023, Ivo of Chartres' *Decretum* from around 1095 and Gratianus' *Decretum* from around 1150 might have been known

---

4. DS #41 = SDHK #224; DS #49 = SDHK #202; DS #50 = SDHK #203.
5. DS #62 = SDHK #221.
6. DS #52 = SDHK #250.
7. DS #41 = SDHK #224.
8. Concerning the *Canones* there is a comprehensive Norwegian research, see S. Bagge et al. (ed.), *Norske middelalderdokumenter* (Bergen, Oslo & Tromso: 1973), 54; O. Sandaaker, 'Canones Nidrosienses – intermesso eller opptakt?', *Historisk tidsskrift* (1988), 2-38.
9. See D. Strauch, *Mittelalterliches nordisches Recht bis 1500. Eine Quellenkunde* (Berlin & New York: 2011), 62-66.

Sweden already in the 12th century in the form of individual *canones* and, if so, how they were received. However, due to the present scarcity of source material, it can be questioned whether it is at all possible to carry through such an investigation regarding Swedish conditions.[10]

Thanks to the fact that fragments of medieval liturgical and Canon law books were preserved in the form of wrappers for royal accounts from around 1530 and 1640 – the books were 'slaughtered' – we get an idea of the amount of Canon law collections and commentaries existing in Sweden. The number of wrappers is great; there are around 23,000, out of which some 11,000 have been identified, belonging to 5,000 different manuscripts. The most part derives from liturgical books (84%) but some of them, approx. 720, are juridical manuscripts.[11] Among them there are fragments of the collections that became *Corpus Iuris Canonici*, normally with each collection's *glossa ordinaria*, furthermore the *Compilationes antiquae* and Hostiensis' *Lectura* and others. However, none of the manuscripts were produced in Sweden. They were all imported, and normally we do not know when they were brought to Sweden neither where the Canon law books were used.[12] Nevertheless, in the light of these facts it is reasonable to assume that the fundamental Canon law collections were spread in Sweden during the second half of the 13th century, i.e. during the period when most of the provincial laws got the wording which we know of today.[13]

Last wills made by Swedish clerics during the period of 1200 till 1330 also give a little hint of the existence of Canon law books in Sweden. Not many last wills, around fifteen all together, the oldest one dating back to 1291. This year the archdeacon Sigtrygg in Linköping made his last will and stated that he owned a number of Canon law books, namely seven books on

---

10. Concerning this complex of problems and the considerable differences in this case between on the one hand Denmark and Norway and on the other hand Sweden, see P. Landau, 'The importance of classical canon law in Scandinavia in the 12th and 13th centuries', in P. Andersen, D. Tamm & H. Vogt (ed.), *How Nordic are the Nordic medieval laws* (Copenhagen: 2011 – 2nd edn), 23-39.
11. J. Brunius, *From manuscripts to wrappers. Medieval book fragments in the Swedish National Archives* (Stockholm: 2013), 34-41.
12. J. Brunius, *From manuscripts to wrappers*, 169-72 = list of the juridical manuscripts to which the fragments belonged; T. Schmid, 'Canon law manuscripts from medieval Sweden', *Traditio* 7 (1949-51), 444-49. Schmid wrote that some of these were in use in Sweden 'at an early date', without any further clarification.
13. The history of the reception of Canon law in Sweden has not yet been written, but Mia Korpiola has the intention of starting such a project, see M. Korpiola, 'On ecclesiastical jurisdiction and the reception of canon law in the Swedish provincial laws', in P. Andersen, D. Tamm & H. Vogt (ed.), *How Nordic*, 207-34, at 234.

The Swedish Ecclesiastical Legislation

the decretal law and one on Gratian's *Decretum*.[14] In the year 1292, a parish priest in Lommaryd in the diocese of Linköping owned Pope Gregory's decretals, C*asus decretalium* (either by Bernhard of Parma or Bernhard of Pavia) and a S*ummula de abstinentia*.[15] In the year 1312 the rural dean in Bollnäs in the diocese of Uppsala willed away Pope Gregory's decretals.[16] Finally, in 1328 the dean Lars of Uppsala cathedral – who is the only known author of Canon law writings in Sweden during the Middle Ages – among several books of different kind gave Gratian's *Decretum* and Pope Gregory's decretals with its *glossa ordinaria* to the Dominicans in Sigtuna, the brothers there promising that he was allowed to keep them as long as he lived. He wrote, among other things, that he was physically weak but had a lucid mind. Therefore he could not manage to live without his books.[17]

Of course, you cannot draw any far-reaching conclusions from the fact that just a little number of priests had some privately-owned books. The representativity is far from satisfying. Still it should be noticed that priests with different types of benefices or prebends owned Canon law manuscripts at the time when a great number of the Swedish provincial laws were written down, and among these manuscripts were – not surprisingly – Pope Gregory's decretals.

Before turning to the sections of church law in the provincial laws, I would like to underline that there was after all ecclesiastical legislation in Sweden which was Swedish in the sense that it was ratified in the domestic context. Thus, it should be pointed out that the church law in the Swedish church province, as in all other church provinces, did not exist only in the form of what we call provincial laws and their sections of church law. In addition, there were statutes issued by the archbishop and his suffragans at the provincial councils as well as by the bishops at the diocesan synods. These decisions and statutes were as essential a part of the medieval church law as was the prescriptions found in the provincial laws, although the statutes normally did not have so great a legal importance for the laypeople. Besides, the provincial statutes and decisions as well as the diocesan ones were confirmed by ecclesiastical legislative bodies only. However, we know that also laymen, i.e. representatives of the secular authorities, to some part exercised influence over the subjects that were dealt with at the provincial councils. In Sweden such councils were often held in connection with the gatherings of the secular authorities. To what extent laymen also had

---

14. DS #1034 = SDHK #1507. H. Lundström, 'Hvilka äro vår äldsta domkapitel?', in H. Lundström (ed.), *Skisser och kritiker. En samling kyrkohistoriska uppsatser och föredrag* (Stockholm: 1903), 33-42 has identified some of the manuscripts.
15. DS #1741 = SDHK #1534.
16. DS #1850 = SDHK #2499.
17. DS # 2672 = SDHK #3550.

influence over the final decisions, formally made by the bishops only, is hard to say, but should be investigated.

The first provincial council in the church province of Uppsala which we know of, was held in 1233, but no statutes have been preserved from this episcopal meeting,[18] the oldest ones instead deriving from the important council of Skänninge in 1248.[19]

The purpose of the provincial councils was partly to implement the juridical decisions made in Rome. The diocesan statutes, on the other hand, mainly contained rather detailed instructions with regard to the liturgy and the sacraments. However, you should not ignore that they were actually also relevant for people outside the limited ecclesiastical circle, i.e. for others than the bishops and the clergy, for instance regarding the sacrament of penance. When asking for the origin of this type of statutes, you can start from a basic idea which is also applicable to the sections of church law in the provincial laws. On the one hand, at least partly, it was about their connection with reality (to put it simplified: 'if there was no crime, there was no prohibition') and on the other hand their regional character[20] (only what happened within the borders of the church province or the diocese was interesting, unless it was about to implement legal ideals coming from Rome).

3. The dating of the Swedish sections of church law

Even though we should not forget the ecclesiastical statutes, we cannot ignore the fact that the provincial laws so far attracted the main attention in research on Swedish medieval history of law.

Nine sections of church law are preserved. Eight of them are parts of provincial laws preserved as a whole. In one case, only the section of church law is left, viz. the Tiohärads law, in force in the province of Småland. In

---

18. DS #281, 1788 = SDHK #494, 2412.
19. On the Swedish provincial councils, see B. Nilsson, 'Medieval province councils in Scandinavia. A preliminary survey', *Annuarium historiae conciliorum* 32 (2000:1), 22-43, at 39-43. Swedish provincial statutes were edited in H. Reuterdahl (ed.), *Statuta synodalia veteris ecclesiæ sveogothicæ* (Lund: 1841); S. Kroon (ed.), *Statuter från svenska medeltida provinsialkoncilier* (Skellefteå: 2010); Swedish diocesan statutes were edited in J. Gummerus (ed.), *Synodalstatuter och andra kyrkorättsliga aktstycken från den svenska medeltidskyrkan* (Uppsala: 1902).
20. See T. Wünsch, 'Partikularsynoden als Normierungsinstanzen am Vorabend der Reformation. (Beispiele aus Böhmen-Mähren, Schlesien und Polen)', in N. Kruppa & L. Zygner (ed.), *Partikularsynoden im späten Mittelalter* (Göttingen: 2006), 289-306, at 291.

The Swedish Ecclesiastical Legislation

the Guta law of the island of Gotland there is no section of church law, but related decrees are found mainly in the first eight chapters of the law. Furthermore, there were two other laws, now totally lost, the Närke law and the Värmlands law. It should also be noticed that decrees with ecclesiastical relevance appear in other parts of the laws, not only in the sections of church law.

How old are they? The question has caused a lot of troubles and led to divergent opinions among scholars during the last two centuries. When trying to make a chronological classification of the mentioned laws you immediately come across a fundamental problem: None of them has been preserved in an original manuscript, i.e. a text which dates back exactly to the day when the law presumably was written down for the very first time. All source material consists of transcripts. Therefore, there are chronological gaps that can only be filled with the question: Did not anything happen with the contents of the law during the gaps of time? The question is legitimate, since there is clear examples that manuscripts of one and the same law sometimes differ in several important respects, also when their time of origin is presumably almost the same.

Thus, the dating has occupied a lot of scholars' thoughts throughout the years. This is true about the manuscripts as well as the endeavours at presenting a point of time when the laws were written down at the earliest. Concerning this problem I will mainly use Dieter Strauch's comprehensive book from 2011 *Mittelalterliches nordisches Recht bis 1500,* where the author also accounts for older opinions about the dating.[21] I have supplemented his information with the recent results presented by some of the members of the *Medieval Nordic Laws* project[22] and some other investigations.

Earlier Swedish scholars used to group the laws into Göta-laws and Svea-laws, respectively, taking into consideration the regions of their validity and to a certain extent also their contents and structure. Such a division is not relevant when only looking at the sections of church law. Certainly, they were in force only within the law districts, but the all-embracing church law, which encountered the local juridical traditions, was not geographically limited with regard to the fundamental claims. It was valid in the church province as a whole or in the different dioceses, and these were not fully identical with the law districts or not at all. Thus, there are two provincial laws with different sections of church law in the dioceses of Uppsala (the

---

21. It is obvious it was written over many years, as the author is not always aware of the latest opinions among scholars.
22. This refers to opinions not yet published from Stefan Brink concerning the Hälsinge law, Staffan Fridell concerning the Tiohärads section of church law, Christine Peel concerning the Västmanna law and Jan Paul Strid concerning the Östgöta law.

Upplands law and the Hälsinge law), Linköping (the Östgöta law and the Guta law) and Västerås (the Dala law and the Västmanna law).

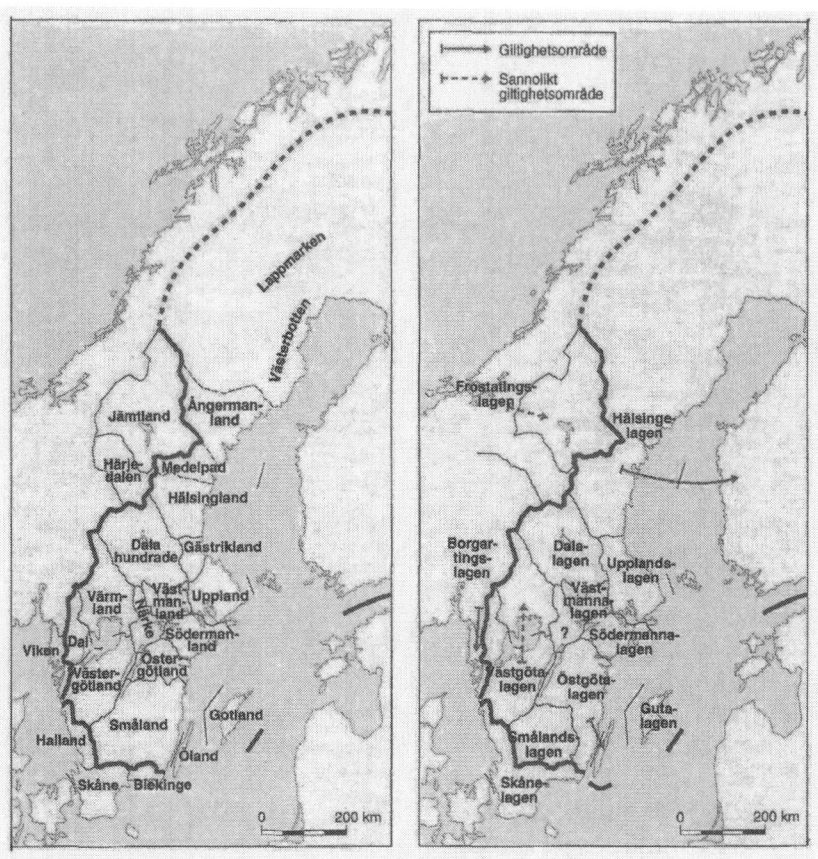

The Swedish provinces (to the left) and the law districts (to the right).

The number of medieval manuscripts containing each law in its entirety is very small. However, there are considerably more manuscripts containing the sections of church law because the Swedish Law of the realm from about 1350 was not provided with such a section. Therefore, the different sections of church law were inserted into manuscripts of the Law of the realm in the different provinces. These manuscripts should be dedicated to a comparative investigation with regard to both dating and contents.[23]

23. There are six separate manuscripts containing the section of church law of the Older Västgöta law, see Å. Holmbäck & E. Wessén, 'Inledning', in Å. Holmbäck & E. Wessén (ed.), *Svenska landskapslagar tolkade och förklarade för nutidens svenskar* 5 (hereafter: SLL) (Stockholm: 1946), xi-cxvi, at xli-xlii; of the Södermanna law more

The oldest section of church law is the one which is part of the *Older Västgöta law* (VgL I). Only one manuscript of the law as a whole is preserved, and it is considered to be a transcript made in the 1280/1290s. A small fragment of the law, which does not contain anything from the section of church law, is, on a linguistic basis dated back to around 1250 at the latest. Some conditions seem to indicate that the law as a whole was written down for the first time during the 1220s. The just mentioned fragment might be as old as that.[24]

The *Upplands law* (UL) occupied a place apart and influenced the other laws. It was compiled by a commission consisting of fifteen members, among others the dean of the cathedral of Uppsala, Andreas And.[25] He had studied in Paris where he took a master's degree. Probably, his education included Canon law. The Upplands law was provided with a royal letter of confirmation on 2 January 1296. There are five medieval manuscripts of the law as a whole, all of them belonging to the middle of the 14th century, except the oldest one considered to be written down during the first half of the 14th century, or maybe at the beginning of the century.[26]

At least four laws contain elements borrowed from the Upplands law, namely the following ones. The only preserved part of the law which once was in force in the law district of *Tiohärad* (TiL) is the section of church law. Only fragments of the rest of the law, sometimes called the Smålands law, remain. The law was mentioned for the first time in a bill of sale in 1299, but the two oldest manuscripts date back to the middle and the end of the 14th century, respectively. The text of the section of church law, as known today, contains elements from the Upplands law as well as the Östgöta law, and, thus, it is considered to have emergerd after 1296 and in the beginning of the 14th century.[27] The *Södermanna law* (SdmL) is preserved in two complete manuscripts from the 14th century; one of them from about 1325/1327, the other from after 1335. A revised version of the law

---

than forty, Holmbäck & Wessén, 'Inledning', SLL 3 (Stockholm: 1940), xi-lxix, at xiii; of the Västmanna law two, Holmbäck & Wessén, 'Inledning', SLL 2 (Stockholm: 1936), xii-l, at xxxiii; of the Östgöta law six, Holmbäck & Wessén, 'Inledande anmärkningar', SLL 1 (Stockholm: 1933), 3-5, at 4; of the Upplands law about one hundred and twenty, Holmbäck & Wessén, 'Inledande anmärkningar', SLL 1 (Stockholm: 1933), 3-4.

24. Strauch, *Mittelalterliches*, 394-400; P.-A. Wiktorsson, 'Inledning', in P.A. Wiktorsson (ed.), *Äldre Västgötalagen och dess bilagor i Cod. Holm. B 59*. Del 1. ([Skara]: 2011), 11-44, at 11-13, 17.
25. The other members were two chief judges of the law district (*lagmän*), two judges and also noble knights and peasants, see Strauch, *Mittelalterliches*, 88-89.
26. Strauch, *Mittelalterliches*, 439-41, 452.
27. Strauch, *Mittelalterliches*, 426-29; Staffan Fridell (manuscript to Bertil Nilsson 24.2.2013).

was ratified in 1326, the revision being made firstly around the year 1300 under the influence of the Upplands law. However, there are elements making the impression that an original recording possibly took place between the years 1279 and 1285. The oldest manuscript probably contains the version of the law before the second revision which took place in 1327/1327, resulting in a royal ratification.[28] The *Västmanna law* (VmL) is preserved in three manuscripts from the 14th century; two of them from the first half of the century and the third one from the second half. To a great extent the law resembles with the Upplands law from 1296 and partly with the Södermanna law from 1327. The years 1327-1347 are usually mentioned as the time of the coming into being of the Västmanna law; the latter year the work on the Law of the realm started. Thus, the two oldest manuscripts might come quite close to the law's earliest version.[29] The *Hälsinge law* (HL) was compiled after the Upplands law 1296 and is obviously influenced by it, but there are also prescriptions considered to contain archaic elements. However, these do not belong to the section of church law. The only preserved manuscript dates back to the time after 1320, probably around 1350. Perhaps it was the archbishop of Uppsala Olof Björnsson (1315-1332) who arranged the law to be written down, but this is not quite sure, and therefore the time space 1296 till about 1350 may be fitting.[30]

The *Östgöta law* (ÖgL) is mainly preserved in fragments from the 14th century; the oldest ones from the first half of the century. The only complete manuscript from the Middle Ages known to us dates back to about 1350. The law was mentioned for the first time in 1303 but might be one or more decades older than the version that we know of.[31]

The only preserved manuscript of the *Dala law* (DL) has been given quite different dating, i.e. the time before 1279 till the time after 1327. Also the time span 1250-1320 was suggested. Furthermore, according to a couple of modern scholars brought up the opinion that it is not even a Dala law but an older version of the Västmanna law, which was in force in both the

---

28. Strauch, *Mittelalterliches*, 463-71.
29. Strauch, *Mittelalterliches*, 479-85; Christine Peel (manuscript to Bertil Nilsson 23.2.2013).
30. Strauch, *Mittelalterliches*, 495-98; S. Brink, 'Hälsingelagens ställning mellan väst och syd, och mellan kung, kyrka och lokala traditioner', *Kungl. Vitterhets historie och antikvitets akademiens årsbok 2010* (Stockholm: 2010), 119-35, at 120-21, 124, 133; Stefan Brink's e-mail to Bertil Nilsson 17.2.2013.
31. Strauch, *Mittelalterliches*, 411-14; Jan Paul Strid's e-mail to Bertil Nilsson 25.2.2013.

provinces of Dalarna and Västmanland, or even the now lost Värmlands law.[32]

The *Gutalagen* (GL) was studied by Christine Peel, who in the 2009 published an English translation of the law and also a source- and text critical introduction and commentaries. The law is preserved in only one medieval manuscript, presumable written down around the year 1350. Peel demonstrated that there are at least four different opinions of when the Guta law was written down for the first time: 1) during the 12th century, 2) 1220-1250, 3) towards the end of the 13th century and 4) during the first half of the 14th century. Without any directly conclusive evidence she suggested a probable dating to around 1220: '[…] a date of ca. 1220 for the earliest manuscript […] seems not unreasonable'. Dieter Strauch seems to be of the opinion that the time interval 1220-1230 is a more plausible one.[33] Perhaps the Canon law expert Archbishop Anders Sunesen of Lund inspired the writing down of the law as well as the narration about the oldest history of Gotland connected with the law and called the Guta saga. He visited the island in the year 1207.[34]

Finally the *Younger Västgöta law* (VgL II). The sources of the laws from the province of Västergötland are unique with regard to Swedish medieval history of law. Apart from the already mentioned Older Västgöta law, there is a younger version which came into being after a thorough revision and far-reaching enlargement. Furthermore, there is a number of ecclesiastical texts from the diocese of Skara, out of which some were given different names during the 19th and 20th centuries. As was recently pointed out, they were not put into the context of the Younger Västgöta law in a satisfactory way by earlier scholars.

When Professor Göran B. Nilsson in 2012 published a pioneering investigation, new light was spread on the history of the coming into being of the younger Västgöta law.[35] He made it very clear that the most elusive source, the so called 'Lydekini excerpts', not at all is excerpts from the Younger Västgöta law, which everyone so far assumed without questioning this

---

32. Strauch, *Mittelalterliches*, 481-83; E. Sjöholm, *Sveriges medeltidslagar. Europeisk rättstradition i politisk omvandling* (Lund: 1988), 328-29. About the Värmlands law, see also Strauch, *Mittelalterliches*, 433-34.
33. C. Peel, 'Introduction', in C. Peel (ed.), *Guta lag. The Law of the Gotlanders* (London: 2009), xxxix; Strauch, *Mittelalterliches*, 505-09.
34. E. Wessén, 'Gutalagen', *Kulturhistoriskt lexikon för nordisk medeltid* 5, 600-02; C. Peel, 'Introduction', in C. Peel (ed.), *Guta saga. The history of the Gotlanders* (London: 1999), vi-lx, at xlix-liii; C. Peel, 'Introduction', in C. Peel (ed.), *Guta lag*, vi-xlv, at xiv-xix, xxxvi-xxxix.
35. G.B. Nilsson, *Nytt ljus över Yngre Västgötalagen. Den bestickande teorin om en medeltida lagstiftningsprocess* (Stockholm: 2012).

'fact'. By using a royal regulation and a number of diocesan statutes from the time of Bishop Brynolf Algotsson, bishop of Skara between 1278 and 1317, Nilsson established that the 'excerpts' in reality must be dated back to the time *before* the Younger Västgöta law was ratified. They contain memoranda, he maintained, with propositions made during the rather long process of legislation, going on between 1295/1300 and 1310/1315 and finally leading to the first ratified version of the law.

Thus, Nilsson was able to give new and adequate names to the most important sources while replacing the older misleading designations and to study the way in which the revision of the law took place with the church of Skara and its representatives as one of the negotiating parties. Furthermore, he managed to divide the legislation process into three fundamental and rather distinct phases. With regard to the dating he established that the Younger Västgöta law as a whole was finished between 1310 and 1315, not in the 1290s as was the former opinion.[36]

Now we can present the dating of the Swedish provincial laws according to suggestions made by different scholars as follows:

Older Västgöta law	1220s-c.1250
Guta law	c. 1220-1230 (11th century-c.1350)
Östgöta law	1280s, 1290s, 1300-1310 (c.1350)
Dala law	before 1279-after 1327
Upplands law	1296
Tiohärads Church law	after 1296, ca.1300-1310
Younger Västgöta law	1310-1315
Södermanna law	c. 1327, 1279-1285, before 1325
Hälsinge law	1320s; 1315-1332; 1296-c.1350
Västmanna law	1327-1347

The overview shows that it is difficult to determine the final enforcement of most of the laws, as well as when they were written down for the first time. This means that the Swedish ecclesiastical prescriptions might have been ratified a number of times within approximately one hundred years when taking all the sections of church law into account. Therefore, it is almost impossible to study the contents of the different sections of church law in a chronological comparative perspective. The uncertainty of the dating is so big that you cannot take the suggested ones as starting-point for such a study. Only the two oldest ones, the Older Västgöta law and the Guta law (maybe), could be compared with the cluster of the others in a reasonable way

---

36. Nilsson, *Nytt ljus,* passim but especially 29-100, 178-94.

In all respects, the question already pointed out manifests itself, viz. whether the text that we know of actually reproduces the sections of church law as they were formulated when they were ratified and written down for the first time. This problem especially becomes obvious regarding the oldest laws, since the time span between the first supposed text and the preserved ones is big, but the same problem is also applicable to the other laws. Göran B. Nilsson's study has proven that more thorough research ought to be done with regard to the manuscripts and their dating in relation to the contents of the laws in their historical context. He also made convincingly clear that you should be very sceptical and questioning concerning older editions and translations with commentaries. When reading his book it becomes overwhelmingly striking how much of negligence, carelessness and rashness he found among earlier scholars with regard to the Västgöta laws.

The fact is that it is not only possible but remarkably fruitful to carry through similar very detailed comparative studies by starting from a selected number of regulations in one section of church law. This was clearly shown when Torgeir Landro published his PhD-thesis at the University of Bergen in 2010. His main results are convincingly contradicting and correcting earlier opinions among scholars concerning the oldest Norwegian ecclesiastical legislation.[37]

The books and articles published by Mia Korpiola during the last decade, mainly on matrimonial law, should also be mentioned here.[38] At the conference at the Carlsberg's Academy ten years ago she was talking about the ecclesiastical legislation in Sweden. On that occasion she was applying a method which is not unusual, namely to start from different themes in Canon law and check if they are represented in the Swedish laws. Furthermore, she related the themes to what ought to be handled within the framework of either ecclesiastical or civil law as well as what was regarded as mixed cases and what should belong to the *forum internum* and *externum*, respectively. Thus, she made a very important exposition of the Swedish ecclesiastical legislation that had not been done before, and she concluded: '[t]he mixture of domestic and international, ecclesiastical and secular

---

37. T. Landro, *Kristenrett og kyrkjerett. Borgartingskristenretten i eit komparativt perspektiv* (Bergen: 2010).
38. To mention just a few recent ones, see for instance, M. Korpiola, *Between betrothal and bedding: Marriage formation in Sweden 1200-1600* (Leiden: 2009); M. Korpiola, 'Marriage causes in late medieval Sweden: The evidence of Bishop Hans Brask's register (1522-1527)', in M. Korpiola (ed.), *Regional variations in matrimonial law and custom in Europe 1150-1600* (Leiden: 2011), 211-49; M. Korpiola, 'The deathbed marriage of Karl Knutsson Bonde: Legitimization by subsequent marriage, property and family strategies in late medieval Sweden', *Tijschrift voor Rechtsgeschiedenis* 80 (2012), 129-55.

shows that medieval Sweden was firmly anchored in the medieval Catholic Church and the larger legal community. Yet, the reception of foreign was by no means automatic, entirely passive or complete.'[39]

Mia Korpiola's results are good enough but still the question can be asked: From a methodological point of view, how do you answer the question of 'How Nordic are the Nordic laws?' in the best way. Is it by identifying elements in the sections of church law that cannot be found elsewhere? Or is it about the structure of the sections of church law which cannot be found elsewhere? Or is it about the language – both the church law terminology as well as the way of expressing things, i.e. a legal language which cannot be found elsewhere? Or is it about church law problems that have got a specific Swedish solution compared to international Canon law or the other Nordic laws? Or is it about all this taken together? In that case it should require an enormous wide reading and knowledge of details appearing in great amounts of source material. However, one thing should be pointed out: There are Swedish elements in the ecclesiastical legislation concerning subjects relevant only very locally, because the prerequisites were only very locally,[40] as for instance prescriptions regarding local cults of saints.[41] But cult of saints was, of course, not itself a local phenomenon.

4. The extent and contents of the sections of church law

When using the rather modern Swedish standard translation and counting pages you get the following results with regard to the extent of the sections of church law:

> The Older Västgöta law = 5 pages;
> The Guta law = 6 pages
> The Dala law = 7 pages
> The Tiohärads section of church law = 9 pages
> The Hälsinge law = 9 pages
> The Södermanna law = 13 pages
> The Östgöta law = 13 pages
> The Västmanna law = 16 pages
> The Younger Västgöta law = 19 pages
> The Upplands law = 19 pages

39. M. Korpiola, 'On ecclesiastical jurisdiction', 234.
40. See Strauch, *Mittelalterliches,* 405-08 (VgLII), 417-19 (ÖgL), 429-31 (TiL), 453-57 (UK), 498-501 (HL), 511-12 (GL) concerning the peculiarities of the different laws, although this only relates to the sections of church law to a very small extent.
41. See for instance SdmL Kk 21.

This way of looking upon the sections of church law from a mere quantitative perspective is, of course, very superficial. Still it is obvious that the shortest ones, the Older Västgöta law and the Guta law, are the ones considered to be oldest in the form that we know of, and the most comprehensive ones, the Younger Västgöta law and the Upplands law, are those about which we know for sure that they have been thoroughly treated in a process of legislation by a commission or the like. Perhaps, it should be seen in this way: The more you conferred and the more profound the competence among the involved expertise was, the more comprehensive became the laws.

When looking at the contents on a general level, you can establish that the most comprehensive sections of church law contain most juridical themes. It is not so, that the shortest ones only were made more precise, but also a number of totally new subjects were added.

You find the most obvious similarities between the sections of church law in the Upplands law, the Hälsinge law, the Södermanna law and the Västmanna law. They are so explicit that there obviously is a connection between them; these sections of church law cannot have come into being independent of each other. The common way to look upon it, and surely also the correct one, is to maintain that the Upplands law was the model.[42] However, from this perspective you can ask yourself why the section of church law in the Hälsinge law is so comparatively short.

We may assume that the sections of church law came into being during shorter or longer processes of legislation in the different law districts engaging representatives of the Church as well as magnates and peasants, although we are not informed as to how the processes went on. However, it is difficult to imagine that all chapters and all paragraphs from the point of view of contents were new creations during the processes made in Sweden as a result of the reception of international Canon law. In what way the legal reception actually took place regarding the different provincial laws was very much discussed within the framework of Swedish history of law when Elsa Sjöholm presented her opinions in a number of books during the 1970s and 1980s strongly opposing the so-called germanistic theory.[43] Recently Dieter Strauch, discussing the question on an overall level with clear examples pointed out the difficulties contained in Sjöholm's lines of argument. In opposition to her theses, he referred to the royal letter of ratifycation of the Upplands law, where it is said that '[...] without urgent reasons

---

42. See Strauch, *Mittelalterliches*, 449, 457-58.
43. E. Sjöholm, *Rechtsgeschichte als Wissenschaft und Politik. Studien zur germanistischen Theorie des 19. Jahrhunderts* (Berlin: 1972); E. Sjöholm, *Gesetze als Quellen mittelalterlicher Geschichte des Nordens* (Stockholm: 1976); E. Sjöholm, *Sveriges medeltidslagar. Europeisk rättstradition i politisk omvandling* (Lund: 1988).

we did not want to change old law and not unduly add new one'. He also made reference to the preface of the same law, where an older law is mentioned, about which it is said that the law commission used the prescriptions from it that were useful for all and excluded what was not useful.[44]

Also Stefan Brink treated the question of reception with regard to the Hälsinge law and drew the same conclusions as most people who discussed Elsa Sjöholm's standpoints, namely that this law '[...] in no way is an 'invention' by someone in the 14th century'. Instead it is about 'older traditions and rules of law, as well as specific documents and lists of importance for the Northern parts of the archdiocese' that were incorporated into the law.[45] This is also my own point of view with regard to all Swedish sections of church law.

When looking at subjects judicially regulated in the shorter sections of church law you realize that they contain apparent similarities both with each other and with the more comprehensive versions. However, obvious variants stand out when scrutinizing the detailed level. For instance, you may ask why the introductory words of the Upplands law and the Hälsinge law, that are identical, got their specific wording. First they contain a *decree* on Christian faith.[46] Nothing is remarkable about this. There are similar decrees in slight different variations in almost every Swedish law, as well as in the older versions of the Norwegian ones, although not in the Danish church laws for the provinces of Sjælland (Sj Kk) and Skåne (Sk Kk), respectively. However, the decrees on Christian faith in the Upplands law and the Hälsinge law are followed by a *prohibition* against heathen cult and belief, where it is also specified what it meant.[47] A more general parallel can be found in the Guta law, where it is also about to 'deny the heathendom'[48] as well as a considerably more exhaustive paragraph on sacrifices (*blot*).[49] Furthermore, there are similar regulations in older legislation on the Con-

---

44. Strauch, *Mittelalterliches*, 457, see also 103-06; H.S. Collin & C.J. Schlyter (ed.), *Samling af Sweriges gamla lagar* 1-8 (Stockholm: 1827-1852) (hereafter: SSGL), at SSGL 3, 3-6, 6-9.
45. Brink, 'Hälsingelagens ställning', 133.
46. UL Kk 1pr., 3, 11: 'A krist skulu allir (kristni) troæ at han ær guþ. oc æi æru guþær flere. æn han æn'.
47. UL Kk 1pr., SSGL 3, 1-2: 'ængin skal affguþum blotæ. ok ængin a lundi ællr stenæ troæ'.
48. GL 1, SSGL 7, 7: 'Þitta ir fyrst upp haf .i. lagum orum þet wir sculum naicca haiþnu oc iatta crisnu'.
49. GL 4, SSGL 7, 14: 'Þet ier nu þy nest et blotir iru mannum mier firj buþni Oc fyrnsca all þaun sum haiþnu fylgir Engin ma haita a huathci a hult eþa hauga. eþa haþin guþ. huatki avi eþa stafgarþa'.

tinent and in England.[50] But why is the prohibition there in the comparatively young Upplands law and Hälsinge law? What made the lawmakers in these provinces insert the prohibition? Sven-Erik Pernler dealt with such questions only slightly in connection with his analysis of the introductory sentences of all the sections of church law but was not able find an answer which he considered entirely satisfying.[51]

In each section of church law there are a number of prescriptions that are unique. In the Guta law it is about an indication of the practice of abandonment of children (*barnutsättning*), the regulation about the priests' families and also three named churches with special rights of asylum. In the Older Västgöta law it is about the payment of capital tithes, in the Dala law about sorcery and in the Tiohärads section of church law about family graves.

It is not my task within the framework of this article to try to explain the variations, differences and similarities, but it might become easier to make more deep going investigations once the project *Medieval Nordic Laws* has reached an end. However, once again it deserves to be underlined that the ecclesiastical legislation was international with regard to fundamental pretensions. So already for this reason only it is natural that the Swedish sections of church law contain similarities. Do they also contain Nordic elements? Are they Swedish in any qualified sense?

Of course, they are Swedish in the commonplace sense of being formulated in Swedish from the very beginning – they are not translated from any other language – and this took place in the different Swedish law districts. However, also regarding their contents in some cases the sections of church law might be considered to be Swedish, seldom when it is about the themes that were the subject of legislation but with regard to the precise wording and the detailed contents that the prescriptions got in Sweden. I will give some examples that may be discussed when taking into account the questions of Swedish and/or Nordic elements.

---

50. Se S.-E. Pernler, 'De svenska kyrkobalkarnas inledningsord', *Kyrkohistorisk årsskrift* (1984), 61-99, at 74.
51. Pernler, 'De svenska kyrkobalkarnas inledningsord', 73-75. He emphasized that one should make a distinction between public and private cult, since the private one might have contained pre-Christian elements even late in the Middle Ages. However, as to why this led the lawmakers to take measures in precisely the two late laws he did not manage to clarify fully.

5. 'Swedish' regulations?

The married priest

In the Guta law there is a regulation without parallels to the other Swedish sections of church law or to the older Norwegian ones and the Danish ones. Only in the Older Eidsivatings law (E) there are prescriptions presupposing the same conditions in its law district as on Gotland, but it is not about any decrees concerning them in the Norwegian case.[52] The example bears witness to the old age of the Guta law regarding Swedish conditions as well as the fact that the law in many important respects was different from the other Swedish laws.

The regulation is about the priest's family, i.e. the priest, his wife and their children. They were to be ranked in the same category as peasants, their wives and children with regard to fines for assault and manslaughter. However, concerning the (grown up) sons of the priest this was true only if they were learned, i.e. belonged to the clergy and, thus, had received at least one of the ordinations within the ecclesiastical hierarchy. A son who did not fulfil this qualification should be punished according to the same penal law as his mother's family.[53]

Thus the Guta law regarded the existence of priest families as self-evident. This fact resembles to what we know about the conditions in the parishes in the rest of Sweden during the first half of the 13th century. When cardinal legate William of Sabina had finished the provincial council of Skänninge in 1248, he wrote a letter addressed to all Christians in Sweden where he by way of introduction called attention to the 'deplorable' fact that almost every priest was married.[54] Referring to decisions made at the second and third Lateran councils in 1139 and 1179, which were taken into Gratian's *Decretum* and the *Liber Extra*, respectively,[55] the cardinal meant that there would be an end of the conditions prevailing in Sweden. However, this was not the case.

Therefore, it is worth noticing that in the oldest manuscript of the Guta law, dating back to circa 1350,[56] there is still the regulation about the priest's family, despite the fact that most part of the chapter where the

---

52. E 49, 53.
53. GL 5.
54. DS #359 = SDHK #613. — On the council, B. Nilsson, 'The provincial council of Skänninge, Sweden, 1248', *Annuarium historiae conciliorum* 38 (2006:1), 115-46.
55. See B. Nilsson, 'A fight against an intractable reality: The efforts at implementing celibacy among the Swedish clergy during the Middle Ages', in P. Krafl (ed.), *Sacri canones servandi sunt. Ius canonicum et status ecclesiae saeculis XIII-XV* (Praha· 2008), 596-617, at 596-98.
56. On dating and stemma, see Peel, *Guta lag,* xiv-xxii.

regulation is found was excluded as to the rest. However, there are no such exclusions in a now lost but in 1587 made transcript of a manuscript from 1470. Exactly how to interpret this fact may be discussed, but if it is so, that they were made in the oldest manuscript at about 1350 because the excluded prescriptions at that time were considered to be without any legal relevance,[57] obviously this was not the case with the ones concerning the priest's family. This is not to say that priests' families were typical only for Gotland, Sweden or Scandinavia, but it appears as Gotlandic that the mentioned regulations can be found in the paragraphs of the Guta law but in no other law and that they still are there undisguised in the middle of the 14th century.

The priest as a layman

Another aspect relating to the just mentioned regulations from Gotland is about the status of the priest in the society consisting of a vast majority of smallholders for which the sections of church law mainly had relevance. In the Guta law, as we have seen, the priest and his ordained sons were ranked in the same category as (free) peasants with regard to penal law. Also in a few other paragraphs in the Swedish laws it is expressly stated that the priest sometimes was regarded as a layman, as a peasant among peasants. I have not been able to find any parallels in other Scandinavian ecclesiastical legislation.

In the Older Västgöta law's section of manslaughter (*Om mandråp*), it is prescribed that if someone killed a foreign priest he should pay a fine as high as for a man from Västergötland, and right after, it is said that the priest should 'be in the peasants' law',[58] i.e. be under the same law as the peasant. It has been discussed whether this last decree was generally applicable or only to penal law concerning manslaughter.[59] Anyhow, the whole paragraph conflicts with the demand for *privilegium canonis* in Canon law according to which a person who used violence against a priest should be subjected to excommunication *ipso facto* and could be absolved from the ban only by the pope,[60] not with the help of a fine. The regulation was later on excluded from the Younger Västgöta law, where instead the requirement for *privilegium fori* was clearly and vigorously expressed with the words 'the bishop shall sentence concerning clerics […]'.[61]

57. Holmbäck & Wessén, SLL 4, 249, note 1.
58. VgL I M 5§5 SSGL 1, 13: 'Præstær skal .i. bondalaghum væræ'.
59. Cf. Holmbäck & Wessén, SLL 5, 47, note 60; G.B. Nilsson, *Nytt ljus,* 121.
60. E. Vodola, *Excommunication in the Middle Ages* (Berkeley, Los Angeles & London: 1986), 28-29; G. Inger, *Das kirchliche Visitationsinstitut im mittelalterlichen Schweden* (Lund: 1961), 41.
61. VgL II Kk 59, SSGL 1, 102: 'Biskuper skal döma vm klærka […]'.

However, according to the last mentioned law the priest was considered layman in other respects. This was the case regarding obligations concerning the matters that the members of the village community had in common. A great number of different types of work was enumerated such as the constructing and maintenance work of gates, bridges, fences and other things,[62] concerning which the vicarage as one of the farms in the village had to participate together with the rest of the peasants.[63] If the priest refused to participate a sentence should be passed by a *nämndeman*, i.e. a layman, not by the bishop.[64] In the section of church law in the Södermanna law this was expressed as clear as here, and it was added that if the priest left his duties in this respect undone he should 'pay a fine according to the law and the law speaker's sentence'.[65] Prescriptions with almost identical wording can be found also in the sections of church law in the Upplands law and the Västmanna law.[66] In the section of the village communities (*Byalagsbalken*) in the Hälsinge law it is expressly said: 'Here is the peasant's law valid for the priest',[67] referring to the obligations concerning common work with bridges and roads. He should pay fines according to the law if he appeared to be neglectful in this case. Thus, in the mentioned paragraphs it was not about that the priest was exempt from the secular jurisdiction.

According to the Tiohärads section of church law *privilegium fori* did not apply to cases concerning buying or selling of pieces of land. In such cases the priest should be 'in the laymen's law', it is said.[68] Here, but not in other laws, the word layman is used with regard to the priest's legal position. Similar regulations with almost the same wording can also be found in the sections of church law in other laws concerning dispute about pieces of land.[69]

With regard to penal law according to the Upplands law and the Södermanna law, there is also a sentence about the bishop.[70] It is said about him that if he did not want to do justice to a peasant, the peasant should appeal to the king with his case. Thus, the peasant could appeal against the

---

62. VgL II Kk 63.
63. Holmbäck & Wessén, SLL 5, 235, note 103.
64. See also G.B. Nilsson, *Nytt ljus,* 122-25.
65. SdmL Kk 2§3, SSGL 4, 13: 'bötin sum lagh sighiæ oc laghmander skil'; Holmbäck & Wessén, SLL 3, s. 28, note 18.
66. UL Kk 2§4; VmL Kk 2§3.
67. HL B 18§1, SSGL 6, 80: 'hær ær præster ii bondælaghum'.
68. TiL Kk 11, SSGL 6, 104: 'thy at j köplaghum oc j iorthælaghum. tha aa præster meth oss wara j lekmannæ laghum'.
69. UL Kk 20; SdmL Kk 19; HL Kk 20.
70. UL Kk 20; SdmL Kk 19.

bishop's decision at the secular authority's court. In the same sphere there is also the prescription in the Upplands law that the priest indeed should be brought before the bishop's court, if he had committed a crime, but if he was convicted he had to pay a fine in accordance with the provincial law.[71] Thus, he should not be imposed with an ecclesiastical punishment in the *forum externum*. According to the Younger Västgöta law, the bishop, in a similar way could be punishable with a fine if he without lawful excuse did not keep to the day which he had fixed for the consecration of a church building.[72]

The sections of church law in several of the Swedish provincial laws counted the priest, and most obviously him, but sometimes also the bishop among those who at times should be punished according to secular law. Thus, the Church's efforts at making clerics and bishops legally a class of their own beside the rest of the society was not fully carried into effect.

Ban

Other phenomena from the ecclesiastical legislation may serve as examples of what possibly can be regarded as Scandinavian or Swedish in relation to the ideals of the international Canon law. First, it is about the right to sentence someone to ban. The ecclesiastical punishment which was designated with the term *forbuþ* (prohibition) in the Scandinavian languages corresponded to *interdictum personale* or *interdictio ab ingressu ecclesiae*. It was usually regarded as having the same consequences as *excommunicatio minor* or the small ban, as it also could be called.[73] Via the decision made by the fourth Lateran council in 1215, the punishment was taken into Pope Gregory's decretals in 1234.[74] The Latin designation of the personal interdict, i.e. *interdictio ab ingressu ecclesiae* tells us more clearly what it was all about – the punished person was not allowed to enter the church building. This meant that he had no right to participate in services, to receive the sacraments or sacramentals and was denied ecclesiastical funeral and a grave in the cemetery.

According to Canon law, the ecclesiastical penal law was completely in the hands of the bishop, or to put it differently: the parish priest had no

---

71. UL Kk 13§1.
72. VgL II Kk 3.
73. P.D. Clarke, *The interdict in the thirteenth century: A question of collective guilt* (Oxford: 2007), 75-76, 81-82.
74. X 5.38.12-13, edited in A. Friedberg (ed.), Corpus Iuris Canonici II, *Decretalium collectiones* (Graz: 1959 – repr.), cols 887-88; P. Hinschius, *System des katholischen Kirchenrechts mit besonderer Rücksicht auf Deutschland* 5 (Berlin: 1895), 13-19; W.M. Plöchl, *Geschichte des Kirchenrechts. 2: Das Kirchenrecht der abendländischen Christenheit 1055-1517* (Wien & München: 1962), 396-97.

iurisdictio externa.[75] Possibly it could be delegated to him momentarily. However, there were different opinions about this in the Canon law commentaries in the way that two of the most eminent commentators of Pope Gregory's decretals during the 13th century, Henricus de Segusia, often called (cardinal) Hostiensis (d. 1270) and Raymundus de Peñaforte (d. 1275), had diametrically opposed opinions. Hostiensis denied that the parish priest already as a consequence of his ministry or his ordination had the power of punishing with the ban, while Raymundus meant that he had that power.[76]

The question was fraught with conflict, and during the latter part of the 12th century and onwards, the leaders of the Church tried to reserve the right of imposing the interdict to the pope and the bishops. However, in England also the rural deans (*plebani*) were given the right to impose this punishment, but ordinary parish priests seem to have been without this right, at least in England.[77]

In the Scandinavian ecclesiastical legislation outside Sweden the personal interdict (with the term *forbuþ*) occurs in the Eidsivartings law and Gulatings law and also in both the Danish church laws.[78] A number of statutes from the Swedish church province from the latter part of the 13th century and the beginning of the 14th century express a standpoint corresponding to the one represented by Hostiensis.[79] The sections of church law in the Swedish provincial laws taken together, however, show a divided picture.

According to the Guta law,[80] which as a consequence of its usual dating cannot have been influenced by the divergent opinions among the decretalists, the priest should impose interdict on those who were guilty of having broken God's holyday. However, it remains unclear exactly what this crime meant, and the law does not use the term *forbuþ* but ban.[81] Possibly, this has to do with the fact that there was some uncertainty as regards the exact definitions in Canon law concerning the ecclesiastical punishments till the

---

75. Hinschius, *System* 5, 291-93.
76. Inger, *Das kirchliche Visitationsinstitut*, 154. There is no modern investigation dealing with the medieval ecclesiastical penal law in Sweden either with regard to legislation or practice.
77. Clarke, *The interdict*, 98-103.
78. E 5; G 2; Sj Kk 17; Sk Kk 15.
79. Inger, *Das kirchliche Visitationsinstitut*, 531, note 1.
80. GL 8§1, SSGL 7, 20: 'prestr a tiþir hepta Oc kirchiu durum atr luca firir allum þaim sum guz helg hafa brutith'.
81. See Peel, *Guta lag*, 82.

promulgation of Pope Gregory's decretals in 1234.[82] Exactly as in the case concerning the breaking of a holyday, the priest had the right of 'closing the church door and cancel the service' for the whole of the parish, if the parishioners (*sockenmännen*) (or some of them?) had not fulfilled their duty of delivering the tithes in due course of time.[83]

The Older Västgöta law, perhaps as old as the Guta law, maintained the opposite opinion, i.e. that the priest was not allowed 'to drive anyone away from the church except the one on whom the bishop had imposed a ban'.[84] Even if it is not said in which cases this punishment could be used, it is obvious that the parish priest did not have the right to impose it, just put it into practice as delegated by the bishop.

In the Younger Västgöta law on the contrary, the conditions are different and the small ban appears in various paragraphs. *Firstly*, the different kinds of crimes were enumerated that led to ban, and, as it appears, varying practices with regard to them. If the cemetery had been polluted through violent crimes, only the bishop should impose the ban, nobody else.[85] Most likely this was due to the fact that the bishop and he alone had the right to restore it to its former condition by means of the liturgical act of cleansing which was called reconciliation.[86] *Secondly*, at the same time as the mentioned prescription in the Older Västgöta law literally was repeated, it was also said that if someone was convicted by a *nämnd*, also the bishop's *ombudsman* was allowed to impose the ban.[87] In the *third* case it was about a person who was in debt to the bishop or a priest and did did not pay after having been reminded three times. Then the bishop should impose the ban.[88] In the *fourth* case it was generally underlined, without the prescription being related to any specific crime, that the bishop's letter was required in order to

---

82. See B. Nilsson, *De sepulturis. Gravrätten i Corpus Iuris Canonici och medeltida nordisk lagstiftning* (Stockholm: 1989), 262, note 32.
83. GL 3§1, SSGL 7, 11: 'En eptir mariu messu þa scal prestr lysa um þria sunnudaga En a fjarþa kirchiu durum atr luca oc tiþr hepta firi kirchiu mannum til þes tima at tiunt ier all fram raid'. Peel, *Guta lag*, 73, 82 considers this punishment to be an *interdictum locale*, but it should not be seen in this way, at least not in GL 8§1 and hardly here in GL 3§1 either, as the interdict in both cases referred to a group of persons; see also Clarke, *The interdict*, 81-82.
84. VgL I Kk 22, SSGL 1, 9: 'Præster ma ængin man fra kirkiu vrakæ. num þen biscopæ havir forboþet'; Holmbäck & Wessén, SLL 5, 22, note 71.
85. VgL II Kk 22.
86. On this, see B. Nilsson, *De sepulturis,* 107-21.
87. VgL II Kk 47, SSGL 1, 97: 'Præster ma ingin v kirkyu uræka vtan þæn biskuper hauer forbuthat. uærther mather aff næmd fælder oc forbuthather aff biskups umbuz manne'.
88. VgL II Kk 70, SSGL 1, 106: 'Hua sum præsti a giælda nokot ælla biskupi at kirkyunna ræt. Hauer han ey guldit þa han ar thrim sinnum minter til. Þær ma biskuper forbuþa til [...]'.

make a priest or a *länsman* able to impose a ban. They should be subjected to the very same punishment if they imposed a ban unlawfully.[89]

It is interesting that not only the priest but also the *länsman* had the same right. Even if it is completely clear that they were only allowed to impose the ban as delegated by the bishop, the question arises: Who was meant by the title *länsman*? Did the person have the same ecclesiastical functions as the one mentioned in the law as 'the bishop's *ombudsman*'?

It appears that the designations the bishop's *official, länspräst, ombudsman, länsman* and rural dean, and in Norway *ármaðr*, just were different designations of the same function in the service of the bishop.[90] However, concerning Västergötland the conditions are more complex because diocesan statutes, issued by Bishop Brynolf Algotsson of Skara on 7 July 1280, contain exactly the same prescription as the section of church law but using the word *laycus* where the law reads *länsman*.[91]

Thus, it seems as if Bishop Brynolf meant that also a layman could be allowed to impose an ecclesiastical punishment, if he did so as delegated by the bishop himself. It appears though that there are no concrete parallels to this phenomenon. The modern handbooks take it for granted that the bishop's officials were clerics,[92] whereas some articles in *Kulturhistoriskt lexikon för nordisk medeltid* contain wordings that seem to implicate that they also were laymen.[93] More profound studies concerning the Swedish conditions are needed.

The rest of the laws that mention the small ban as a punishment differ a little, but the question is what significance the differences might have. The Tiohärads section of church law and the Östgöta law just mention the bishop as the one who imposes the ban, and so far there is no problem. The wordings of the Dala law do not make it clear who is imposing the ban, the bishop or the rural dean. The Södermanna law and the Västmanna law mention the bishop and the priest with the bishop's permission. The Upplands

---

89. VgL II Kk 71, SSGL 1, 106: 'Ængin præster ælla lænsman ma forbutha vtan biskups breff. forbuthar han vskællika uæri sua længe i forbuthi sum bonden war'.
90. Holmbäck & Wessén, SLL 5, 237, note 125; T. Dahlerup, 'Official, alment' 'Official, Danmark', *Kulturhistoriskt lexikon för nordisk medeltid* 12, 528-32; H. Schück, 'Official, Sverige och Finland', *Kulturhistoriskt lexikon för nordisk medeltid* 12, 532-36; L. Hamre 'Official, Noreg', *Kulturhistoriskt lexikon för nordisk medeltid* 12, 536-39; G. Hafström, 'Lensman, Sverige', *Kulturhistoriskt lexikon för nordisk medeltid* 10, 510-12; T. Dahlerup, 'Provst', *Kulturhistoriskt lexikon för nordisk medeltid* 13, 537-40.
91. Gummerus (ed.), *Synodalstatuter*, 64: 'Item si quis sacerdos vel laycus interdixerit aliquem sine litteris episopi et trina monicione, sit ipse interdictus tanto tempore sicut ille fuit quem interdixit'.
92. See for instance, Plöchl, *Geschichte des Kirchenrechts* 2, 152.
93. Dahlerup, 'Official', 530; Schück, 'Official', 533.

law mentions the bishop and the priest but not the bishop's permission, and the Hälsinge law mentions the priest only.[94] Anyhow, it should be considered special and hardly in accordance with international Canon law that a parish priest, as it appears in some of the laws, already by force of his ministry was allowed to impose the minor ban, as well as the fact that a layman had the right of performing this function, although it in his case it was a consequence of delegation.

The appointment of parish priests

Almost every section of church law contains prescriptions concerning the appointment of parish priests. Regulations are missing only in the two oldest laws, the Guta law and the Older Västgöta law.[95] There are similar prescriptions also in all of the older Norwegian sections of church law as well as in the two Danish church laws.[96] This is not surprising; the topic must be considered both fundamental and important.

In the light of the fact that there were proprietary churches during the early Middle Ages in Northern Europe and England and that the laymen who had founded the churches therefore possessed almost total influence over the appointment of priests, there was a reaction through the Gregorian reform movement from the end of the 11th century with its requirement that the Church should be liberated from such influence. The requirement was even more emphasized by decisions made by the two first Lateran councils in 1123 and 1139, respectively. Among other things it was decided that laymen had no right what so ever to interfere in ecclesiastical matters, and nobody was allowed to receive ecclesiastical benefices from a layman.[97] In line with this, also Gratian dismissed the thoughts of a church owner as the one who should make appointments to ecclesiastical benefices. At the same time he and the commentators of his *Decretum* presented the legal basis for

---

94. TiL Kk 13§4; ÖgL Kk 25§1; DL Kk 15; UL Kk 13§2; SdmL Kk 10§2; VmL Kk 12§2; HL Kk 13§1.
95. Possibly a very short prescription in the Older Västgöta law referred to, among other things, the appointment of priests, VgL I Kk 11, SSGL 1, 6: 'Scill sopn valdi þer sum flere æru' (If the parish is at variance those who are more should rule). Thus, the will of the majority should prevail. See also W. Sjögren, 'De fornsvenska kyrkobalkarna' *Tidsdkrift for retsvidenskap* 17 (1904), 125-76, at 133, who takes it for granted that the prescription concerns the appointment of priests. No matter what, no conclusions can be drawn with regard to the bishop's influence in such matters from this regulation.
96. E 31; G 15, B 12; F 11; Sj Kk 3; Sk Kk 2.
97. Generally on proprietary churches, see Susan Wood's monumental investigation *The proprietary church*. For a classical definition of 'proprietary church', see Wood, *The proprietary church*, 1 f.; c. 8, conc. Lat. I, edited in N.P. Tanner (ed.), *Decrees of the ecumenical councils* 1 (London & Washington D.C.: 1990), 191; c. 25, conc. Lat. II, edited in Tanner (ed.), *Decrees* 1, 202.

Bertil Nilsson

what would become the *ius patronatus*. It involved the church owner's right to present a candidate to the ministry for the bishop.[98] The patronage was later on ratified by no less than thirty-one decretals in the *Liber Extra*, mainly issued by Pope Alexander III.[99]

The patronage, as defined in Canon law, was clearly mentioned but still in passing and with almost the same wording only in the Upplands law and the Södermanna law. Both laws used the Latin term *ius patronatus*. It is evident that this right was considered a possible alternative to the right which belonged to the peasants collectively at their parish churches.[100] However, in the rest of the Swedish legislation, it is only about the relation between the parishioners and the bishop with slight variations in a way that does not appear in the international Canon law.

In the Dala law[101] the question of appointing the priest appears already in the first chapter. The prescription is not fully transparent, but it seems to presuppose two different procedures. First, it is stated that after the peasants had built their church and it was ready to be consecrated, the parish sent a *nämnd* consisting of twelve people to the bishop in order to ask for a priest. Thus: The first priest was appointed by the bishop at the request of the peasants. In the future, when a new parish priest was about to be appointed, they had the right to elect the one they wanted within six months. If this did not happen, the bishop appointed the priest that he wanted.

In the Tiohärads[102] section of church law there is a comparatively detailed prescription which with regard to its basic contents can be found also in other laws. However, the text in this law is not fully transparent. The starting-point is that a priest himself came to the parish and asked to become

---

98. P. Landau, *Jus patronatus. Studien zur Entwicklung des Patronats im Dekretalenrecht und der Kanonistik des 12. und 13. Jahrhunderts* (Köln & Wien: 1975), 5-7.
99. See X, tit. de iure patronatus, edited in Friedberg (ed.), *Corpus Iuris Canonici* 2, 609-21.
100. UL Kk 5, SdmL Kk 4pr. Of, course, one can discuss whether also peasants who collectively had built a church and provided it with the required economic basis could be considered the church's *patronus*, see Wood, *The prorietary church*, 651-58 concerning the Continent during the early Middle Ages.
101. DL Kk 1, SSGL 5, 3: 'Nu ækirkia war gior. oc till wigslæ boyn. þa giorþu þeer tolf næmpdæ men til biscops. at beþas præst æfti þy sum ræt ær. Aghin böndir wald at wælia præst slikan þær þe wilia innan sæx manaþa. Siþan vti æru sæx manaþa. hawi þa biscopir wald at fa þem præst slikan þær han wil'.
102. TiL Kk 4pr., SSGL, 6 , 98-99: 'Nw kan præster koma oc hænna bethæs. thet monn ræet wara the at taka thær allom sæmber aa. Tha agho the meth hanom till biscops fara. biscoper scal scutha kunna hans. oc wiixlæ breef hans. han scall ey doblare ekker drinkare. ey puto mathe eller portkunw. renn a rhen wara. guthi scal thiæna'. — In one of the manuscripts there is the addition: 'there might be one to choose' (can een j uali uara).

parish priest. If the peasants were unanimous they had the right to choose him. Then they should go to the bishop, who should test the priest with regard to his knowledge, and he should show his ordination letter. Here the law also pointed out the moral requirements which were demanded concerning the one who wished to be parish priest.[103] If the parish was not unanimous concerning who should be appointed, the bishop should participate. He should draw up a nomination list consisting of three names and appoint the one whom the parishioners agreed about. If the parishioners did not agree about one of them, the majority should be followed, and if the number of votes were equal the bishop had the casting vote.[104]

No doubt that the bishop's power in this case was subordinated to the one of the parishioners. His task was only to examine the priest's qualifications and appoint the one elected by the peasants either unanimously or by the majority. Thus, the peasants held the decision in their hands. This procedure is hardly in line with the *ius praesentandi* of Canon law.

Also according to the Östgöta law the peasants, with the law's wording should 'rule the election'. If they were unanimous, the bishop should appoint the one they wanted. Otherwise, the peasants drew up a nomination list with three priests out of whom the bishop appointed the one he wanted.[105] Probably the regulations in the Södermanna law should be interpreted in the same way even though they are not as clear as the ones just mentioned.[106]

103. It was suggested by some scholars that the expressed moral requirements and also the procedure of probation might have been inspired by a letter written by Pope Alexander III some time during his pontificate (the letter cannot be attributed to a specific year) to the archbishop of Uppsala and his suffragans. Among other things, the letter contains the corresponding requirements regarding the priest as the Tiohärads law. The pope also maintained that it had occurred that even people who were not ordained had practiced the priestly ministry (DS #54 = SDHK #209; Holmbäck & Wessén, SLL 5, 438, note 3). If the assumption of influence from this papal letter is correct it sheds interesting light upon the process of legislation in the Tiohärad's district and in the diocese of Växjö as well as upon the fact that the contents of a papal letter, at least a hundred years old, was preserved when the law was written down.
104. See Holmbäck & Wessén, SLL 5, 438-39, note 4. However, the manuscript B dating back to the middle of the 14th century contains another prescription which ascribed the decision to the bishop, if the parishioners were not able to agree. This is only one of many examples that illustrate how different manuscripts of the same law diverge and, thus, shed light upon the problem which I have pointed out before: Did not anything happen with the contents of the laws between the first for us unknown time when they were written down and the coming into being of the first manuscripts that we know of today? See above.
105. ÖgL Kk 4pr.; Holmbäck & Wessén, SLL 1, 23, note 15.
106. SdmL Kk 4pr.; Holmbäck & Wessén, SLL 3, 29, note 25.

According to the Västmanna law, the bishop should appoint the one whom the parishioners had proposed unanimously. If they did not agree, they should make a proposal list, not the bishop, but the bishop should choose one of them mentioned in the proposal, not the parishioners.[107] The Upplands law also contained the same prescription, although a sentence surely has fallen out of the manuscript.[108] Thus, in this case it was not a question of a decision made by the majority. Instead, the bishop had stronger influence than in the section of church law in the Tiohärads law. Also according to the Hälsinge law unanimity in the parish was enough in order to make the bishop appoint the priest whom the parishioners wanted. However, if they did not agree, no proposal should be made either by the peasants or the bishop, but he should appoint the one he wanted but with the consent of the parishioners.[109] The Younger Västgöta law established that the decision by the majority in the parish should prevail, if the parishioners were not unanimous, but after three weeks the bishop had the right to appoint the one he preferred.[110] This prescription is very short and not fully clear, but the formulation about the bishop's right should possibly be interpreted as has been done here: if no election had been held in the parish within three weeks, the bishop alone had the right to make the appointment.[111]

Thus, we can see that there were variations within the different law districts with regard to the relative strength between the bishop and the peasants/parishioners. When looking at the Swedish church province as a whole, it becomes obvious that the local variation was considerable in its turn depending on to what extent the parishioners managed to assert themselves in relation to the bishop. To give an answer as to why the parishioners in some law districts had stronger influence on the appointment of the parish priests than in others would require a more profound investigation into the different provincial laws when also other factors were taken into account. Anyhow, the peasants' position in this case should be considered a Scandinavian phenomenon.

Capital tithes

Finally, a problem which only concerns the Västgöta laws. It is considered to be a mere Nordic phenomenon, thus missing in the international Canon

---

107. VmL Kk 4.
108. UL Kk 5; Holmbäck & Wessén, SLL 1, 36, note 21.
109. HL Kk 5pr.
110. VgL II Kk 21; Holmbäck & Wessén, SLL 5, 227, note 31.
111. Sjögren, 'De fornsvenska kyrkobalkarna', 133.

law, namely the obligation to pay so-called capital tithes.[112] Yet, it was still about a form of tithes taxation.

The phenomenon appears in several paragraphs in the Nordic legislation, for instance in all of the older Norwegian laws,[113] but on the other hand not in the Danish church laws. According to the Older Västgöta law capital tithes should be paid at the consecration of a church building and also at the reconsecration of a church, if ten winters had passed since the peasants last time paid capital tithes. Tenants were exempt from this obligation at a reconsecration. They should pay this type of tithes only once, except if they wanted to or had committed a capital sin.[114] The capital tithes were later on the subject of a detailed regulation in the section of church law in the Younger Västgöta law, where all the occasions when capital tithes should be paid are enumerated: distribution of an estate, marriage with the exception of those who had not inherited anything, consecration of a church building and after having committed a capital sin.[115]

In the year 1220 Pope Honrious III (1216-1227) confirmed for the bishop of Skara his and his successors' right to get capital tithes and underlined that the parishioners of the diocese had taken on this fee voluntarily.[116] This type of taxation of economic capital is regarded to have lost its compulsory position and become a voluntary gift when the Church was consolidated. Then the yield taxation in the form of crops tithes and tithes of the living (animals and fish) successively came into use.[117] Even though you find legal decrees on capital tithes in the Västgöta laws only, it is supposed that a wording in the Östgöta law on the consecration of a church building and one in the Upplands law on donation of inherited land might originate from the fact that capital tithes once upon a time were compulsory in great parts of

---

112. From what objects it specifically should be paid and which importance it really had was the object of a discussion in Sweden during 2010 and 2012, see J. Runer, 'Huvudtionde, odal och prästgårdar' *Historisk tidskrift* 132 (2012:4), 595-623. However, the discussion has no relevance as to the question of Nordic or not Nordic, so I leave it at that. A clarifying analysis of the problems concerning capital tithes is given in G.B. Nilsson, *Nytt ljus,* 238-50.
113. E 48; B 11; G 18 in some additions to some of the manuscripts; F II:17.
114. VgL I Kk 3, 4.
115. VgL II Kk 72.
116. DS #189 = SDHK #384.
117. L. Hamre, 'Tiend, Norge', *Kulturhistoriskt lexikon för nordisk medeltid* 18, 280-87, at 280; L. Hamre, 'Donasjon', *Kulturhistoriskt lexikon för nordisk medeltid* 3, 224-29, at 227; H. Schück, 'Tiend, Sverige', *Kulturhistoriskt lexikon för nordisk medeltid* 18, 295-99, at 295-96.

the Swedish church province.[118] However, there is no papal confirmation making this assumption probable with regard to the other Swedish dioceses corresponding to Pope Honorius's for the diocese of Skara.

In his investigation of the Västgöta laws Göran B. Nilsson made it clear that the capital tithes surely was a field of negotiation filled with conflicts between the representatives of the Church and the peasants when drawing up the section of church law of the Younger Västgöta law. The prescriptions in this law were softened in comparison to the requirements posed by the Church during the negotiations about the law at the same time as there were considerably harsher requirements with regard to efficiency when capital tithes actually should be paid. The set term for payment at weddings and deaths was shortened from three years to thirty days.[119]

So, why was there still capital tithes in the legislation in Västergötland even during the 14th century? The question is legitimate, but cannot be easily answered. Generally seen it might be a question of an early medieval Nordic phenomenon which is only fragmentarily hinted at in the late Swedish legislation without having been adopted there, apart from in the section of church law in the Younger Västgöta law. If the assumptions of a great diffusion of the capital tithes in Sweden, as well as of an origin in the early Christian period in the North, are correct we deal with a phenomenon which gained papal acceptance in the 1220s. As a consequence of the fact that the requirements of yield tithes as found in Canon law were successively implemented, the capital tithes lost their importance and thus disappeared from the ecclesiastical legislation. In this perspective the sections of church law in the Västgöta laws appear as the most typical of all Swedish ones in comparison to international Canon law.

6. Conclusions

During the first phase the requirements of the international Canon law successively became known in Sweden through papal letters sent to bishops and kings in the realm. How the requirements were received from a Swedish point of view is to a great part not possible to determine. After the council of Skänninge, in 1248, also the Canon law collections that became parts of the *Corpus Iuris Canonici* with *glossa ordinaria* respectively were available in the Swedish church province. Exactly in which ways these legal sources arrived in Sweden is not possible fully to determine, neither their diffusion

---

118. ÖgL Kk 9pr.; UL Kk 14pr.; Holmbäck & Wessén, ÖgL SLL 1, 26, note 26; Holmbäck & Wessén, UL SLL 1, 40, note 61; Holmbäck & Wessén, SLL 5, 12, note 13; Schück, 'Tiend, Sverige', 295-96.
119. G.B. Nilsson, *Nytt ljus,* 244-47.

within the realm. In some cases, however, the manuscripts were owned by individual canons or parish priests. Therefore, it can be maintained that Canon law was know of, on the one hand through these manuscripts, and, on the other hand through provincial- and diocesan statutes at the time when most part of the provincial laws with their sections of church law were written down, i.e. mainly during the period of 1280 to 1350, and that Canon law influenced their contents. However, it was not about a one-sided reception of Canon law, but compromises were reached during negotiations between on the one hand the representatives of the Church and, on the other hand great men and peasants' communities. Despite this fact, it is difficult to identify individual elements in the sections of church law that should be regarded genuinely Swedish or Nordic in a qualified sense. As examples I have pointed out the married parish priest, the parish priest's right to impose the minor ban, the tensions between the parishioners and the bishop concerning the appointment of parish priests and also the obligation of paying capital tithes. If anything these examples should be regarded as Swedish solutions of problems caused by the requirements of international Canon law. Such requirements could be received in similar or other ways in other church provinces. Thus, concerning the sections of church law, fundamentally it is all about problems that derive from Canon law, and, consequently, the question of 'How Nordic are the Nordic laws' might be regarded as unessential with reference to the Swedish ecclesiastical legislation. It was not genuinely Swedish in any important respect.

HOW NORDIC ARE THE BIBLICAL SOCIAL IDEALS AS EXPRESSED IN THE EARLY SCANDINAVIAN CHURCH LAWS?

Torstein Jørgensen

1. Introduction

To trace and identify features that meet the criteria of being Nordic in early medieval Scandinavia is an unsteady exercise. To distinguish cultural elements sprung from pure Nordic soil from aspects coloured and shaped by foreign impulses will always be a matter of approach and definition. It should be enough here to refer to the long discussion among scholars as to whether the Old Norse religion as we know it today was a product of pure Nordic or Germanic roots, or whether it was some kind of a mixture with a variety of Christian thoughts and motifs baked into it.[1] Perhaps the aspect of being open and inclusive to impulses from abroad was in itself a very Nordic feature at the time.

In this article we will throw a closer look at the early Scandinavian church legislation. In order to sharpen the focus and to go more into details with special texts, we will limit our analysis to the Norwegian provincial laws, in particular the Christian section of the Gulathing law.

There is broad consensus that the early medieval Norwegian provincial laws on ecclesiastical affairs came into being as the result of joint efforts by king and church. For the king the cooperation with and support of the expertise of the learned clergy was a crucial factor in the shaping of a Norwegian kingdom in line with contemporary Christian kingdoms in

1. See for instance, G. Steinsland, 'Hedendom mot kristendom i norrøne myter', in I.M. Ruud & S. Hjelde (ed.), *Enhet i mangfold? 100 år med religionshistorie i Norge* (Oslo: 1998), 81-92.

England and on the continent.² And for the church the same relation was a most useful factor for the realization of its aim of a speedy and efficient inclusion of the country into the sphere of Western Christendom. Among the earliest surviving texts that document direct contact between the papacy and Norwegian kings in the 11th century is a papal diploma from Pope Gregory VII to King Olav Kyrre from 1078 which gives some evidence of the process of increased central ecclesiastical impact from the papacy on Norwegian legislation in this particular period. In this letter the pope, by showing to the fact that

> ... you who live in the outskirts of the world ... have fewer men to teach you the Christian religion...' asks the king to '... send some young and noble men from your country to the Apostolic See that they under the wings of the apostles Peter and Paul in a proper way can be taught the holy and divine laws...' and after their training these men can '... preach to you what is required in the order of Christianity.³

The letter gives an indication of how the contemporary Gregorian ambitions during the investiture controversy and the related impetus on Canon law in learned centres like Bologna and Paris from this time onwards put their marks also on the distant North.⁴ And it gives a likely picture of how learned ecclesiastical personnel had a hand on the Norwegian legislation process in the period.

The question about the provenance of these laws, and of the Christianization of Norway in broader terms, has been a matter of a long debate among scholars. Since Absalon Taranger⁵ in the late 19th century pointed to English 10th and early 11th century legislation as the main model of Norwegian laws, this has remained a dominant perspective in later Norwe-

---

2. S. Bagge, *From Viking Stronghold to Christian Kingdom: State Formation in Norway, c. 900-1350* (Copenhagen: 2010), 137-65, 179-227.
3. *Diplomatarium Norvegicum* (hereafter: *DN*) 5, no. 1194. The full text of this passage goes as follows: 'Rogamus uos sicut et regi Danorum denuntiauimus ut de iuonioribus et nobilibus terr/e/ uestr/e/ ad apostolicam aulam mittatis quatenus sub alis apostolorum Petri et Pauli sacris ac diuinis legibus diligenter edocti, apostolic/e/ Christian/e/ religionis ordo postulauerit apud uos non quasi rudes aut ignari sed lingua ac scientia moribusque prudentes digne deo predicare.'
4. J.V. Sigurdsson et al., 'Making and Using the Law in the North, c. 900-1350', in G. Lottes et al. (eds.), *Making, using and resisting the law in European history* (Pisa: 2008), 37-60.
5. A. Taranger, *Den angelsaksiske kirkes indflydelse på den norske* (Kristiania: 1890); F. Birkeli, 'The Earliest Missionary Activities from England to Norway', *Nottingham Medieval Studies* XV (1971), 27-37; K. Helle, *Gulatinget og Gulatingslova* (Leikanger: 2001), 177-82.

gian research on the topic. In recent years Torgier Landro[6] has presented convincing evidence that also impulses from the Continent, especially from Burchard of Worms need to be taken into account. Landro's new perspectives have been supported by Sverre Bagge.

The preserved text of the Gulathing law[7] reveals two stages of the formation of the text, i.e. the Olav provisions, referring to promulgations allegedly agreed upon by King Olav the Saint (1015-30) and his missionary bishop, Grimkell, as early as at the council of Moster in 1024,[8] and the Magnus provisions added by King Magnus Erlingsson (1156-84) in agreement with Archbishop Eystein Erlendsson and Earl Erling Ormsson the Crooked.[9] This means that the Gulathing law had its historical *Sitz im Leben* in one of the front zones of Western Christendom, in a period of organizational establishment and consolidation stretching from the beginning of the 11th until the latter half of the 12th century.

There can be no doubt that the text of this law bears the marks of the hands of qualified theological expertise. Either these persons came from abroad themselves or they brought back home learnings and traditions from longer stays abroad. The main questions in this article will therefore be: What kind of visions did these clerics have for the formation of a Christianized Norway? From which sources did they draw their ideas? And, to what extent can we trace evidence that these experts brought with them models of similar visions expressed in legislative texts from elsewhere?

In our investigation of the texts in focus in this article we have found that the sources of inspiration of the clerical legislators in Norway in this period seem to have been mainly two, namely 1) The Bible, in particular the Old Testament religious order of society, and 2) 9th and 10th century English and Continental laws.

---

6. T. Landro, *Kristenrett og kyrkjerett: Borgartingsretten i eit komparativt perspektiv* (Unpublished PhD-dissertation, University of Bergen: 2010), 227-29.
7. The standard edition of the Old Norse version of the Gulathing law (hereafter: GuL) is to be found in R. Keyser & P.A. Munch (ed.), *Norges Gamle Love indtil 1387* I (Christiania: 1846), 1-118. Translations into English in this article are by T. Jørgensen.
8. For reference here see GuL I.10: 'The next thing is that we shall maintain all those churches and observe all those decrees about Christianity which Holy Olav and Bishop Grimkjell laid down at the Moster assembly.' See also GuL I.15.
9. GuL I.2.: 'Here are the new ordinances adopted in accordance with the guidance of King Magnus, Archbishop Eystein, Earl Erling and all the wisest men in Norway.'

2. Biblical motifs

There are no explicit references whatsoever in the Gulathing law, neither to particular passages from the Bible nor to foreign laws. The only references to foreign legislation that one can find in the texts are of a very general nature, by formulations such as 'violating articles of Christian law'.[10] However, biblical ideals and expressions of a biblical ethos seem to lie behind as some kind of a backdrop and on some points also coming to the surface in more clear terms. Motifs are taken from both the New and the Old Testaments. But there is a difference between the two that we need to note. Whereas the laws of the Old Testament had their historical application area in the state of old Israel, with the aim of forming a theocratic society in accordance with religious and divine norms, the community of the church, which was the context of New Testament ideals, was of a different, more spiritual kind, consisting of believers in the Christian faith regardless of political citizenship or ethnic belonging. During the period when the texts of the New Testament were composed in the first and second centuries AD, Christianity stood in no formal relation to any state or political authorities. Thus, the parallelism of the Nordic provincial laws was in many ways closer to the Old Testament historical setting than that of the New Testament in the fact that they were meant to form a civil-religious society under a common king, *in casu* a Christian kingdom. Of course, the laws contain a long row of particular *Christian* provisions: impositions about baptism, instructions about the ecclesiastical year, building and maintenance of churches, priest's duties and much more. After all, it was not Judaism the legislators wanted to introduce. But on many points we see that features from the Old Testament do stand as model.

From this more general outlook we will now move on to give some examples to illustrate the presence of biblical perspectives in the Gulathing law.

3. Illustrating examples

Bowing to the East
The opening words of the very first provision of the Gulathing law read: 'That is the beginning of our laws that we shall bow to the East and pray to the Holy Christ for good harvest and peace.'[11]

---

10. GuL I.33: 'misgort einnhvern lut i kristindoms brote'. For original text see Keyser & Munch (ed.), *Norges Gamle Love indtil 1387* I, 20.
11. GuL I.1.

A more advanced understanding of the symbolism embedded in the concept of the East was probably something that was confined to the clergy and perhaps to the better oriented among the laity. But at the point of time when this motif was included into Nordic laws, the idea of the East had a long tradition throughout the history of the Church with roots all the way back to the Old Testament. According to the Old Testament the East was the cardinal direction from which God's glory was expected to come.[12] Accordingly, the expectation of the coming of Messiah included the perspective of his appearing from the East. Thus the temple in Jerusalem was built in an East-West direction from the Temple Square towards the Mount of Olives.

During the time of the Ancient Church and early Middle Ages baptism rituals, in accordance with this basic biblical idea, instructed the catechumens first to renounce the devil by turning to the West and then, by turning to the East, profess their faith in Christ. An excerpt from the Byzantine rite shows this very illustratively:

> ... after this he [the priest] says to them [the baptism candidates]: Turn to the West, raise your hands, what I say, you say also: I renounce Satan and all his works and all his service and all his angels .... Then again he says to them: Turn to the East and lower your hands, behave with reverence, what I say, you say also: I adhere to Christ ....[13]

Similar formulas seem to have been a common feature in most of the baptismal rituals from these centuries, for instance, from the Syrian-Orthodox rite: 'The priest dips the child into the baptismal font facing East, the child facing West', and from the Armenian rite:

> Next he orders the catechumen to turn to the West, and he adjures him three times to say as follows: We renounce you, Satan, and all your deceitfulness and your wiles, and your service and your paths and your angels .... Then he shall turn towards the East, confessing the one Godhead of the Holy Trinity.[14]

In the Nordic setting this perspective of geographical orientation is also reflected in the new practice of Christian burials, according to which the dead bodies were to be placed on their back in the grave with their head pointing westwards and feet eastwards, so that on the day of Christ's return they could sit up facing his coming. Also the erection of church buildings in

---

12. Ezechiel 43:1-5, especially v. 4: 'And the glory of the Lord came into the house, by the way of the gate whose prospect is toward the East.' The Hebrew word *kedem* means East, origin.
13. E.C. Whitaker, *Documents of the baptismal liturgy* (London: 1960), revised ed. by M.E. Johnson, 2003, 110-111.
14. Whitaker, *Documents of the baptismal liturgy*, 94 and 75-76.

early medieval Norway adopted the general east-west construction of Christendom with the altar, which represented God's presence in the church, placed at the eastern end, and the congregation facing it with their backs towards the West.

The same formulation about bowing to the East also introduces the Borgarthing law[15], but we have found no direct parallels in English or Continental legislation from the early Middle Ages. Or is it possible that we in this motif find a piece of influx from the Viking contacts with Byzantium through their travels in *austerveg*[16] through Russia?

Baptism

The main expression of a person's conversion to Christianity was baptism. Ever since New Testament time, baptism was the very initiation rite for people who wanted to adopt the Christian religion – understood as it was as a sacramental unification with Christ in his atoning death for men's sin and in his resurrection to a new life. As St. Paul wrote in his letter to the Romans:

> By our baptism, then, we were buried with him [Christ] and shared his death, in order that, just as Christ was raised from death by the glorious power of the Father, so also we might live a new life.[17]

All the four Norwegian laws state in explicit terms the invariable obligation for every child born in the realm to be baptized. The wording of the Gulathing law on this point reads: 'Every child born in our country shall be nurtured ..., brought to church and baptized.'[18]

Although the faith-related content of baptism is definitely New Testament and Christian, the procedures and formalities around it, as promulgated in the law, contain some striking parallels to Old Testament society. One aspect here is the fact that baptism is imposed as an initiation rite for everyone within the borders of the kingdom to submit to, in the same way as circumcision was in the Jewish society of the old covenant. And it was supposed to take place within certain rather short deadlines after birth, in the Old Testament eight days[19], in the Norwegian laws within set time limits in the course of the ecclesiastical year. According to the Gulathing law these were:

15. Borgarthing law (hereafter: BoL), Keyser & Munch (ed.), *Norges Gamle Love indtil 1387* I, 337-72. For this reference see BoL I.1.
16. Toward the East.
17. Rom 6:4.
18. GuL I.21.
19. Gen 17:10-14.

> And every child who is born after Christmas night shall be baptized before Septuagesima. And if it is born during Lent, it shall be baptized at Easter. And if it is born after Easter, it shall be baptized before St. John's Mass [June 24th]. And every child who is born after St. Michael's Mass [Sept. 29th] shall be baptized before Christmas night.[20]

So, like circumcision in the Old Testament baptism was in the Norwegian legal context more than an initiation into a spiritual community of co-believers. It was also an entrance into a political society.

The parallelism between Old Testament legislation and that of the medieval Norwegian laws can also be observed in the provisions about expulsion from the country of those who did not comply with the law on this point, whether they were indigenous people who simply neglected the deadlines or they were pagan strangers in the land who did not accept circumcision or baptism. The formulations of the two text units are, in fact, both quite definite on this point. The Old Testament text reads: 'Any uncircumcised male who is not circumcised in the flesh of his foreskin shall be cut off from his people, he has broken my covenant.'[21]

And the Gulathing text reads:

> If a man keeps an unbaptized person in his house for twelve months, then he has forfeited every penny of his property ... and they will both have to leave the country.[22]

Liberation of slaves

Another issue in the Gulathing law with a biblical parallel applies to the liberation of slaves, in Old Norse called thralls. Both in biblical time, in the antique world and in most early medieval western societies the class of slaves found themselves at the bottom of rather hierarchical societies. Full abolition of slavery was, however, something to be implemented *after* the period of the law formation process we are dealing with here. So, what we observe in the Gulathing law is a quite modest legal measure of granting freedom for one slave every year. Provision four of the Gulathing law prescribes that this shall take place on the first Sunday of the annual assembly of the law district. The wording of the law is this:

> The next thing is that every year we shall give one slave his freedom here in Gulen .... And that man shall be given his freedom on the first Sunday of the Gulathing session.[23]

20. GuL I.21.
21. Gen 17:14.
22. GuL I.22.

Nothing is said as to how the person should be selected, but the costs are instructed to be shared equally among the delegates by a joint amount of six *aurar* which equalled half the price of a slave. The other half was supposed to be paid by the slave himself.[24] In provisions four and five it is stated that the same should be implemented also in each *fylki*, i.e. the sub-districts of the Gulathing,[25] and that the release should be executed before Christmas Eve every year. The fact that failing to comply with the law entailed a fine to the bishop (of 12 *aurar*) is a clear indication of this being basically an ecclesiastical promulgation. The text reveals nothing about the motives behind this act. But, the act seems to have been understood as some kind of benefaction, or merit, by which one obviously wanted to introduce these assemblies.

When it comes to the Bible, we again have to turn to the Old Testament to find similar legal provisions. But the differences are also apparent. Whereas the Norwegian law deals with one slave every year from certain districts, and as it seems, regardless of their ethnic origin, the Old Testament legal rule is limited to apply only to Hebrew slaves who are all to be set free in the seventh year of their service. The promulgation is included in several places in the Old Testament,[26] but the main text of Ex 21:2f, from the so-called Book of Covenant, is formulated as follows:

> When you buy a male Hebrew slave, he shall serve six years, but in the seventh he shall go out a free person, without debt. If he comes in single, he shall go out single, if he comes in married, then his wife shall go with him.

The reason for the regulation is expressed in Deut 15:15: 'Remember that you were a slave in the land of Egypt, and the Lord your God redeemed you; for this reason I lay this command upon you today.'

But, according to the wider context, the rationale of the Hebrew law has also to do with the idea of the Sabbath, which did not only apply to the seventh day of the week, but also to the sequence of years, according to which every seventh year should be a year of rest in the land.[27] Of this motivation we find no resonance in the Norwegian law.

Tithes

The next point we will focus on deals with tithes. The paying of tithes was a principle that only gradually got a foothold in the teaching and practice of

---

23. GuL I.4.
24. GuL IV.6.
25. Or county.
26. Lev 25:47-54; Deut 15:12; Jer 34:12-19.
27. Lev 25:1-7.

How Nordic are the Biblical Social Ideas?

the church. And again we see, as far as the Bible is concerned, that the Old rather than the New Testament stands as model. Among the many places where tithes are mentioned in the Old Testament,[28] Lev 31:30-32 is probably the most central:

> All tithes from the land, whether the seed from the ground or the fruit from the tree, are the Lord's, they are holy to the Lord .... All tithes of herd and flock, every tenth one that passes under the shepherd's staff, shall be holy to the Lord.

In the two mentioned layers, i.e. the Olav text and the Magnus text of the Gulathing law, as expressed in provisions eight and nine, we can observe a change from the old so-called *reiða*-system[29] into a system of tithes, by which the Norwegian church was brought in accord with churches abroad on the point of ecclesiastical funding. There seems to be a general agreement among scholars that the change took place during the reign of King Sigurd the Crusader who reigned from 1103-1130.[30] The Magnus ordinance reads as follows:

> We have made an agreement with our bishop that he shall provide us with his service, and we shall reward it by paying the full tithe, both of all harvest and stock, and of all rightful catch of fish and game.[31]

The law also prescribes how the payment should be divided:

> And it [the tithe] shall be divided such that the bishop takes one fourth of it, and the poor one fourth, the church one fourth and the priest one fourth.[32]

The former of these two quotations is very similar to the quoted text from Lev 31, and may have stood as a model, at least indirectly via continental and English laws, and Gratian's *Decretum*.[33] We shall return to this later.

---

28. See also Gen 28:22; Num 18:26; Deut 14:22; 2 Chron 31:5.
29. A payment system according to which the church officials were paid for their different services on the basis of given tariffs, and by which the different needs of the church, such as maintenance of church buildings etc., were covered by defined duties shared among members of the relevant community.
30. K. Helle, *Gulatinget og Gulatingslova*, 41.
31. GuL I.8.
32. GuL I.8.
33. 'Decimas a populo sacerdotibus ac Leuitis esse redendas, diuinae legis sanxit auctoritas'. c. 47 C. XVI. qu. 1, edited in A. Friedberg (ed.), *Corpus Iuris Canonici* I, *Decretum Magistri Gratiani* (Graz: 1959 – repr.), col. 775. The code is attributed to Pope Paschal II (1099-1118).

In the New Testament we find no ordinances about tithes. But also the community of the earliest church was in need of some kind of proper support for the clergy, as stated in St. Paul's first letter to the Corinthians:

> ... those who serve the altar shall live by the altar. In the same way the Lord has decided that those who preach the Gospel shall live by the Gospel.[34]

But in the New Testament provisions the sacred ministers were instructed to be supplied by spontaneous offerings, as St. Paul prescribed in his second letter to the Corinthians: 'Each of you must give as you have made up your mind, not reluctantly or under compulsion, for God loves a cheerful giver.'[35]

Forbidden food (Gulathing law and Borgarthing law)[36]

The last example we will comment upon regarding ordinances in the Norwegian laws as examples of reflections of biblical texts applies to forbidden food, especially meat from unclean animals. Again Old Testament regulations appear more relevant. Two provisions of the church section of the Gulathing law deal with this matter. Article 20 provides a general prohibition against eating horse meat and imposes quite heavy sanctions on violators: in general a fine of three marks[37] to the bishop, but in cases when horse meat was eaten during Lent, the punishment was confiscation of all one's property and expulsion from the country. When it comes to dogs, the wording of the law is more indirect. It says that, if a person finds himself in a desperate situation without any other food, he may eat flesh from the dog during Lent because '... it is better for him to eat the dog than that the dog eats him'.[38] If we look at the Bible, the Old Testament reckons as unclean and forbids eating food from 'Every animal that has hoofs but is not cleft footed or does not chew the cud ...' and '... all that walk on their paws...'.[39] These prescriptions would include horse and dog.

In the other provision about forbidden food, the subject is animals which, to quote the law, '... die of themselves and nobody knowing the reason'.[40] On this point the Old Testament is categorical, as stated in Deut 14:21: 'You shall not eat anything that dies of itself.' But the impact of Old

---

34. 1 Cor 9:13b-14.
35. 2 Cor 9:7. See also 1 Cor 16:1-2.
36. See also Landro, *Kristenrett og kyrkjerett: Borgartingsretten i eit komparativt perspektiv*, 92-149.
37. 1 mark silver = 214,3 grams, divided in 8 *aurar* or 24 *ertogar* or 240 *penningar*. The price of a slave was 6 *aurar*.
38. GuL I.20.
39. See Lev 11:26-27.
40. GuL I.31

Testament regulations in the Gulathing text on this regulation, and even more in Norwegian provincial laws in general, is ambiguous. The interpretation of the term 'died of itself' – or *morticina* which is the Latin term – is not the same. The Gulathing law allows eating meat from animals that 'wolves bite', 'the bear strikes or dogs bite'.[41] The same is forbidden in the Old Testament Book of Covenant, saying: '... you shall not eat any meat that is mangled by beasts in the field, you shall throw it to the dogs.'[42]

The regulations about clean food, as we can read them in the Old Testament, were not included in the New Testament. At the famous council in Jerusalem, where all the leading apostles were present, and which is referred in Acts 15, it was decided that, when it came to Old Testament prescriptions about unclean food, Christians were only instructed to '... abstain from what has been sacrificed to idols, and from blood and from what is strangled.'[43]

And St. Mark is even less reserved by lifting the subject to a spiritual level: 'Do you not see that whatever goes into a person from outside cannot defile, since it enters, not the heart, but the stomach, and goes out into the sewer.'[44]

The issue of forbidden food illustrates, however, to the full the very long road that existed from the historical setting of the Old and New Testaments to that of the 11th and 12th century Norwegian provincial laws.[45]

4. Biblical models of law in other European legislation

This leads us over to the second section of this article in which we will make a brief outlook on possible parallels – or perhaps even models – in other European legislation of the time. We will confine ourselves to two points: First, we will give some reflections on the role and status of the Old Testament as a societal model in early medieval European history in more general terms based on observations from other scholars. And second, we will illustrate this with a few examples from foreign legislation.

---

41. GuL I.31.
42. Ex 22:31.
43. Acts 15:29.
44. Mk 7:18f. See also Col 2:16.
45. For a wider discussion of the ecclesiastical food prescriptions in the early Middle Ages, such as in penitentials, see Landro, *Kristenrett og kyrkjerett: Borgartingsretten i eit komparativt perspektiv*, 83-91, and A. Sanmark, 'Dietary Regulations in Early Christian Norway', *Viking and Medieval Scandinavia* 1 (2005), 203-24.

Torstein Jørgensen

In his commentary on tithes, which extends the perspective to the construction of an early medieval Christian European society in more general terms, R. Kottje writes:

> Der Wunsch nach allgemeiner Anerkennung und Befolgung des Zehntgebotes reiht sich ein in eine Bewegung, in der in West-Europa im 6. und 7. Jahrhundert in breiter Front die Aufnahme alttestamentlicher Sitten und Gebräuche propagiert wurde ... eine Massnahme, durch die das Leben der christlichen Gemeinde dem Vorbild des Volkes Israel nachgestaltet werden sollte.[46]

And about the Torah or the Pentateuch, which in the Middle Ages was presumed to have been written by Moses, W.R. Cook and R.B. Herzman present the following observation:

> A significant portion of these books ... is taken up with legal material and ritual prescriptions .... It captured the interests of medieval writers, and several long allegorical commentaries on details of ritual and law were composed and widely known.[47]

On the application of the Pentateuch within the legislation context of the Christian West, P. Wormald continues in the same track:

> The Bible was the lawbook of the heavenly kingdom, and Christ was of course regularly depicted as a judge holding a book. Moreover, the Bible contained, in the Pentateuch, what King Alfred called 'seo æ' (The Law), the model legislation which Moses had derived from God. Thus barbarian *lex scripta* could emulate Moses, could testify to the new status of kings as Christian rulers, and could identify their subjects as another holy people like the Israelites.[48]

There is also a general agreement among scholars that the learned class of clerics, not surprisingly, played a significant role in this, as stated by Wormald:

---

46. R. Kottje, *Studien zum Einfluss des Alten Testaments auf Recht und Liturgie des frühen Mittelalters* (Bonn: 1964), 68.
47. W.R. Cook & R.B. Herzman, *The Medieval World View: An Introduction* (New York & Oxford: 1983/2004), 5.
48. P. Wormald, *Legal Culture in the Medieval West: Law as Text, Image and Experience* (London & Rio Grande: 1999), 32.

> Thus we could say that the Church, with its commitment to, and its effective monopoly of literacy, played the same part with later barbarian legislation as did Roman government officials earlier.[49]

So, a general picture of the formation of Christian kingdoms in the Early Medieval West is that regulations for the order of society as expressed in the Bible, and in particular those of the Old Testament Pentateuch, seem to have stood as model for much of Continental and English legislation. Our above analysis of the church section of the Norwegian Gulathing law should show that this same principle was also implemented in the Norwegian legislative process in the 10th and 11th centuries.

A brief look at some texts from English laws shows how the mentioned aspects were realized in practice.

Perhaps the most striking example is to be found in the law of King Alfred the Great (ca. 871 - ca. 900). This law is introduced by a long first section with altogether 49 articles which covers approximately one third of the law and consists entirely of translations of the ten commandments and many other passages from Exodus 20-23, i.e. the already mentioned Book of Covenant, texts from the Acts of the Apostles, and finally, in provision 49, a presentation of references to promulgations of church law from different church councils.[50] There has been a discussion among scholars as to what extent these articles really were part of the law, and whether they were ever used in court. But in any case they do render an illustration of the fact that these most central pieces of Old Testament law lay at the bottom as some sort of an ideological fundament when this great English king designed his law.

In the legislative body of King Æthelstan (ca. 925 - ca. 939), i.e. the six series of preserved laws issued by him, the biblical background is also visible in quite clear terms. In series I, article 2, the text of the law about tithes does not only refer to, but also quote text passages from the Bible:

> Let us remember how Jacob the Patriarch declared: "*Decimas et hostias pacificas offeram tibi*" and how Moses declared in God's Law: "*Decimas et primitias non tardabis offere Domino*".[51]

The quotations are not quite exact, but in content and also in formulation very close to Gen 28:22 and Exodus 22:29. And if we turn to Gratian's

---

49. Wormald, *Legal Culture in the Medieval West: Law as Text, Image and Experience*, 32.
50. F.L. Attenborough (ed. & trans.), *The Laws of the Earliest English Kings* (New York: 1963), 34.
51. Attenborough (ed. & trans.), *The Laws of the Earliest English Kings*, 123.

Decretum, we find more or less the same formulation, quoted from the Council of Mainz of the year 813: '*Decimas Deo et sacerdotibus Dei dandas, Abraham factis, Iacob promissis insinuate, et omnes sancti sacerdotes conmemorant.*'[52]

A resonance of the very wording of Lev 31:30-32, about tithes from the fruit from ground and livestock, can be read in the preamble to Æthelstan's series I,[53] and as we have already noted, also in article I.8 of the Gulathing law. And with similar formulations to be found in early medieval church councils, it seems that some line of textual tradition must have combined at least some of the different West European laws on this point.

Other examples of parallels between Nordic and English legislation reflecting regulations from the Bible deal with baptism within set time limits which in Ine's law was 30 days,[54] abolition of heathen cult and practices,[55] maintenance of peace in places dedicated to God,[56] and the general obligation to serve and be loyal to God and king.[57]

5. Conclusions

As already mentioned we have found no specific references made in the Norwegian provincial church laws neither to specific passages in the Bible nor to particular texts or promulgations of foreign law. In English legislation, or at least in some of it, we have seen that this is different. But the overall picture, also in English and Continental legislation, is that the presence of biblical regulations of people's lives and society in the texts of these laws were of a more indirect nature, and related to content more than formulation. And this was certainly the case in the Norwegian laws.

---

52. c. 6 C. XVI. qu. 7, edited in Friedberg (ed.), *Corpus Iuris Canonici* I, *Decretum Magistri Gratiani*, col. 802.
53. '… in the first place that ye render tithes of my own property, both in livestock and in the yearly fruits of the earth.' Attenborough (ed. & trans.), *The Laws of the Earliest English Kings*, 123.
54. Ine's law 2. Attenborough (ed. & trans.), *The Laws of the Earliest English Kings*, 37.
55. Edward's and Guthrum's laws 1 and 11, in Attenborough (ed. & trans.), *The Laws of the Earliest English Kings*, 103, 109; Æthelred' law V.1,34, VI.1,7., in A.J. Robertson (ed. & trans.), *The Laws of the Kings of England from Edmund to Henry I* (Cambridge: 1925/2009), 79, 89. 91, 93.
56. 1 Sam 1:51f, 1 Kings 2:28, Ine's law 6.1, Alfred's law 2, in Attenborough (ed. & trans.), *The Laws of the Earliest English Kings*, 39, 65, 67; Edmund's law I.2, Æthelred's law VIII.1, Canute's law I.4, in Robertson (ed. & trans.), *The Laws of the Kings of England from Edmund to Henry I*, 9, 117, 159.
57. Canute's law I.1, in Robertson (ed. & trans.), *The Laws of the Kings of England from Edmund to Henry I*, 155; GuL I.1.

Still, we have shown that biblical, and in particular Old Testament, ordinances of law and standards of social life are very much present also in the Norwegian texts. Our explanation as to why the Old Testament was chosen as model rather than the New Testament is that the aim of the Nordic laws, like those of the Old Testament and also of other European legislation of the time, was to organize a civil-religious society as a political unit, whereas the community of the New Testament was of a more spiritual nature.

The Gulathing Church law, as we have it today, is a product of a historical process as stated in the law itself to reflect two layers. The historical role of King Olav the Saint and Bishop Grimkell in the promulgation of the Gulathing law has, in our mind rightly, been questioned.[58] But the fact that the church laws mainly were the product of joint efforts from king and learned clerical experts can hardly be questioned. The role of other legal experts, such as a man named Atle, mentioned in the Gulathing law about land defence,[59] was probably restricted to the civil parts of the law. Archbishop Eystein Erlendsson, referred to in the King Magnus text of the Gulathing Church law, was an obvious figure in the mid-12th century legislative process. The members of the higher clergy, many of them with longer periods of study abroad at reputed schools behind them, were the natural resources for the kings to rely on when the ecclesiastical laws of the country were to be formed.

So, what is our concluding answer to the question raised in the title of this article? To what extent would it be relevant to describe biblical societal ideas as found in the text of the Gulathing law as Nordic? We mentioned at the beginning that the answer to this will be a matter of definition. From one perspective an obvious conclusion will be that they were not Nordic at all. Ideals from the Bible, which as we have seen also played a central role in similar legislation abroad, were of course altogether imported stuff. But Norway was, in line with the rest of Scandinavia, a country in transition and change during the actual period, with open ports to manifold contacts and impulses from a bigger world. And from this point of view we could perhaps say that the process of law formation, on the basis of the models from foreign sources that took place in this particular period of time, was indeed a very Nordic feature.

---

58. For the discussion, see Landro, *Kristenrett og kyrkjerett: Borgartingsretten i eit komparativt perspektiv*, 189-91.
59. GuL XIII.21. See also Helle, *Gulatinget og Gulatingslova*, 41.

THE ORIGINS OF THE SWEDISH MEDIEVAL LAWS – A STATE OF THE ART, FROM MY PERSPECTIVE

Stefan Brink

1. Introduction

My relation to the Swedish and for that matter the Scandinavian medieval laws go twenty-five years back in time. Being not a trained lawyer or legal historian, my approach to the laws was instead by using them as sources for the study of settlement history and landscape studies, hence trying to squeeze out historical information from them. And also, as a trained philologist, I became instantly caught by the legal language and terminology, which then falls under the label of an old research field, *Rechtsphilologie*. With this background it is not surprising that I immediately became interested in the development of the laws, their background, chronological aspects and the possibility of using them as historical sources for an early medieval society in Scandinavia.

2. Elsa Sjöholm and Swedish laws

I was brought up in the shadow of reading Elsa Sjöholm's overview of the Swedish laws, *Svenska landskapslagar* (1988), and Gudmund Sandvik's long article 'Norsk rettshistorie i mellomalderen' in the journal *Jussens venner* (1989),[1] which, when talking to academic senior lawyers and legal historians at that time, were more or less the accepted foundation to stand on when approaching the Old Swedish and also the Old Norwegian laws. My perception of these laws was thence that they were fairly useless for squeezing out historical information from, instead they were seen as emanating from a power struggle amongst king and aristocracy in the 13th and 14th centuries, mirroring only a societal situation of that particular historical period, and being heavily dependent upon continental law.

Disturbing for this picture was however a couple of reviews of especially Sjöholm's work by the Danish legal historian Ole Fenger,[2] the Norwegian historian Sverre Bagge[3] and the Swedish historian Thomas Lindkvist,[4] who all three wrote rather, or in some cases, very critical reviews of her book, accusing her to be too dogmatic and rigid in her approach to the laws.

It is therefore impossible to neglect Sjöholm on an occasion like this and her, as we shall see, very black-or-white view of the Old Swedish laws. Here we have a scholar who does not hesitate; she has a very firm opinion regarding the background of the earliest laws.

1. E. Sjöholm, *Svenska landskapslagar: europeisk rättstradition i politisk omvandling* (Stockholm: 1988); cf. E. Sjöholm, *Rechtsgeschichte als Wissenschaft und Politik: Studien zur germanistischen Theorie des 19. Jahrhunderts* (Berlin: 1972); E. Sjöholm, *Gesetze als Quellen mittelalterlicher Geschichte des Nordens* (Stockholm: 1976); E. Sjöholm, 'Rättshistorisk metod och teoribildning', *Scandia* 44 (1978), 229-56; E. Sjöholm, 'Sweden's medieval laws: European legal tradition – political change', *Scandinavian Journal of History* 15 (1990), 65-87; G. Sandvik, 'Norsk rettshistorie i mellomalderen', *Jussens Venner* 6/7 (1989), 281-310. Another scholar who was very critical of finding older layers in the early Scandinavian laws was Klaus von See, who was of the opinion that for example customary law was unknown in Scandinavia before the concept *consuetudo*, emanating from, in his opinion, the Roman law, was introduced by the Church. K. von See, *Altnordische Rechtswörter. Philologische Studien zur Rechtsauffassung und Rechtsgesinnung der Germanen* (Tübingen: 1964), 100-02, 249-55. This is, again, one of these Catch-22 arguments which have flourished in Scandinavian legal historical research during the 1960s, 1970s and 1980s. von See's statement has been refuted, in my opinion correctly, by K. Lunden, 'Norsk tronfylgjerett i seinmellomalderen og lovgjevingssuvereniteten', (*Norsk*) *Historisk Tidsskrift* 65 (1986), 393-419.
2. O. Fenger, [Review of E. Sjöholm, *Svenska landskapslagar*], (*Dansk*) *Historisk Tidsskrift* 89 (1988), 443-46; cf. E. Sjöholm's reply in (*Dansk*) *Historisk Tidsskrift* 91 (1991), 340-42.
3. S. Bagge, [Review of E. Sjöholm, *Svenska landskapslagar*], (*Norsk*) *Historisk Tidsskrift* 69 (1989), 500-07.
4. Th. Lindkvist, 'Medeltidens lagar', (*Svensk*) *Historisk tidskrift* 109 (1989), 413–20; cf. Sjöholm's reply, 'Marxistisk propagandaseger?', (*Svensk*) *Historisk tidskrift* 110 (1990), 259-71, and Th. Lindkvist's reply to Sjöholm's reply, 'Svar till Elsa Sjöholm', (*Svensk*) *Historisk tidskrift* 110 (1990), 558-59.

In an article from 1991 she summarized her stance and I will quote her extensively to paint the picture of her view of the Old Swedish laws,[5] which hence – I have to iterate – presents the position many scholars take as a foundation for these laws today and during the last couple of decades.

Sjöholm starts by criticising two history handbooks of that time,[6] the first one by the historians Sten Carlsson and Jerker Rosén.[7] Their handling of the laws is in her opinion flawed by the fact that they see a development from a, during especially the 1980s, refuted concept of *ättesamhälle*, a society founded on the family or kin, which in the Middle Ages develops into a state. This means that the book, in her opinion, becomes a useless overview because it is founded on false premises. This refuting of a kind of *ättesamhälle* was so profound in the research of the 1970s, 80s and 90s, where we, studying this field, instead of analysing the matter in a constructive way based our understanding of this early society on the – in principle sound – criticism and ideas by some influential scholars like Elsa Sjöholm, Christer Winberg and David Gaunt,[8] who all dismissed the existence of an *ättesamhälle* as important for early society.[9] Especially David Gaunt's refuting of a collective society based on kins (*ätter*) played an important role; he looked upon it as a myth. Instead he stressed that the early society was based upon nucleus family groups (*kärnfamiljer*).[10] Was it? We all could see the elephant in the room, but cowardly no one dared to mention it! Christer Winberg had however a more mediating approach, in that he analysed land and inheritance in the medieval laws, but refrained from having an opinion for earlier periods.[11] It would have been interesting to have him contrasting his insights with the evidence from the runes stones

---

5. E. Sjöholm, 'De svenska medeltidslagarna som historiska källor', *Historielärarnas förenings årsskrift* (1990/91), 36-41.
6. Sjöholm 'De svenska medeltidslagarna som historiska källor', 36-37.
7. S. Carlsson & J. Rosén, *Svensk historia. Tiden före 1718* (Stockholm: 1962).
8. C. Winberg, *Grenverket. Studier rörande jord, släktskapssystem och ståndsprivilegier* (Stockholm: 1985); D. Gaunt, *Familjeliv i Norden* (Stockholm: 1983).
9. Cf. for example, M. Widgren, 'Individuellt och kollektivt ägande i bondesamhället?', in M. Widgren (ed.), *Äganderätten i lantbrukets historia* (Stockholm: 1995), 10 (and also *passim* in this volume).
10. Gaunt, *Familjeliv i Norden*, 208-10.
11. Winberg, *Grenverket*, 25-30. A mediating and – in my opinion – constructive view regarding the role of the *ätt* (kin) and family in early Scandinavian is hinted at by Sverre Bagge in his review of Elsa Sjöholm's *Sveriges landskapslagar* (1988), in (*Norsk*) *Historisk Tidsskrift* 69 (1989), 504-05, and in the same way Janken Myrdal points out that Elsa Sjöholm (and her followers) goes too far in the refuting of the importance of the kin (*ätt*) in early Scandinavia, J. Myrdal, *Boskapsskötseln under medeltiden. En källkritisk studie* (Stockholm: 2012), 33.

and the concept of *oðal*.[12] The situation today concerning this elusive concept of *ätt*, German *die Sippe* (and *ättesamhälle*), is not so black-and-white any more as it was during the 1980s. In a recent analysis Thomas Lindkvist has in a constructive way analysed the concept of *ätt* and the elusive – and in my opinion, as it was assumed by researchers in the past – certainly never existing *ättesamhälle* and he has stressed that the kin (*ätt*, *Sippe* etc.) *was* important in the Viking Age and in the Middle Ages, but the kin was not the *only* important collective in society.[13]

A somewhat later handbook on medieval history by Kurt Ågren and Thomas Lindkvist[14] is also swiftly dismissed by Sjöholm,[15] because the authors are accused of being Marxist scholars, which, according to her, means that they are unaware of source criticism. Their book is labelled 'unsuitable for academic teaching' (*otjänlig för vetenskaplig undervisning*; p. 37). The sad state, according to Sjöholm (*ibid.*), is that these two handbooks are 'indoctrinating' students in a totally obsolete view of the laws.

Sjöholm's own theory is that the earliest Scandinavian laws, hence not just the Swedish ones (and one must assume she also includes the Icelandic *Grágás*), are from the time when Scandinavia was 'colonized', which is the word she uses (Sw *koloniserad*), by the Catholic Church.[16] There are no traceable layers or reminiscences of Old Nordic law in them, according to her, although she admits she can identify layers in the laws. They are

12. Cf. e.g. K. Robberstad, 'The Odal Right according to the old Norwegian Laws', *Universitetet i Bergen. Årbok. Hist.-Antikv. Rekke* (1955), 34-40; A.J. Gurevic, 'Edda and Law. Commentary upon *Hyndlolióð*', *Arkiv för nordisk filologi* 88 (1973), 72-84, at 77-84; S. Brink, 'Law and Legal Customs in Viking Age Scandinavia', in J. Jesch (ed.), *The Scandinavians from the Vendel Period to the Tenth Century: An ethnographic perspective* (Woodbridge: 2002), 103-05.
13. 'Ätten, släkten, *die Sippe*, var inte någon stat i staten. Men släktskap, biologiskt eller artificiellt, var en viktig grund för skilda typer av kollektiv under det vi i Norden brukar kalla vikingatid och tidig medeltid. [...] Ätten var inte den enda grunden för samhörighet eller den enda grunden för att konstituera ett kollektiv, inte ens under ättesamhällets tid.' ('*Ätten*, the kin, *die Sippe*, was not a State in the State. But kinship, biological or artificial, was an important basis for different types of collective during what we in Scandinavaia usually call the Viking Age and Early Middle Ages. [...] The kin was not the only basis for affinity or the only basis to constitute a collective, not even during the time of the *ättesamhället*', my trans.). Th. Lindkvist, 'I stället för ättesamhälle?', in H.J. Orning, K. Esmark & L. Hermanson (ed.), *Gaver, ritualer, konflikter. Et rettsantropologisk perspektiv på nordisk middelalderhistorie* (Oslo: 2010), 299.
14. Th. Lindkvist & K. Ågren, *Sveriges medeltid* (Stockholm: 1985).
15. Sjöholm, 'De svenska medeltidslagarna som historiska källor', 36-37.
16. Sjöholm, 'De svenska medeltidslagarna som historiska källor', 37.

The Origins of the Swedish Medieval Laws

therefore products of the mid and late 12th and especially the 13th centuries. She then takes a case, conveniently for her, namely the Church law of the law of Scania, where she finds a law rule which is supposed to show a new agreement between bishop and farmers, because the older law (*sic*) was considered, she assumes, too harsh.[17] The farmers are supposed to have rebelled and the bishop had to compromise. This case can be used, according to Sjöholm, to explain all the legal agreements in Scandinavia found in the laws. The laws are therefore to be seen as a result of a struggle between competing interests, and it is the power situation at each time which decides which party has the upper hand.

Furthermore the laws' primary function was to be normative, according to Sjöholm;[18] she looks upon the laws as constructions of how it *should* be. This position has recently been discussed and contradicted by Marie Johansson in her analysis of the legal process in the Östgöta law,[19] and her conclusion shows for example that the law rules demanded so many witnesses, in some cases up to 42 men plus 12 men, hence 54 men, to take oaths, and the total number in settling a case could count up to 96 men, which must mean, according to Johansson, that not only the upper strata in society were involved, but that more or less all men in the hundred (*härad*) must have been participating in the legal process, which means that rules and structures of the law must – at least to some degree – have been anchored among people in society. Johansson ends her analysis by stating: 'you cannot look upon the [medieval] laws as something that merely reflects a construction of how a society *should* look like. The rules and structure of the laws must at least to some degree have been anchored among people in society'.[20]

When the Old Scandinavian laws got their codification and were written down, this was, according to Sjöholm, influenced and made out from the continental legal tradition, and therefore got a *judicial form*, which are the words she uses,[21] which we find in the continental laws, especially the

---

17. Sjöholm, 'De svenska medeltidslagarna som historiska källor', 37.
18. Sjöholm, 'De svenska medeltidslagarna som historiska källor', 38.
19. M. Johansson, 'Att stämma till ting – om rättegångssystemet i Östgötalagen', *Scandia* 64 (1998), 161-93.
20. 'man [kan] inte betrakta lagarna som något som bara återspeglar en konstruktion av hur samhället *borde* se ut. Lagarnas regler och strukturer måste åtminstone till en viss del ha varit förankrade hos människorna i samhället'; Johansson, 'Att stämma till ting…', 189. (My trans.)
21. Sjöholm, 'De svenska medeltidslagarna som historiska källor', 39.

Stefan Brink

Lombarda.²² This influence was, according to her, channelled through the archdiocese of Lund, beginning, one then has to assume, sometime after 1103. And in this respect she has the rather astonishing remark that due to this fact, or rather, this idea of hers, the archbishop of Lund's work with what was to become the law of Scania, was meant to be used all over his ecclesiastical jurisdiction, hence all over Scandinavia. Thus the law of Scania was meant to be not a, but *the* pan-Scandinavian law. And more impressively, all law in Western Europe builds, according to Sjöholm, on the law of Moses, and in the Pentateuch, according to Sjöholm, we find the whole programme for the medieval penal law in the western world and the foundation for the organisation of our societies.²³

Then Sjöholm goes on to dismiss an oral tradition for the laws, not the fact that there must have been an oral tradition in the earlier culture in Scandinavia, but that it is impossible to *prove* that we have reminiscences of an oral tradition in our laws, due to the fact that we don't have any earlier written sources which can prove this;²⁴ hence a classical Catch-22 situation. The only way forward to understand the creation of the Scandinavian laws is instead, according to Sjöholm, to accept her 'reception theory', that our laws come from 'learned' continental law.²⁵ Oral, handed down customary law, is according to her a myth, a figment of imagination, impossible to prove.

Sjöholm's idea is that when this learned law was used in Scandinavia, it was not a word-for-word copying of the continental laws, it was adjusted to political realities in Scandinavia, which sounds reasonable. Whether these

22. For an interesting discussion on the mixed origin of and the spread and usage of the Lombard law, see N. Everett, 'How territorial was the Lombard Law?', in W. Pohl & P. Erhart (ed.), *Die Langobarden. Herrschaft und Identität* (Vienna: 2004), 347-62.
23. Sjöholm, 'De svenska medeltidslagarna som historiska källor', 38.
24. Sjöholm, 'De svenska medeltidslagarna som historiska källor', 37-40. For a discussion of possible oral (even early oral) law in the medieval laws of Scandinavia, see e.g. C.I. Ståhle, 'Om Dalalagens ålderdomlighet och ålder – och Kopparbergsprivilegiernas oförbätterliga "sik biwiþär"', in *Nordiska studier i filologi och lingvistik. Festskrift tillägnad Gösta Holm på 60-årsdagen den 8 juli 1976* (Lund: 1976), 392-401; P. Foote, 'Oral and literary tradition in early Scandinavian law: aspects of a problem', in H. Bekker-Nielsen et al. (ed.), *Oral Tradition – Literary Tradition* (Odense: 1977), 47-55; P. Foote, 'Some lines in Lögréttuþáttr. A comparison and some conclusions', in *Sjötíu Ritgerðir helgaðar Jakobi Benediktssyni 20. Júli 1977*, vol. 1 (Reykjavík: 1977), 198-207; J. Øyrehagen Sunde, '"De skal vera samde menn". Ei vitskapleg fundering og spekulasjon over den eldste norske processen', *De lege. Juridiska fakulteten i Uppsala årsbok* (2007), 305-22; S. Brink, 'Oral Fragments in the Earliest Old Swedish Laws?', in M. Mostert & P.S. Barnwell (ed.), *Medieval Legal Process. Physical, Spoken and Written Performance in the Middle Ages* (Tunhout: 2011), 147-56.
25. Sjöholm, 'De svenska medeltidslagarna som historiska källor', 38.

laws were also adjusted to local customs and agricultural and environmental preconditions, she never discusses, she only conducts a discussion on a political level, hence neglecting to discuss large parts of the laws dealing with such matters.

The – for Sjöholm – important analysis of the power structure in society, mirrored in the laws, she exemplifies with the Uppland law.[26] This was not, according to her, a step towards a united Swedish kingdom, which many have suggested, but instead a detaching of the province of Uppland vis-à-vis the central power. The king's power was heavily reduced and so was the power of the Church. It was the secular aristocracy that became the dominant party. *Nota bene*, this is a law which was commissioned by the king, ratified by the king and where one member of the law committee (probably the secretary), preparing for the new law, was the dean in the archbishopric at the cathedral in Uppsala, Andreas Andreæ And, educated in theology and Canon law in Paris, a councillor to the king and the cousin to the man in charge of preparing for the new Uppland law, the Lawman Birger Persson to Finsta (who, besides this function, was also the father to Saint Birgitta of Vadstena).[27] I have huge difficulties in following Sjöholm here.

3. Reception and criticism of Sjöholm

One good thing about Sjöholm's books and articles on the matter was that they provoked Ole Fenger, Sverre Bagge and Thomas Lindkvist to write extensive and in-depth reviews.

Ole Fenger did review and comment on several of Sjöholm's books and articles in *(Dansk) Historisk Tidsskrift*. I will here concentrate on his review of her book *Sveriges medeltidslagar* (1988).[28] Firstly he is obviously irritated at the parsimonious use by Sjöholm of the Danish and Norwegian research in legal history, past and ongoing, something she claims is lacking especially regarding power struggles during the period of the writing of the early laws. He then asks why Sjöholm has not tried to contextualize her analysis in a societal situation, especially regarding the earlier laws in order to understand the background to an early phase of Scandinavian laws, something that Sjöholm stated was a useless task due to the lack of sources. Fenger however points to the possibility that it might be rewarding to use comparative sources to grasp what might have happened and points to the potential of legal sociology (*retssociologi*). However, the general criticism

---

26. Sjöholm, 'De svenska medeltidslagarna som historiska källor', 40.
27. See K.B. Westman, 'Andreas Andreæ And', *Svenskt biografiskt lexikon* 1 (1918), 648.
28. O. Fenger, [Review of E. Sjöholm, *Sveriges landskapslagar* (1988)], *(Dansk) Historisk Tidsskrift* 15:4 (1989), 443-46.

that is permeating Fenger's review – more so between the lines than explicitly stated – is, in his view, the rigid stance that Sjöholm takes in her analyses, and he ends his review by accusing Sjöholm of not having an open mind in her research for counter-ideas, demurs and remonstrance.

Sverre Bagge spends eight dense pages in *(Norsk) Historisk Tidsskrift* on his review of Elsa Sjöholm's *Sveriges medeltidslagar*, and he points out several important aspects of our medieval laws of general importance to future research in our old laws. He gives Sjöholm credit where she deserves good press, but he is astonished that it is possible in 1988 to publish something so antiquated that one hardly believes one's own eyes (*så antikverte at man knapt tror sine egne øyne når man finner dem i en bok fra 1988*). Sverre Bagge starts by commenting on Sjöholm's *lidenskapelige angrep*, i.e. passionate attack, on old key figures such as Montesquieu, Savigny, Hegel and others, which according to Bagge, hence, seems odd in a book from 1988, and he notes that this obsolescence regarding methods and problems is a continuing theme in her book. Both Fenger and Bagge note that Sjöholm is heavily influenced by the Weibull brothers,[29] and their source-critical theory, which they developed in the beginning of the twentieth century with the aim of searching for an absolute secure foundation to stand on in their analysis of the available written sources. The criticism to this, in principle, sound position is, according to Bagge, that this is not only a methodological principle for Sjöholm, it has become her world view (*virkelighetsoppfatning*). This leads to the contradictive situation that it presupposes on the one hand law-givers who mechanically (*slavisk*) copy foreign law, and on the other hand these law-givers, being rational operators, consequently create their laws out from their personal interests. Bagge scrutinizes Sjöholm's theoretical and methodological ideas and gives her credit for her attempt at a power analysis of the medieval Swedish society (which may have been quite different from the Norwegian and especially the Icelandic society), but cannot follow her regarding her other major theory, the one of reception.[30] Bagge's final, in my opinion accurate, verdict of Sjöholm's overall analytical method is therefore: with this method you can prove in principle anything (*med denne metoden kan man bevies omtrent hva som helst*).[31]

---

29. See e.g. L. Weibull, *Kritiska undersökningar i Nordens historia omkring år 1000* (Lund: 1911) and *Historisk-kritisk metod och nordisk medeltidsforskning* (Lund: 1913).
30. For a definition of *reception* as a legal term, see E. Levy, 'Reflections on the First 'Reception' of Roman Law in Germanic States', *The American Historical Review* 48 (1943), 20-29, at 20.
31. Bagge, [Review of Sjöholm], 500-07. A likewise balanced verdict of Sjöholm's book, similar to the one presented by Bagge here, was given by P. Norseng, 'Lovmaterialet

Thomas Lindkvist's review in (*Svensk*) *Historisk tidskrift* 1989 is very moderate, restrained and polite. He highlights several aspects in Sjöholm's book, and gives her credit for many observations and new perspectives. However, the main results he cannot support. His main criticism is that with the perspective, or method, Sjöholm has taken, she disregards any political and social context, hence she is not able to contextualise these laws in a contemporary society and political situation – similar to the criticism formulated by Fenger. Moreover she disregards any other discussion that has taken place in the field, apart from stating that she has produced an analysis diametrically opposed to all other research before her, as if that was one specific tradition. Furthermore, Sjöholm's declared belief that it is impossible to know or say anything about law and a legal society before the time we have the earliest laws actually disregards a lot of research in this field.[32] With the stance Sjöholm has taken in her research she places herself in a historiographical vacuum, Lindkvist notes, paying no interest in others' research, more than criticising a 'Germanic' theory developed in the 19th century.[33]

Symptomatic for this pugnacious scholar, Sjöholm writes in the next volume of the journal a sharp and critical review of Lindkvist's review, claiming that he has totally misunderstood her book, and that this misunderstanding depends on Lindkvist's adopted political perspective; the retort has the title 'A Marxist Victory of Propaganda?' (*En marxistisk propagandaseger?*).[34]

4. Scandinavian laws and the question of external influence

Since my first area to venture in my research was northern Sweden, I started to read and analyse the medieval law of this region, the Hälsinge law, never mentioned by for example Sjöholm in her overview, and when reading about the law in handbooks, it was obvious that that law was seen as pretty uninteresting, being a mere copy of the Uppland law from 1296, so it was said. However, having spend a decade or so reading this law and compared it to other provincial laws, I had come to the insight that the background to

      som kilde til tidlig nordisk middelalder', in G. Karlsson (ed.), *Kilderne til den tidlige middelalders historie. Rapporter til den XX nordiske historikerkongres Reykjavík 1987*, vol. 1 (Reykjavík: 1987), 66.
32. Th. Lindkvist, 'Medeltidens lagar', (*Svensk*) *Historisk tidskrift* 109 (1989), 413-20, at 418.
33. Lindkvist, 'Medeltidens lagar', 419.
34. Sjöholm, 'En marxistisk propagandaseger?', 259-71; in its turn followed by a short comment in the same volume by Thomas Lindkvist (pp. 558-59).

the law must be more complicated than being just a simple copy of the Uppland law. And in the discussion of the background to the earliest laws in Scandinavia in the 1980s and 90s, where the stance in the research at that time was a heavily influence from Continental jurisprudence and the uselessness of using the laws for any period earlier than when they were written down, a question like 'How Nordic are the Nordic laws?' had the obvious answer: 'not particularly'.

As I have dealt with before and written about recently, my analysis was that a law like the one for Hälsingland deviates in many respects from what was discussed in research at that time, in the 1980s and 90s. The law was not commissioned by a king and no aristocracy was involved in the process. What I hope I have been able to show is that the law is composed from different sources, one is the Uppland law, which was used as a palimpsest, an inclusion of a *kirkiubalker*, a Church law, very close to the one found in the Uppland law, legal rulings found over more or less the whole of Scandinavia, but also layers in the law which were unique, very often with a legal language which was something of its own, showing clear correspondence with Norwegian legal custom and language. My conclusion was, when I did a close reading of the law, that the Hälsinge law was built up of many different layers and that in several respects it differed from other Scandinavian and even Swedish laws.[35] The picture that emerged for me was that the provincial laws in Scandinavia, although from the outside looking very similar in composition and legal rulings, when reading them more closely for understanding their background, commissionaires and influences, became more heterogeneous, and so not just for the Swedish laws.[36]

This observation of a, so to say, 'regionality' found in these laws has recently been given interesting support by the agrarian historian Janken Myrdal. In his – as always – thorough study of, in this case, the grazing culture of medieval Sweden, and in doing so having close-read the provincial laws, Myrdal found how the legal rules, covering the same phenolmena, have adapted to the special conditions for their specific regionnal preconditions and environments. It is hence obvious that the laws had to be

---

35. S. Brink, 'Hälsingelagens ställning mellan väst och syd, och mellan kung, kyrka och lokala traditioner', *Kungliga Vitterhets Historie och Antikvitets Akademiens årsbok* (2010), 119-35; S. Brink, 'The Hælsinge Law between south and west, King and Church and local customs', in S. Brink & L. Collinson (ed.), *New Approaches to Early Law in Scandinavia* (Turnhout: 2014).

36. See also S. Brink, 'The creation of a Scandinavian provincial law: how was it done?', *Historical Research* 86 (2013), 432-42. For a balanced stance as to the question of old customary law or newly created law, see H. Vogt, *The Function of Kinship in Early Legislation* (Leiden & Boston: 2010), 61-63.

The Origins of the Swedish Medieval Laws

functional for their specific region and its natural preconditions. One example Myrdal gives is the way the cultivation of fields was conducted: in areas where the farmers used arder for tilling the soil, arder (*årder*) and ploughing with an arder (*ärjning*) are found in the laws, but where ploughs were used, ploughs and ploughing are found in these law with rules regulating the cultivation of fields. Another example is the rule about acorn trees, which is found in all laws, except the Hälsinge laws, for the obvious reason that no oak trees grow in these northerly regions.[37] His results link up in an interesting way with the analyses that Annette Hoff has described for medieval Denmark, analysing the Danish medieval laws.[38] This means that the laws for the different regions were not mechanically receptions of some foreign legal palimpsest, the law rules had to be adapted to local conditions, otherwise they would certainly not be used and accepted by the people in that regions.

In this new State of the Art we have today, it is obvious that the earliest Swedish laws are not *in toto* transferred customary law from the Viking Age, neither total new inventions during the time of the writing down of laws. The picture is much more complex. The influence of Canon law is evident and does not have to be questioned or discussed. But what about influence from Roman law?

In this case the 'window' for influence is perhaps more narrow, since according to Anders Winroth it can only have started in the 1130s,[39] and especially after the middle of this century. However, as an interesting case of departure Tore Iversen has analysed the Gulathing law in this respect. He finds several instances in the law which, more or less certain, can be attributed to an influence from Roman law. One interesting case is the right to matrimony for unfree individuals, which his analysis shows does not follow Canon law, in the form of Pope Hadrian's decretal (1154-1157), but instead the Summa of Stephan of Tournai from 1160. Iversen shows, to me convincingly, that Archbishop Eysteinn was the one who was responsible for the revision of this law, which then resulted in an Olav and a Magnus redaction, which must have been created in late 12th century, during King Magnus Erlingsson's reign (1161-1184). This must mean, according to Iversen, that the Olav redaction from the time of King Olav Kyrre (1066-

---

37. J. Myrdal, *Boskapsskötseln under medeltiden* (Stockholm: 2012), 35.
38. A. Hoff, *Lov og landskab: Landskabslovenes bidrag til forståelsen af landbrugs- og landskabsudviklingen i Danmark ca. 900–1250* (Aarhus: 1997).
39. A. Winroth, 'The teaching of Law in the Twelfth Century', in H. Vogt & M. Münster-Swendsen (ed.), *Law and learning in the Middle Ages* (Copenhagen: 2006), 41-62, at 41.

139

1093) bears no trace of Roman law.[40] I think this observation is applicable also to a situation in Sweden during this period. These kinds of analyses, finding cases going back on Roman law, or in other cases back on Canon law, are important to find, but equally important, in my opinion, are the cases, such as the one Tore Iversen has revealed in his analysis, of layers in the laws which are not to be seen as emanating from Canon or Roman or Continental law, but seems to be older and even indigenous, perhaps dealing with local or regional customs. These are the kind of cases I am interested in and collecting.

Thus, with the angle I have taken in my research, trying to understand the background to the earliest Scandinavian laws and finding arguments for older layers in the laws, it is notable that during the last decades few lawyers and legal historians have found this research perspective interesting, something, which in the words and opinion of Elsa Sjöholm, of course, is a totally futile enterprise. However, we have the occasional observation. In an important and often referred article by Per Norseng, he discusses in what way it is possible to use our laws as sources for early medieval Scandinavia.[41] By way of introduction Norseng notes that many of the early laws in Scandinavia explicitly mention that older laws are included and do this by referring to older 'law books', so for example in the Frostathing law and in the Uppland law it is stated in the preamble that something called *Vighers flockar*, which is said to be older laws, was used when making the new law, but, as Norseng concludes, it has not been possible to reconstruct such older laws.[42] Norseng's meticulous discussion of the research up to the late 1980s ends in a sigh that even if it is difficult to use the laws as a source for early medieval Scandinavia, such an approach is, however, probably not totally in vain and he ends with his fist in the air, stating that 'It is hopeless, and we never give up' (*Det er håpløst, og vi gir oss ikke*).[43]

But we can continue on this path. Recently Jørn Øyrehagen Sunde has written a really interesting article, which relates to the legal procedure, but then we have to go to Norway again.[44] In this article Sunde analyses the legal procedure called *trygdamål* in the older Gulathing law, hence a kind of agreement form (*avtaleformular*), regulating future peaceful coexistence between two parties which have had a legal dispute. Sunde's departure is that this might be a reminiscence of an old procedural order, full of religious

---

40. T. Iversen, 'Some examples of Roman Law in the Gulathing Law – could Archbishop Eysteinn (1161–88) possibly be the mediator?', in T. Iversen (ed.), *Archbishop Eystein as Legislator. The European Connection* (Trondheim: 2011), 103-22.
41. Norseng, 'Lovmaterialet som kilde', 48-77.
42. Norseng, 'Lovmaterialet som kilde', 51.
43. Norseng, 'Lovmaterialet som kilde', 69.
44. Øyrehagen Sunde, 'De skal vera samde men', 305-22.

The Origins of the Swedish Medieval Laws

references, which was obsolete when it was written down in the Rantzau manuscript ca. 1250, and that this was part of an old legal and widespread custom of using such agreement forms (*avtaleformular*). In this rather ingenious analysis, using the version of *trygdamål* in the Icelandic *Grágás* to supplement the Gulathing law by some, for me, convincing arguments, this leads him to place the origin of the law rule in Western Norway. Analysing what is said in the actual rule suggests to him that the rule should be placed in a time where Christians and pagans lived side by side in society, again a speculative idea, but which actually can be substantiated in the law rule itself in an interesting way.

A couple of years earlier, but obviously unaware of each other's research and conclusions, the legal philologist Bo Ruthström has the following verdict of the agreement form *trygð*, which he calls *förverkandeformel*, and also the related *grið/gruþ* 'peace, asylum' etc.: 'The alliterated *förverkandeformel* which is tied to the crime breaking of *grið/gruþ* and of *trygð* found in all Norwegian laws and in the Swedish Västgötalagarna was probably created in Norway at the latest in the beginning of the 10th century'.[45]

The kind of law which emerges out from this analysis is bound by its form, and it also paints a poetic picture: The one who breaks the agreement sets himself outside of society and shall be chased like a wolf. For this kind of formulaic, poetic constructed law rule it was, according to Sunde and many other scholars, important to give the agreement a form which was memorable and easy to remember.

We then enter into a rather confused discourse, so hotly debated in the 1970s in Sweden, namely whether we can see these kinds of poetic, formalistic, mnemonic devices, suitable for an oral society, such as a poetic form, alliteration, end rimes etc., typical for early law or if it was an invention introduced and used by the editors of the laws in the 12th and 13th centuries, hence literary devices typical for and to be dated to the Middle Ages. Scholars like Elsa Sjöholm and Gudrun Utterström took the latter position,[46]

---

45. B. Ruthström, *Land och fæ. Strukturellt-rättsfilologiska studier i fornnordiskt lagspråk över beteckningar för egendom i allmänhet med underkategorier* (Lund: 2003), 150: 'Den allittererade förverkandeformel som är knuten till brotten kränkning av *grið/gruþ* och av *trygð* i alla norska lagtingslagar och i de svenska västgötalagarna skapades sannolikt i Norge senast i början av 900-talet och kan troligen inte ha kommit in i västgötskt lagspråk senare än i början av 1000-talet.'
46. Sjöholm, *Svenska landskapslagar: europeisk rättstradition i politisk omvandling*, *passim*; G. Utterström, 'Die mittelalterliche Rechtsprache Schwedens. Einige quellenkritische und sprachliche Beobachtungen', in K.H. Dahlstedt (ed.), *The Nordic Languages and Modern Linguistics, vol. 2, Proceedings of the Second International Conference of Nordic and General Linguistics ... Umeå ... 1973* (Stockholm: 1975);

whereas Peter Foote and Carl Ivar Ståhle advocated the former possibility,[47] in vain, one should add, in the discourse climate of that time. I have lately in two articles hopefully given arguments that open up – again then – the possibility of these kinds of mnemonic devices having been used also in early law, since we for example find it in formulaic runic inscriptions.[48] And now I also feel being backed up by Jørn Øyrehagen Sunde and his analysis of *trygdamål* on this issue.

Now someone might argue that this kind of legal procedural form is also found in Roman law and could have that background. Sunde mentions this possibility, but adds in my opinion a very important remark, namely that this kind of legal process is typical for *all* early laws, where form was tied to rituals, something that we find in most early and oral legal societies. Sunde states that the simplest form of this kind of legal ritual is – hence – the agreement form (*avtaleformular*). To sum up the discussion of the *trygdamål*, Jørn Øyrehagen Sunde argues that we here find indications that the king or kingship had not yet established itself as an executive power and that the law rule, the agreement form, has all the qualities which one would expect in an early, oral legal society.

In the title of Sunde's article we find the word 'speculation'. So it is, but in my opinion his analysis results in an interesting, plausible hypothesis, backed up by some rather solid arguments. Further than this we are normally not able to go, since we are dealing with a period with no or very few written sources. Some of us can live with this uncertainty; some have problems, and therefore refrain from speculations. With the stance I have taken in my research, I have to live with this uncertainty, and I do.

An interesting contribution to the old Swedish laws are two philological works, doctoral theses, by Nils Jörgensen, on the syntax and the textual structure in medieval Nordic laws (1987), and by Bo Ruthström, on the terminology of movable and immovable property (2003),[49] and most

---

G. Utterström, 'Ålderdomlighet utan ålder?: en replik om Dalalagen', *Arkiv för nordisk filologi* 93 (1978), 199-204.

47. C.I. Ståhle, *Syntaktiska och stilistiska studier i fornnordiskt lagspråk* (Lund: 1955); C.I. Ståhle, 'Lagspråk, in *Kulturhistoriskt lexikon för nordisk medeltid* 10, 167-77; Ståhle, 'Om Dalalagens ålderdomlighet och ålder', 392-401; Foote, 'Oral and literary tradition in early Scandinavian law: aspects of a problem', 47-55; Foote, 'Some lines in Lögréttuþáttr. A comparison and some conclusions', 198-207.
48. S. Brink, '*Verba Volant, Scripta Manent?* Aspects of Early Scandinavian Oral Society', in P. Hermann (ed.), *Literacy in Medieval and Early Modern Scandinavian Culture* (Odense: 2005), 59-117; Brink, 'Oral Fragments in the Earliest Old Swedish Laws?', 147-56.
49. N. Jörgensen, *Studier över syntax och textstruktur i nordiska medeltidslagar* (Uppsala: 1987); Ruthström, *Land och fæ*.

The Origins of the Swedish Medieval Laws

important as a bi-product of his work, Ruthström presents us with a relative chronology for these legal terms.

Jörgensen's main result can be said to be that from a syntactical point of view, laws such as the Svea laws show a much more archaic structure and composition than for example the Icelandic *Grágás*, which has a much more modern, technically and syntactically skilful language,[50] being more literary advanced so to say. Peter Foote has also remarked upon the lack of rhetorical formulas in the Icelandic *Grágás*, noting that the Swedish laws are 'more primitive and less literary than the Icelandic',[51] although the Swedish ones are much later.

In Ruthström's case he is able to show that the legal terminology for movables has changed during the Middle Ages, so that some earlier terms have been exchanged with younger ones. This change, Ruthström's plausible conclusion is, comes with the Church and the introduction of Canon law.[52] Again we have here a scholar who is able to trace the background to what we find in our Old Swedish laws even before the Middle Ages, and this not by clinging to some *Germanischen Urrecht* theory, but by analysing the legal terminology.

Not directly relating to the Swedish provincial laws, Gabriela Bjarne Larsson has in her thesis discussed secular statutes in Sweden between 1350 and 1500, and how the royal power and the aristocracy used statutory legislation to obtain political and economic power in late medieval Sweden. She has also discussed how these statutes may have influenced the Swedish National Law of King Magnus Eriksson (ca. 1350) and the National Law of King Christopher (1442).[53] Christine Ekholst has analysed how men and women were looked upon as legal subjects during the Middle Ages, as criminals and as victims. She finds that female legal responsibility for serious crimes was emphasized, but that there was a differentiation regarding death penalties for men and women. Ekholst sees this as a royal initiative to make women more into legal subjects.[54]

New light has recently been shed on the assumed oldest of the Swedish laws, the two Västgöta laws. Per-Axel Wiktorsson has produced a new edition of the manuscript B59ab, containing these laws, which is a welcome and solid foundation to stand upon for future research. Furthermore, Göran B. Nilsson has dived into the manuscript and been able to rewrite the history

50. Jörgensen, *Studier över syntax och textstruktur i nordisk medeltidslagar*, 102-03, 167.
51. Foote, 'Oral and literary tradition in early Scandinavian law: aspects of a problem', 48; cf. Foote, 'Some lines in Lögréttuþáttr. A comparison and some conclusions', 207.
52. Ruthström, *Land och fæ*, 135-47.
53. G. Bjarne Larsson, *Stadgelagstiftning i senmedeltidens Sverige* (Lund: 1994).
54. C. Ekholst, *För varje brottsling ett straff. Föreställningar om kön i de svenska medeltidslagarna* (Stockholm: 2009).

143

of especially the younger Västgöta law (*Yngre Västgötalagen*).[55] His book is constructed as a kind of personal vendetta against older authorities (e.g. Carl Johan Schlyter), who, according to Nilsson, became too dominating in the field, wherefore no one dared to evaluate their research. Nilsson convincingly demonstrates that the younger Västgöta law was developed during much longer time than normally believed, and that it is a radically different law from the older law. The notes and extracts, which have been labelled the *Lydekini excerpter*, are according to Nilsson to be looked upon as notes done by the law commission for the revision of the law. The book gives interesting insights into the law-making process in medieval Sweden.

5. Looking into the future

I will end this paper by looking into the future. To accompany the overviews of our earliest laws, which we find in for example *Kulturhistorisk lexikon för nordisk medeltid*,[56] we now have a new Stand-der-Forschung with the German lawyer Dieter Strauch's *Mittelalterliches Nordisches Recht bis 1500* from 2011,[57] which is more a kind of a database than a theoretical speculative contribution but all the same very useful. And in a near future there will be new introductions to the earliest laws, which at the moment are in the process of being written within a project entitled *Nordic Medieval Laws*,[58] where all the earliest Scandinavian laws are being translated into English. This will hopefully open up also an international research into the medieval Nordic laws.

---

55. G.B. Nilsson, *Nytt ljus över Yngre Västgötalagen. Den Bestickande Teorin om en medeltida lagstiftningsprocess* (Stockholm: 2012).
56. *Kulturhistoriskt lexikon för nordisk medeltid från vikingatid till reformationstid*, 22 vols (Malmö, København & Oslo: 1956-78).
57. D. Strauch, *Mittelalterliches Nordisches Recht bis 1500: eine Quellenkunde* (Berlin: 2011).
58. See http://www.abdn.ac.uk/medieval-nordic-laws/

LAW, LANGUAGE AND CRIME IN DENMARK AND ENGLAND: A COMPARATIVE APPROACH

Jenny Benham

1. Introduction*

Significant amounts of ink have over the years been spilt by historians investigating the laws of England and Scandinavia in the period of the Viking invasions and settlement in England. For the 12th and early 13th centuries, however, much less attention has been paid to the comparative legal history of these geographical entities, with those scholars researching English law and practice, in particular, focusing more on developments and influence from the Continent and Rome than on comparisons with Scandinavia, deeming it peripheral after the events of 1066. Furthermore, historians have tended to pay most attention to inheritance and property while much less has been written about crime. This paper is an attempt to redress some of this balance by looking at crime and language in the laws of England and Denmark in a comparative context and to consider some of the problems and possibilities of such an approach.

One of the first things to note is that it is not always easy to define crime in the laws of the 12th or early 13th centuries. In the modern world criminal law defines social conduct and bans and punishes threatening, harming, or otherwise endangering the health, safety, and moral welfare of people. It differs, at least in the UK, from civil law, which is more focused on dispute resolution and on the compensation of victims than on punishment. Charles Donahue Jr. has further commented that 'the distinction between crime and tort, and between criminal and civil procedure, are subdivisions of a wider distinction between public law and private law.'[1] In modern times, crime is thus a matter of public law – an offence against the state or the public generally – it is usually pursued by a public official and if convicted it leads to a state-imposed punishment. Tort, or civil procedure, is an offense against a private individual, it is frequently pursued by the victim, and a judgment favourable to the plaintiff in such a case usually results only in compensation being paid to the victim.[2] For most of the 12th century, 'crime' was not usually grouped under a single term, and offences like killing, rape, theft, and so on, which we think of as crimes today, were often not distinct from civil law.

John Hudson has commented 'the word *crimen* was familiar in the Anglo-Norman period, but its meaning was more flexible, often more extensive, than the modern notion of crime... Nor were the other words used to describe offences which we would call crime solely applicable to a clearly defined category of acts'.[3] At the beginning of the 12th century, the *Leges Henrici Primi*, composed at some point in the second decade of the 12th century, contained some clauses relating to 'criminal causes' and lists these as theft, murder, betrayal of one's lord, robbery, offences punishable with outlawry, *husbreche* (lit. 'house breaking'), arson and counterfeiting.[4] At this point, the author does not specifically state if these were offences that were punished or paid for but an earlier chapter stated that some pleas could not be compensated for with money and these are then listed as: *husbreche*, arson, open theft, palpable murder, treachery towards one's lord, and violation of the peace of the church or the protection of the king through the commission of homicide.[5] One interesting thing about these two lists is that robbery, like theft, was a crime, but unlike theft it was not listed as being unemendable, despite the fact that the author himself thought that both offences could occasionally be amended with a payment, and the chronicler John of Worcester noted for the year 1108 that Henry I 'constituted ... such

---

*   I would like to thank the conference organisers for extending a cordial welcome and for providing such a convivial atmosphere in which to discuss legal history. My thanks also to Ditlev Tamm and Helle Vogt for inviting me to work on the Danish laws and for the many stimulating discussions that have ultimately led me to produce this article. Any mistakes shall, alas, remain my own.

1. Ch. Donahue Jr., 'The Emergence of the Crime-Tort Distinction in England', in W. Brown & P. Górecki (ed.), *Conflict in Medieval Europe: Changing Perspectives on Society and Culture* (Aldershot: 2003), 220.
2. Donahue, 'The Emergence of the Crime-Tort Distinction', 220.
3. J. Hudson, *The Formation of the English Common Law. Law and Society in England from the Norman Conquest to Magna Carta* (London: 1996), 56.
4. L.J. Downer (ed.), *Leges Henrici Primi* (Oxford: 1972), c. 47.1.
5. Downer, *Leges*, c. 12.1a.

a law that if anyone was caught in theft or robbery, they were hanged'.[6] The *Leges* also listed some offences, which we would think of as crimes, such as wounding or *hamsocn* (the offence of one assaulting another in his own home), by setting out a system of fixed levels of compensation – much like earlier Anglo-Saxon laws.[7] Evidently, there is plenty that is ambivalent in the *Leges* about whether crimes should be punished or paid for. In addition to the various lists of pleas, the author seems to have considered that if a person unintentionally committed a crime, such as killing, one should make amends but preferably through a reconciliatory settlement.[8] Furthermore, there were also some pleas that placed a man in the king's mercy, and here we find some further inconsistencies. For instance, coiners of false money would lose a hand and could not redeem it in any way and anyone who fought in the king's dwelling would forfeit his life, while the outcome for violence done to a virgin or a widow is not specified.[9] What is clear from this is that some offences were regarded as more serious than others, but how they were dealt with was seemingly not applied with absolute consistency.

2. Formalizing distinctions

The more formal distinction between civil and criminal pleas began to enter into English law in the late 12th century, under the influence of Roman and canon law.[10] The *Dialogue of the Exchequer* of the late 12th century noted that 'the greatest or heinous offences' were paid for in the guilty person's life or limbs. These were pleas that could only be heard before the king or his justices and they became known as the pleas of the crown. The *Assize of Clarendon* of 1166 named these serious crimes as robbery, murder, theft, or a receiver of a person who had committed such a crime.[11] Ten years later, in 1176, the *Assize of Northampton* further added arson and forgery to the list of such crimes, making it fairly similar to that in the *Leges Henrici Primi*.[12]

---

6. Downer, *Leges*, c. 12.3; R.R. Darlington & P. McGurk (ed.), *The Chronicle of John of Worcester*, 3 vols. (Oxford: 1995-1998), iii, 112.
7. Downer, *Leges*, c. 93.1-36.
8. Downer, *Leges*, c. 5.28b, 70.12b, 90.11-11a.
9. Downer, *Leges*, c. 13.3, 13.6-7.
10. Hudson, *The Formation of the English Common Law*, 56; Donahue, 'The Emergence of the Crime-Tort Distinction', 220-02.
11. N. Vincent (ed.), *Assize of Clarendon*, Early English Laws project: http://www.earlyenglishlaws.ac.uk/laws/texts/ass-clar/view/#edition,/apparatus, c. 1 (Accessed 15.12.2013).
12. N. Vincent (ed.), *Assize of Northampton*, Early English Laws project:

From the *Assize of Clarendon* we know that twelve law-abiding men ('legaliores homines') from each hundred should swear whether any man in the hundred was accused or publicly suspected of one of the more serious crimes.[13] This panel was then expected to present any suspects for trial and those who could not be arrested were condemned to outlawry.[14] The assizes of Clarendon and Northampton seem to relate instructions to justices travelling through the country, so-called justices of the eyre, and they created a more centralised system for the whole of the English kingdom.[15] Another legal text from the late 12th century is the treatise commonly known as *Glanvill*. It is often referred to as a legal manual and attributed to Ranulph Glanville, chef justiciar of England during Henry II's reign, even though it is uncertain whether he actually wrote it, and it is dated to the late 1180s.[16] *Glanvill* contains fourteen chapters, thirteen of which are concerned with the common pleas and only the 14th and shortest chapter relates to crime. From *Glanvill* it is clear that any accused was to appear at court, where he would either confess or provide proof of his innocence. If he confessed, he was adjudged to have 'no law', although exactly what this meant is not specified: it could refer to death or to outlawry or to something else entirely. I hesitate to interpret it as outlawry primarily because usually outlawry is stated very clearly. If the accused denied the offence, he would have to provide proof. According to the assizes, this was done by the ordeal of water. However, we know from court records and from *Glanvill* that proof was commonly provided through an offer of battle. Curiously enough, neither the *Assize of Clarendon* nor *Glanvill* is particularly specific about

http://www.earlyenglishlaws.ac.uk/laws/texts/ass-nor/view/#edition,/hv-image, c. 1. (Accessed 28.11.2013).

13. *Assize of Clarendon*, c. 1.
14. *Assize of Clarendon*, cc. 2–14, 19; W. L. Warren, *The Governance of Norman and Angevin England 1086–1272* (London: Edward Arnold, 1987), 109.
15. J. Hudson, 'Kings and Crime: Ideology and Practice in the Tenth and Twelfth Centuries', in Ph. Chassaigne & J.-Ph. Genet (eds.), *Droit et Société en France et en Grande-Bretagne (XIIe–XXe siècles)* (Paris: 2003), 17; R.C. Van Caenegem, 'Criminal Law in England and Flanders under King Henry II and Count Philip of Alsace', in R.C. Van Caenegem, *Legal History: A European Perspective* (London: 1991), 40. Both *The Laws of Edward the Confessor* and the *Leges Henrici Primi* emphasize that in the early 12th century there were still significant regional differences in the law, in particular between the Danelaw area and that area covered by English (that is, West Saxon) law. Downer, *Leges*, c. 6.2; B. O'Brien (ed.), *The Laws of Edward the Confessor*, Early English Laws project: http://www.earlyenglishlaws.ac.uk/laws/texts/ECf2/, c. 10.1, 12.4–5, 18.4, 20. (Accessed 31.12.2013).
16. G.D.G. Hall (ed.), *The Treatise on the Laws and Customs of the Realm of England Commonly Called Glanvill* (Oxford: 1993), i–xxv.

what punishment was meted out if the accused was found guilty.[17] The *Assize of Northampton*, on the other hand, states that anyone found guilty of the serious crimes would lose a foot and his right hand and abjure the realm, that is, he would leave the kingdom within forty days through a specified port.[18]

Despite the fact that the assizes and *Glanvill* differentiated between crimes and other pleas, the exact distinction was not absolute. For instance, beating someone was not considered among the criminal pleas but instead among the common or civil pleas and it was usually paid for with compensation. However, if a man beat another so that it led to a wound, then it would be considered a criminal plea. This distinction with regard to wounding we know of not from the laws but from the court records made by the king's justices. With the court records of the early 13th century, the historian is fortunate to have access to a plethora of evidence about crime in England. There are a number of different rolls containing legal matters dating from this period, but here I shall primarily deal with material from the eyre rolls, cases heard before the itinerant justices of the eyre. The eyre heard all pleas; both pleas of the crown, matters of crime and administration and finances which concerned the king; and common pleas, referring to disputes concerning land, money, personal injury and inheritance.[19] The rolls are problematic when it comes to crime, however. For example, from the rolls it would be easy to assume that the only outcome for someone who had committed a serious crime was outlawry, primarily because the accused had fled. However, one of the biggest problems with the rolls is that it is not a record of all cases that came to court but rather of those cases that involved or could involve a financial transaction in which the king was the main beneficiary. Outlawry was of course followed by the confiscation of the accused's property, which the king would retain and reap all rewards from for a year. If an accused was propertyless and had no chattels, this is also recorded in the rolls because to reverse outlawry one had to pay a fine to the king.[20] A very small number of cases in the rolls, mainly robbery and wounding, show that one could pay a fine and thereby avoid both any punishment and outlawry. In one case from Yorkshire of 1218, a certain

---

17. For a discussion of some of the punishments in the early 12th century, see J. Hudson (ed.) *The Oxford History of the Laws of England, volume II: 871-1216* (Oxford: 2012), 399-415.
18. *Assize of Northampton*, c. 1.
19. S. Stewart, 'Outlawry as an Instrument of Justice in the Thirteenth Century', in J.C. Appleby & P. Dalton (eds.), *Outlaws in Medieval and Early Modern England: Crime, Government and Society c. 1066–c. 1600* (Farnham: 2009), 39.
20. Hudson, *The Oxford History of the Laws of England*, 724-27; Stewart, 'Outlawry as an Instrument of Justice', 40, 48, 51.

Adam de Mora was accused of wounding Swan of Upton in his head. The case was initially dismissed because the correct procedure had not been followed, but once the case had been renewed, Adam was taken into custody and eventually paid a fine of ten shillings for his act.[21] In another case, from Gloucestershire, Baldwin de Blechesdune killed John Hurt and was captured and imprisoned at Gloucester. He had chattels worth four shillings, for which the sheriff had to answer. No mention is actually made of what happened to Baldwin, apart from the fact that he seemingly forfeited his chattels.[22] The rolls are full of little inconsistencies like these and in addition we know that some settlements were made with the permission of the justices. Barbara Hanawalt, having investigated criminal prosecutions based on the assize roll for Lincolnshire of 1202, concluded that cases were rarely prosecuted according to the letter of the law.[23] Be that as it may, what seems clear is that despite attempts to distinguish between criminal and civil cases, there were small but significant ambiguities in practice, and only a small proportion of accusations reached conviction and execution.[24]

The blurring between criminal law and civil law is perhaps more noticeable in the Danish laws than in the English. The laws mention a number of offences, which we would consider to be crimes in the modern world, most of which are not punished but paid for with compensation. To take one example, the first clause of King Cnut VI's ordinance of homicide, issued in 1200, states: 'If it happens that someone commits homicide, he shall not receive the kinsmen's part ('etheboth') from them [referring to the kin], until he has paid one instalment ('sal') of the wergeld himself, and that is one third. After that he shall convoke the paternal kinsmen and with them find out how much each of them shall pay together with him.'[25] Parts of this ordinance also made it into the *Law of Scania* (*Skånske Lov*), which was compiled shortly after 1200 and at least before 1218, and this particular clause is repeated almost word for word in there.[26] The ordinance mentions other serious crimes including wounding and gang crime (*hærwirki*), e.g. a

---

21. D.M. Stenton (ed.), *Rolls of the Justices in Eyre for Yorkshire in the Year 3 Hen. III (1218–19)*, Selden Society, 56 (London: 1937), no. 553.
22. F.W. Maitland (ed.), *Pleas of the Crown for the County of Gloucester before the Abbot of Reading, 1221* (London: 1884), no. 327.
23. B. Hanawalt, 'Justice without Judgement: Criminal Prosecution before Magna Carta', in J.S. Loengard (ed.), *Magna Carta and the England of King John* (Woodbridge: 2010), 120.
24. Hudson, *The Oxford History of the Laws of England*, 740.
25. C.A. Christensen et al. (ed.), *Cnut VI's Ordinance on Homicide*, in *Diplomatarium Danicum. 1. række*, 7 vols. (Copenhagen: 1957-1990), iv, no. 24, c. 1.
26. J. Brøndum-Nielsen & P.J. Jørgensen (eds.), *Skånske Lov*, in *Danmarks gamle landskabslove*, vol. 1 (Copenhagen: 1933), c. 85.

Law, Language and Crime

man goes to another man's house with intent and removes goods or he beats the householder or his wife while he is in the house.[27] For killing a man one would pay a full man's worth in compensation, although it is not specified exactly how much this was. For gang crime, a fine of forty marks was paid to the king by the leader of the gang, a further forty marks was paid to the kinsmen, and those who were with him in the gang paid three marks each to the king and another three marks to the kinsmen.[28] There are a number of forty-mark cases mentioned in the various laws, which were clearly regarded as the most serious crimes, and they include willingly setting fire to another's house, fighting at the assembly, taking a woman or maiden by force and breaching the peace at the market place.[29]

However, clearly some offences were punished, that is, they were what we would regard as crimes. For instance both the ordinance and the *Law of Scania* mention that if a man seizes something surreptitiously, that is not openly, he would be hanged at the law assembly just as if he had committed theft.[30] A number of the laws record how hanging was the punishment meted out to thieves who had stolen goods worth half a mark or more.[31] If the stolen goods were worth less, the thief would be whipped or lose a limb.[32] The *Law of Jutland* (*Jyske Lov*), decreed by King Valdemar II in 1241, sets down that regardless of how little was stolen, the culprit would receive a 'thief's mark' (*thiwfs mærk*) – be branded or have his ears or nose cut off – and would also pay a fine and compensate the householder.[33] This particular law further details that a second offence, regardless of value, resulted in hanging, as well as compensation and forfeiture of land.[34] Another offence that was so serious that it was punished is murderous arson, for which a guilty person was 'burned or broken on the wheel', according to *Erik's Law of Zealand* (*Eriks Sjællandske Lov*).[35] Note, however, that in the *Law of Jutland*, the guilty not only forfeited his life but also had to pay

27. *Cnut VI's Ordinance on Homicide*, cc. 6-7; *Skånske Lov*, c. 87. Note that in the *Law of Scania* an additional offence, also regarded as gang crime, is the taking by force of a virgin or wife in a field or at home in a house, for which see *Skånske Lov*, c. 218.
28. *Cnut VI's Ordinance on Homicide*, cc. 4, 6-7; *Skånske Lov*, c. 87-8.
29. J. Brøndum-Nielsen (ed.), *Valdemars Sjællandske Lov. Danmarks gamle landskabslove* 8 (Copenhagen: 1941), cc. 57, 63; E. Kroman (ed.), *Eriks Sjællandske Lov. Danmarks gamle landskabslove* 8 (Copenhagen: 1941), Bk. II, cc. 14, 17, 20, 22; P. Skautrup (ed.), *Jyske lov. Danmarks gamle landskabslove* 2 (Copenhagen: 1933), Bk. III, c. 22.
30. *Cnut VI's Ordinance on Homicide*, c. 2; *Skånske Lov*, c. 85.
31. *Skånske Lov*, c. 151; *Jyske Lov*, Bk. II, c. 87
32. *Skånske Lov*, c. 151; *Valdemars Sjællandske Lov*, c. 87.
33. *Jyske Lov*, Bk. II, c. 89.
34. *Jyske Lov*, Bk. II, c. 89.
35. *Eriks Sjællandske Lov*, Bk. II, c. 15.

compensation.[36] Both arson and theft are listed among those offences that were unemendable in English laws, and although this must have been the case also in Denmark, judging by the punishments, they are not specifically referred to as such. Here we are hindered by language and terminology, as well as the problem of criminal-civil distinction. The Danish laws were set down in the vernacular, while in England the laws were increasingly being translated into and set down in Latin, although certain terms were retained in the vernacular. There is no specific word for crime or criminal law in the Danish laws and the only offence that is specifically set out as being different from those for which compensation was paid is the so-called *Orbotæ mal*; often translated as 'heinous' or 'unemendable crimes' but where the second part of the phrase, *mal*, is perhaps better reflected in English as 'case' or 'plea' rather than 'crime'.[37] These cases are listed as killing a man in his own home, shed, stable, barn, churchyard, or at the assembly (the OE equivalent of *hamsocn*), and killing a man after compensation has been paid. All of these instances are indeed heinous but from the laws it is much less certain if they were unemendable. The laws relating to *Orbotæ mal* were originally set down in the late 12th century but later became incorporated into first *Valdemar's Law of Zealand* (*Valdemars Sjællandske Lov*), compiled around 1222, and then *Erik's Law of Zealand*, compiled at some point after 1241.[38] The first of these laws relates the matter in the following way: 'they [referring back to the list] are *orbotæ mál* and [in such cases] the king will take all of their capital lots and all the valuables that they own, except their land, because they are the leaders in those deeds. The king cannot receive the peace buy from the men and cannot rightfully give them their peace, unless he receives the consent of those who are the closest relatives of the killed [man] and [they] are of full age and can rightfully receive promise of compensation'.[39] Judging by this then, the punishment was a partial forfeiture of chattels and, crucially, if the kin gave their consent, compensation and a payment for the guilty man to be brought back into the king's peace. Furthermore this particular law claims that a man who had killed another would pay three marks to the king to buy his peace and would then put the case before three successive provincial assemblies. If the killed man's family did not by the third assembly declare the case unemend-

36. *Jyske Lov*, Bk. III, c. 66.
37. H. Vogt, *The Function of Kinship in Medieval Nordic Legislation* (Leiden: 2010), 127-30; P. Andersen, *Legal Procedure and Practice in Medieval Denmark* (Leiden: 2011), 71-2.
38. On the dates of *Valdemar's Law of Zealand* and *Erik's Law of Zealand*, see discussions in Vogt, *The Function of Kinship*, 64-71; Andersen, *Legal Procedure*, 77-8.
39. *Valdemars Sjællandske Lov*, c. 53.

able, then he would pay compensation for the killing.[40] The assembly (*thing*) and kinsmen seem to have had significant sway over how an offender was dealt with also in other cases. For instance, *Valdemar's Law of Zealand* stipulates that if a man 'catches a thief with half a mark or more, then he should bring him to the assembly and the men of the assembly can either order him to hang or to the king's estate (i.e. to enslavement) or to have his hide whipped, and it shall be [done] with the consent of the one from whom he stole'.[41] The *Law of Jutland* further stipulates that those who heard a criminal case, such as homicide, could decide if the guilty should pay compensation or be declared an outlaw.[42] With regard to the *orbotæ mál*, it is clear that the consequences of being found guilty shifted slightly over time. In *Erik's Law of Zealand*, the statement about what happened to a person found guilty had been amended somewhat from the earlier law: 'And everything except land which belongs to the one who has killed is in the king's power, and he himself flees as a *frithløs* man'.[43] This seems closer to being 'unemendable' in that there is no mention here of the guilty being able to compensate for his crime or pay a fine to be received back into the king's protection. What is evident from all of this is that just like in England in the early 12th century the evidence from the Danish laws indicate that there were more serious offences, but in Denmark most were paid for rather than punished, and even those that were punished frequently included also the payment of a fine and compensation to the victim. The kind of attempted division between criminal and civil pleas that we find in the assizes, *Glanvill*, and the court records in England are not, according to Helle Vogt, apparent in Denmark until the late 13th century with the abolishment of collective payment of compensation from both the guilty person and his kin.[44]

Something can perhaps be said here about outlawry, which features strongly in the court records and in the laws of both Denmark and England. Outlawry, or *utlaga*, is, of course, a word of Norse origin, which quickly came to mean a person 'outside the law' in Old English.[45] That is how it is

---

40. *Valdemars Sjællandske Lov*, c. 50. This role of the assembly and kin was later given to the king, for which see *Eriks Sjællandske Lov*, Bk. II, c. 9.
41. *Valdemars Sjællandske Lov*, c. 87.
42. *Jyske Lov*, Bk. II, c. 12.
43. *Eriks Sjællandske Lov*, Bk. II, c. 5. On the word *frithløs*, see below.
44. H. Vogt, 'Nye perspektiver på familierettens historie. Nordisk middelalder – Individ, familie, slægt', in M.J. Jareborg & M. Kumlien (eds.), *De lege: årsbok 2011 från juridiska fakulteten i Uppsala: Rätten och rättsfamiljer i ett föränderligt samhälle – rättshistoriskt och komparativt: Vänbok till Rolf Nygren* (Uppsala: 2011), 259-261.
45. S.M. Pons-Sanz, *Norse-derived Vocabulary in Late Old English Texts. Wulfstan's Works, a Case Study* (Odense: 2007), 80, 122.

used in late Anglo-Saxon texts and also in texts from the early 12th century. Once the laws came to be written in Latin, from the early 12th century onwards, the word *utlaga* was still usually retained in its Old English forms (or Latinised versions) and on those rare occasions that it is translated, it appears as 'ex lege' (outside the law). The word seems to have referred to someone who had been expelled from the community and therefore had forfeited his possessions and his right to protection.[46] As noted, outlawry is also a feature in the Danish laws but despite *utlaga* being a word of Norse origin, the word in the Danish laws, as also in the Swedish laws, is *frithløs*, which literally translated means 'peaceless' or 'without peace/protection' and not 'outside the law'. It might be significant that the word used in England is *utlaga* even though the Old English *friðleas*, a loan translation from Old Norse *friðlauss*, did exist in earlier Anglo-Saxon laws. Scholars have usually translated both *utlaga* and *friðleas* as outlaw/outlawry in modern English, and Sara Pons-Sanz is the latest to do so, justifying this decision on the fact that *friðleas* occurs in one manuscript of the Wulfstan corpus together with the word *flyman* (fugitive) and the fact that in the *Instituta Cnuti*, of the early 12th century, it is translated as 'expulsus' ('expelled').[47] As noted above *utlaga* is usually translated into Latin as 'ex lege' not 'expulsus', but apart from this, it is possible that 12th-century usage of *utlaga* and *frithløs* reflected a small difference in concept and practice of what outlawry actually meant in the two kingdoms.

In the second quarter of the 13th century, Bracton wrote in his *On the Laws and Customs of England* that after a proclamation of outlawry 'henceforth they bear the wolf's head and in consequence perish without judicial inquiry; they carry their judgment with them and they deservedly perish without law who have refused to live according to law. This is so if they take to flight or resist when they are to be arrested; if they are arrested alive or give themselves up, their life and death will be in the hands of the lord king'.[48] This is clearly referring back to the *Laws of Edward the Confessor*, in which an outlaw was also said to bear a wolf's head and would be surrendered to the king and placed in his mercy, if he was caught,

---

46. Pons-Sanz, *Norse-derived Vocabulary*, 80.
47. Pons-Sanz, *Norse-derived Vocabulary*, 130. Some of this had already been noted by Steenstrup at the end of the 19th century. J.C.H.R. Steenstrup, *Normannerne*, 4 vols. (Copenhagen: 1876-1882; repr. 1972), iv, 252.
48. G.E. Woodbine (ed.), *Bracton On the Laws and Customs of England*, 4 vols., trans. with revisions and notes by S.E. Thorne (Cambridge, MA: 1968-1977), ii, 354. The alliteration 'they deservedly perish without law who have refused to live according to law' has a curious similarity with reference to a *frithløs* man in *Erik's Law of Zealand*: 'then he shall always be without peace [*frithløs*] until he has redeemed his peace'. *Eriks Sjællandske Lov*, Bk. III, c. 46.

or killed, if defending himself.[49] The *Leges Henrici Primi* had, furthermore, set out that anyone who suffered outlawry would forfeit his bocland to the king.[50] What is clear from these texts and also from the assizes and the court records is that outlawry was pronounced once someone had fled, and it was not a punishment for being caught or found guilty of committing a crime.[51] It would also seem that although an outlaw was outside the law, he was in certain circumstances, such as travelling to and from the king's court to pay the fine to revoke the outlawry, allowed the king's peace.[52] Thus one could seemingly be outside the law but this did not necessarily mean that one was completely outside the peace and protection of the king.

In Denmark it is not clear if being a *frithløs* man always indicated outlawry in the way we think of it in England in the same period, i.e. as a pronouncement made because a person had fled and refused to answer an accusation of a serious crime. *Valdemar's Law of Zealand* certainly seems to anticipate that this was the case. It states that if a man had been accused of theft and failed to appear at successive assemblies, then his personal peace (*man hælæct*) would be taken and thereafter he would be 'a cowardly and *frithløs* man'.[53] However, two of the provincial laws, the *Law of Scania* and the *Law of Jutland*, set out different provisions. According to the *Law of Scania* 'if a man kills another man after compensation has been paid, he shall go *frithløs* and never gain his peace, and the king shall take all that he has except his land'.[54] Some forty years later, the *Law of Jutland* detailed that if a man had killed another man and was sworn *frithløs* and the person who made the accusation did not want to accept compensation, 'then he [the accused] will flee the province before a day and a month. If he does not flee, the king can seize his goods and the king should not receive peace buy (*frith køp*) from him until he is reconciled with the kin of the dead man'.[55] The same law also sets out that a board of 'truth men' had the option of swearing

---

49. O'Brien, *The Laws of Edward the Confessor*, c. 13.1. Steenstrup noted that the expression probably derives from Salic law, for which see Steenstrup, *Normannerne*, iv, 252-54.
50. Downer, *Leges*, c. 13.1.
51. There is one exception in the *Leges Henrici Primi* under the ecclesiastical pleas belonging to the king, where if a man kills another 'he shall be outlawed'. Downer, *Leges*, c. 11.11b. Despite this some historians have considered outlawry a punishment for crimes. For one example, see C. Saunders, 'The Medieval Law of Rape', *The King's College Law Journal* (2001), 28.
52. For some examples of how certain individuals revoked outlawry, see Stewart, 'Outlawry as an Instrument of Justice', 42-53.
53. *Valdemars Sjællandske Lov*, c. 87. The Law of Scania also has an example of this, for which see *Skånske Lov*, c. 145.
54. *Skånske Lov*, c. 90.
55. *Jyske Lov*, Bk. II, c. 22.

that an accused had committed an offence 'without cause' (*sakløøs*), for which he should then be declared *frithløs*.[56] In these examples, becoming *frithløs* was not an effect of fleeing an accusation, but a punishment of being found guilty. Furthermore, a *frithløs* man seemingly always had the option of buying back his peace (*frith*), the so-called 'peace buy' (*frithkøp*).[57] *Erik's Law of Zealand* explains that whoever kills a man must pay six marks for the peace buy in addition to a fine to the king and compensation. It continues, that if a guilty man cannot afford to pay for all of these, 'then he shall always be *frithløs* until he has redeemed his peace'.[58] This is significant, I think, because while the *frithløs* person was without peace, he was seemingly not outside the law, because the law stated that he could always buy his peace back. In England this is not explicitly stated in the law texts, merely that the person fell under the king's mercy if captured, although it is clear from the court records that an acceptable way to be brought back inside the community was to pay a fine to the king. In any case, what seems evident is that if we apply the modern English word outlaw/outlawry to both *utlaga* and *frithløs*, we miss some of the subtle differences between the laws in Denmark and England.

3. Crime in warfare as an example

Most of what I have outlined so far is well-known and has been better said, and also in more detail, by historians such as John Hudson concerning England and Helle Vogt and Per Andersen concerning Denmark. However, one aspect that has perhaps attracted less attention among both scholars interested in English law and those researching Danish law is law and crime in the king's troops. As both the Danish and English kings were involved in a significant amount of warfare in the 12th and early 13th centuries, it seems likely that there were measures in place for dealing with crimes, such as theft or killings, committed while in the king's service. The *Law of Jutland*, for instance, contains two small paragraphs relating to this particular aspect of crime and punishment. The first one states that if a man kills another while in military service, he should always pay forty marks to the kin and also to the king, in addition to paying the appropriate man worth.[59] Another paragraph details that if a man in the military service is accused of theft by a steersman or anyone else from among the ship's crew, then he shall defend himself with the two men who are closest to him on the thwart – that is,

---

56. *Jyske Lov*, Bk. II, cc. 12, 14, 16.
57. On the peace buy, see Vogt, *The Function of Kinship*, 130-31.
58. *Eriks Sjællandske Lov*, Bk. III, c. 46.
59. *Jyske lov*, Bk. III, c. 22.

Law, Language and Crime

those who sit next to him at the oars – and six others of the ship's crew. If he is found guilty, 'then fare with him as with other thieves and he has forsaken both the goods he has there and the capital lot at home'.[60] Among the English laws there are some similarities to the first of these paragraphs. The *Leges Henrici Primi* states that 'if anyone commits homicide in the house or court or fortress or castle or army or personal troop of the king, he shall be in the king's mercy with respect to his property or his limbs'.[61] It also sets down that 'anyone who breaks the peace in the king's troop (*hostico*) shall lose his life or pay compensation in the amount of his wergeld'.[62] It is curious that the provisions in Denmark (or at least Jutland) were more specific than those found in the *Leges Henrici Primi*, although both laws clearly encouraged payment of compensation as the main form of punishment for homicide. It is also curious that only the Danish laws make provisions for theft in military service even though this offence must surely have been more common than homicide.

Nevertheless, what is evident from the Danish provisions is that matters in military service were expected to be resolved in a similar way to when a man was not in military service, with some slight variations in the number of witnesses; that is, if found guilty one's fate would be decided by a board who could either swear you to compensation or to something infinitely more horrible. By contrast, on the one occasion when we have a more specific ordinance about crime in military service from England, it is very different to what usually happened. In a short law issued by Richard I, possibly in June 1190, to those of his subjects who were about to accompany him on the Third Crusade Richard stated that: 'Whoever slays a man onboard a ship shall be bound to the dead man and thrown into the sea. But if he shall slay him on land, he shall be bound to the dead man and buried in the earth. If anyone, moreover, shall be convicted through lawful witnesses of having drawn a knife to strike another, or of having struck him so as to draw blood, he shall lose his hand. But if he shall strike him with his fist without drawing blood, he shall be dipped three times in the sea. But if any one shall taunt or insult a fellow man or charge him with hatred of God: as many times as he shall have insulted him, so many ounces of silver shall he pay. A robber, moreover, convicted of theft, shall be shorn like a hired fighter, and boiling tar shall be poured over his head, and feathers from a cushion shall be shaken out over his head, so that he may be publicly known; and at the first land where the ships put in he shall be cast on shore'.[63]

60. *Jyske lov*, Bk. II, c. 114.
61. Downer, *Leges*, c. 80.1.
62. Downer, *Leges*, c. 13.8.
63. W. Stubbs (ed.), *Chronica magistri Rogeri de Hovedene*, 4 vols., Rolls Series, 51 (London: 1868-1871), iii, 36.

None of these provisions bear similarities to provisions in the English laws for dealing with killings, wounding or robbery. The text is interesting at a number of levels, not least the curious mention of tarring and feathering. Scholars think that this is the first appearance in history of this peculiar punishment, which of course is more commonly known from the early history of North America or at least forever more given to posterity in comics series such as Lucky Luke, who was said to be able to draw his pistol faster than his own shadow and whose opponents frequently ended up tarred and feathered.[64] On a more serious note, there might of course be very good reasons why Richard's short law on criminal crusaders looks very different from other laws. Lots of rowdy men in confined space for a longer period of time may have required some specific measures. Richard's law on criminal crusaders later became incorporated into the laws of Oléron and subsequently into the Admiralty Black Book, both of which were collections of statutes dealing specifically with matters related to the sea, navigation and maritime trade rather than crimes and warfare.[65] Nevertheless, it is curious that there are very few other provisions for military service in the English laws, and it may be that this points to some fundamental differences in how society was organized but also in the nature of warfare. One such example is that the Danish fleet was still supposed to gather every spring, and there are plenty of examples in the work of the Danish late 12th-

---

64. E.F. Henderson, *Select Historical Documents of the Middle Ages* (London: 1896), 4, 135; W. Sayers et al., 'The Early Symbolism of Tarring and Feathering', *Mariner's Mirror* 96:3 (2010), 317-36. For some of the historiography surrounding tarring and feathering in North America, see B. Levy, 'Tar and Feathers', *The Journal of the Historical Society* 11 (2011), 85-110; D. Grimsted, 'Rioting in Its Jacksonian Setting', *American Historical Review* 77 (1972); C.E. Prince, 'The Great "Riot Year": Jacksonian Democracy and Patterns of Violence in 1834', *Journal of the Early Republic* 5 (1985), 1-19; A.E. Young, 'English Plebeian Culture and Eighteenth-Century American Radicalism', in J.R. Jacob & M.C. Jacob (eds.), *The Origins of Anglo-American Radicalism* (London: 1991), 184-212. For an example from Lucky Luke, see R. Goscinny, *La Ville fantôme* (Marcinelle: 1965).
65. On the origin of the laws of Oléron and the Admiralty Black Book, see T. Twiss (ed.), *The Black Book of the Admiralty*, 4 vols., Rolls Series 55 (London: 1871-1876), i, lvi-lxxi; P. Studer, trans., *Oak Book of Southampton*, 2 vols. (Southampton: 1910-1911), ii, xxxv; T.J. Runyan, 'The Rolls of Oleron and the Admiralty Court in Fourteenth-Century England', *American Journal of Legal History* 19 (1975), 96-99; E. Frankot, 'Medieval Maritime Law from Oléron to Wisby: Jurisdictions in the Law of the Sea', in J. Pan-Montojo & F. Pedersen (eds.), *Communities in European History: Representations, Jurisdictions, Conflicts* (Pisa: 2007), 159.

century historian, Saxo Grammaticus, of naval warfare, neither of which is seen very often in England in the 12th and early 13th centuries.[66]

4. Concluding remarks

In a collection of essays derived from a conference where the theme was to ask how Nordic the Nordic medieval laws were, it is imperative, I think, to compare some of the laws mentioned above, not just to other laws in Scandinavia or to developments of Roman and canon law, but also to those of the other polities of the medieval West. England and Denmark provide a particularly good basis for making such comparisons. For instance, the two kingdoms shared a common cultural background and, of course, a similarity in language. We know, furthermore, that in this period England was divided into two legal areas, one under English, that is West Saxon law, and another under Danish law. Although some of Henry II's legal reforms of the late 12th century were intended to eradicate some of these differences, it is clear that customary law continued to play a large role in English legal culture, and there are also significant regional differences to be found in the court records.[67] In addition, the 12th century in England and the late 12th and early 13th centuries in Denmark saw not only much lawmaking but also changes in legal procedure and in language. There are significant commonalities in the laws of both kingdoms, in particular relating to language and procedure, but most of these have not received widespread attention, especially among Anglophone scholars unfamiliar with Old Danish, and hence the new translations of the medieval Danish laws into English by Ditlev Tamm and his team will be invaluable. Of course, there are differences too. For instance, crime is not necessarily defined in the same way in the laws of both kingdoms, and some crimes, such as the gang crime that we find in the provincial laws of Denmark, do not exist in England.[68] Furthermore, the seeming departure from the system of compensation in England and the separation of civil and criminal pleas and the fact that England had a very bureaucratic system with a king and an administration well able to enforce

---

66. For just a few examples of naval warfare during the Danish conquest of the Slavs in the late 12th century, see E. Christiansen (ed.), *Saxo Grammaticus, Danorum Regum Heroumque Historia. Books X-XVI: the Text of the First Edition with Translation and Commentary*, 3 vols. (Oxford: 1980-1981), ii, 616-21.
67. For one example, see J. Benham, 'Wounding in the High Middle Ages: Law and Practice', in C. Warr & A. Kirkham (ed.), *Wounds in the Middle Ages* (Farnham: 2014), 241.
68. Vogt makes the point that even across the Scandinavian laws, the heinous crimes are often different. Vogt, *The Function of Kinship*, 129-130.

the laws are significant differences. Thus comparing the two kingdoms is never going to be a comparison of like for like. However, this does not for that reason render the whole exercise useless. Indeed, one would face a similar array of obstacles if comparing English law and legal practice to that of any of the other medieval kingdoms of this period.

How Nordic were the Nordic medieval laws? In attempting to answer this overarching question, it is perhaps not possible to provide a wholly satisfactory answer. Judging by the approach taken in this paper, one could conclude that the Danish laws, at least, may well have been Nordic but had significant commonalities with the English laws of the same period. However, the comparative basis provided here is on a very small aspect of the law codes, namely crime, and it is not one that is commonly studied by scholars, who are mostly interested in property and inheritance. Despite this, a thorough investigation of the laws of England and Denmark in the 12th and 13th centuries could yield some interesting results and provide us with some further pointers for future research. In particular, the language of the laws contains peculiar similarities, for instance in the alliterations about living within or without law and peace, and undoubtedly a wider investigation could provide others. It is hence fortunate that on both sides of the North Sea there are ongoing projects to edit, translate and comment, upon both the Nordic medieval laws and the early English laws, providing scholars and students alike with the tools to make further comparative studies.[69]

---

69. For instance, the recent work by Alice Taylor on Scotland shows that there are some interesting comparisons to be drawn on law and crime with this kingdom too. See A. Taylor, 'Crime without Punishment: Medieval Scottish Law in Comparative Perspective', *Anglo-Norman Studies* 35 (2013).

INDIGENOUS OR UNIVERSAL? A COMPARATIVE PERSPECTIVE ON MEDIEVAL (FRISIAN) COMPENSATION LAW

Han Nijdam

1. Introduction

The pursuit of reconstructing a common Proto-Germanic law system (as part of a wider 'Proto-Germanic culture') was very popular during the 19th century and the first half of the 20th century. After World War II it was frowned upon by scholars for a long time – and for good reason. During the last decade or so, however, the topic has cautiously and in various guises re-emerged on the agendas of medieval and legal historians. This did not happen, however, before the influences of Roman and canon law upon the various medieval European law systems had been laid bare.

In this chapter, I will first present my own research into medieval Frisian compensation (damages). In order to explain how and why compensation worked I took refuge to cognitive sciences and the study of human universals. This proved to be very rewarding. The theories and methods developed in these fields can, I believe, help scholars to compare cultural traits – in this case aspects of medieval law systems – and to distinguish indigenous, imported or universal aspects. Second, I hope to show that by means of these theories and methods, it will be easier to reinvestigate certain aspects of what was once called 'Germanic culture'.

2. Medieval Frisian law

Throughout its history, medieval Frisia has been a region of contact and exchange. It consisted of the coastal zone of what are now the Netherlands and Germany, roughly situated between the Belgian and Danish borders. Not all these regions were called Frisian all the time or even at the same time. Being coastal dwellers, the Frisians have always been seafarers and traders. For this reason, the North Sea was called *Mare Frisicum* ('Frisian sea') during the early Middle Ages.

Although Roman historians and annalists, such as Tacitus, already mention the Frisians as a tribe living along the borders of the North Sea, the Frisians from the Roman period were not the same people that inhabited the region a few centuries later. During the age of the Great Migration (3rd and 4th centuries), most of the original – assumedly Celtic – Frisians left. From the 5th century onwards new people colonised the Frisian coastal area. This happened during the same migration waves that brought Jutes, Angles and Saxons to England. Archaeologists have now convincingly shown that some of those same people settled in Frisia.[1] For some reason they were called Frisians, after the original inhabitants.[2]

Archaeological evidence and written sources both point to an especially strong link between Kent and Frisia during the early Middle Ages.[3] Unfortunately, the Frisian archaeological record is far less well preserved than the English, since a large amount of the artificial mounds the Frisians lived upon to keep their feet dry from the sea was dug up for its fertile soil and sold commercially in the 19th and early 20th centuries. Although effort

---

1. J. Nicolay, 'Een politiek machtscentrum in noordelijk Westergo', in E. Kramer, I. Stoumann & A. Greg (ed.), *Koningen van de Noordzee, 250–850* (Leeuwarden: 2003), 55-74; J. Nicolay, 'Nieuwe bewoners van het terpengebied en hun rol bij de opkomst van het Friese koningsschap. De betekenis van gouden bracteaten en bracteaatachtige hangers uit Friesland (vijfde-zevende eeuw na Chr.)', *De Vrije Fries* 85 (2005), 37-103; J. Nicolay, 'Een koninklijk machtscentrum in vroegmiddeleeuws Friesland? De interpretatie van goudvondsten uit de late zesde en vroege zevende eeuw na Chr.', *De Vrije Fries* 86 (2006), 33-94.
2. J.G.A. Bazelmans, 'The early-medieval use of ethnic names from classical antiquity. The case of the Frisians', in T. Derks & N. Roymans (ed.), *Ethnic Constructs in Antiquity. The Role of Power and Tradition* (Amsterdam: 2009), 321-37.
3. For connections between Kentish and Old Frisian law, see H.H. Munske, *Der germanische Rechtswortschatz im Bereich der Missetaten. Philologische und sprachgeografische Untersuchungen. I. Die Terminologie der älteren westgermanischen Rechtsquellen* (Berlin & New York: 1973).

was undertaken to rescue finds that were unearthed during these commercial enterprises, these objects lacked all archaeological context.[4]

A few Frisian kings are mentioned in the written sources of the 7th and 8th centuries. The most famous of them is called Radbod / Redbad. These Frisian kings were in conflict with the Merovingian and Carolingian kings, due to the northward expansion of the Franks. Eventually, Charles Martel was successful in conquering the Frisians halfway the 8th century. Because the Frisians had become part of the Carolingian empire and because Charlemagne wanted to have the law of each *gens* within his realm on paper, Frisian law was written down for the first time at the end of the 8th century. This is fortunate for modern scholars, since the *Lex Frisionum* ('Law of the Frisians') yields extensive information on early medieval Frisian law.[5]

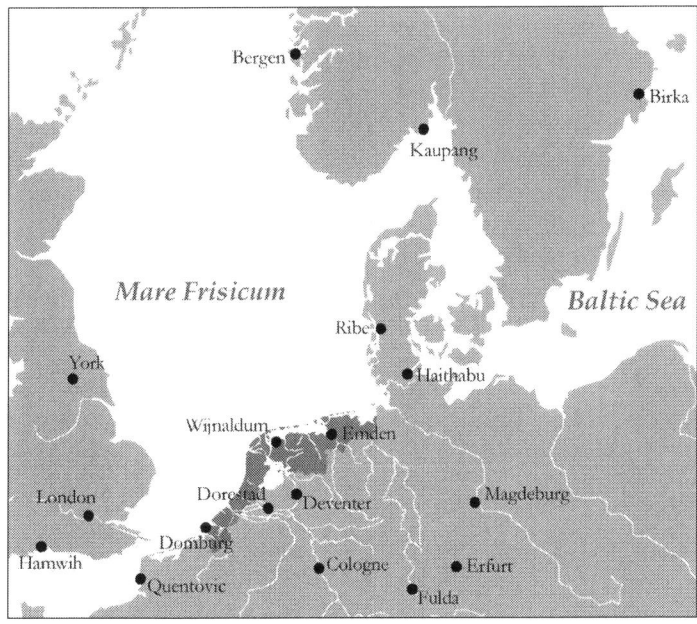

Early medieval Frisia within the larger North Sea area (map created by Arjen Versloot)

4. L. Verhart, 'Terug naar het land van herkomst. Over archeologen, terpen, ruzies en lege handen (1)', *De Vrije Fries* 92 (2012), 9-36; L. Verhart, 'Terug naar het land van herkomst. Over archeologen, terpen, ruzies en lege handen (2)', *De Vrije Fries* 93 (2013), 27-52.
5. H. Siems, *Studien zur Lex Frisionum* (Ebelsbach: 1980).

The *Lex Frisionum* divides the Frisian region into three parts: a central part between the rivers Vlie and Lauwers (the present-day province of Friesland in the Netherlands), a western part between the rivers Zwin and Vlie (thus comprising of the provinces South and North Holland in the Netherlands), and an eastern part between the rivers Lauwers and Weser (i.e. Groningen in the Netherlands and Ostfriesland in Germany). The law varied somewhat in these three regions. The fact that the river Lauwers constitutes a very old dialect border yields further evidence that the three regions, which the *Lex Frisionum* distinguishes between, were indeed different cultural zones.

During the 9th century, Danes again entered the Frisian scene. As Vikings, they periodically plundered the Frisian coastal area. Later, during the reigns of Louis the Pious (778-840) and Lothar (795-855), Danish warlords were bestowed with certain parts of Frisia. They received these lands in fief and thus entered into a feudal relation with the Frankish kings. In return they were expected to defend the Frisian coasts against other Vikings.

All this time, the Frisians continued to trade around the North Sea. This meant the Vikings not only looted the Frisians, but also traded with them and probably even went on Viking expeditions with them.[6] Evidence for all these forms of exchange and contact can be found. A few rune stones in Sigtuna raised by members of the 'Guild of the Frisians' testify of extensive trade contacts. Influence of Frisian traders has further been attested archeologically in Ribe and Kaupang.

Furthermore, an 11th century silver arm ring, found on the Norwegian island of Senja, contains a runic inscription which reads: furu* trikia frislats a uit auk uiks fotum uir skiftum.[7] A transcription to Old Norse (Old Icelandic) yields: *Fórum drengja Fríslands á vit, ok vígs fötum vér skiptum*. Two interpretations have been given. The traditional translation 'We paid a visit to the lads of Frisia, and we it was who split the spoils of battle' interprets the event referred to in the inscription as one where Vikings raided Frisians. More recently, however, new interpretations have been offered. Judith Jesch underscored the trading relations between Vikings and Frisians by translating the sentence to: 'We visited our trading-partners in Frisia and bought / sold / exchanged war-gear'. Kees Samplonius interpreted the inscription as evidence of mutual raiding activity by Vikings and Frisians, and opted for this translation: 'We visited the lads/warriors of Frisia and together we split the war-booty'.[8]

---

6. N.L. IJssennagger, 'Between Frankish and Viking: Frisia and Frisians in the Viking Age', *Viking and Medieval Scandinavia* 9 (2013), 69-98.
7. For an overview of the discussions of this arm ring and the interpretation of its runic inscription, see IJssennagger, 'Between Frankish and Viking'.
8. K. Samplonius, 'Friesland en de Vikingtijd: de ring van Senja en de Vierentwintig Landrechten', *It Beaken* 60 (1998), 89-101.

Indigenous or Universal?

Interestingly, the younger Frisian vernacular law texts (on which more below) also contain a few stipulations which refer to Viking contact. One says that if a Frisian is captured by Vikings, taken off with them and forced to fight and plunder in his hometown, he cannot be persecuted for these offences after his release and return. This text thus indirectly corroborates Samplonius' interpretation of the runic inscription on the Senja arm ring.

After the Vikings stopped their raiding activities in the North Sea region, in the 11th and 12th centuries, the Saxon counts of the house of Brunswick had a claim to Frisia east of the river Lauwers, while the counts of Holland and the bishops of Utrecht simultaneously claimed the western and central regions.[9]

From the 12th century onward, Frisia between Vlie and Weser (i.e. the old central and eastern regions in the *Lex Frisionum*) began to deviate from its neighbouring regions. The various counts who had a claim to Frisia did not succeed in establishing a suzerainty (German *Landesherrschaft*).[10] Instead, the various autonomous Frisian communities ruled themselves, only paying relatively small tithes and taxes to church and worldly lord, but keeping direct control at bay. These autonomous lands or *terrae* had their own laws and seals. The Frisian elite, calling themselves 'Free Frisians' (OFris. *fria Fresa*), chose judges-administrators from amongst their midst. This office circulated on a yearly basis.

In order to explain their extraordinary political situation the Frisians developed a few mythic narratives, which can be found in the Frisian law manuscripts from the 13th to 15th centuries. The most important of these roughly went thus:

> One day the inhabitants of Rome capture Pope Leo, said to be the brother of Charlemagne, and poke out his eyes. Upon this Charlemagne edicts a call to arms. Knightly armies from various countries travel to Rome to assist him. The Frisians also answer Charlemagne's call. Until that time, they have been under the rule of the Viking Danes. As a token of their serfdom, they wear a wooden neck band. In this state they arrive at the battle scene, before the city of Rome: as naked slaves.
>
> As the battle begins, they are placed as cannon fodder in the front lines. Contrary to everyone's expectations, however, they fight very bravely and actually succeed in conquering Rome for Charlemagne. The Frisian hero Magnus plants the Frisian banner on the highest tower in the city. At this point

---

9. D.J. Henstra, *Friese graafschappen tussen Zwin en Wezer. Een overzicht van de grafelijkheid in middeleeuws Frisia* (ca. 700-1200) (Assen: 2012).
10. H. Nijdam, *Lichaam, eer en recht in middeleeuws Friesland. Een studie naar de Oudfriese boeteregisters* (Hilversum: 2008), 107-19; O. Vries, 'Geschichte der Friesen im Mittelalter: West- und Ostfriesland', in H.H. Munske et al. (ed.), *Handbuch des Friesischen. Handbook of Frisian Studies* (Tübingen: 2001), 538-50.

Charlemagne realizes he will have to bargain with the Frisians to be given entry to Rome. He offers them gold and beautiful textiles, but to no avail. The Frisians want privileges and freedom from their serfdom. Charles reluctantly gives in. Henceforth they are free and equal to Charles' highest vassals and knights. As a token of this, the wooden band is removed from their necks and replaced by a golden necklace. As a further token of their newly acquired status, their hair is shaven around their ears, leaving hair only on the tops of their heads.

The most important of the other privileges the Frisians ask for themselves are a high degree of tax exemption, an exemption from military expeditions, and the right to choose and uphold their own system of law. All these privileges are put to writing and the seals of both pope and emperor are attached at the bottom of the charter which is drawn up for this purpose. With this precious freedom charter the Frisians return to their home country.

From this story, a socio-political model consisting of a set of dichotomies can be distilled. In this model, the left column represents the negative elements, which pertained to the Frisians before they became free. The right column consists of positive elements applicable to the Free Frisians. The last two terms are the two types of tax the Frisians had to pay: *klipskelde* to the Vikings before they became free and *huslotha* to the Carolingians after their liberation.[11]

SOCIAL

enslavement	freedom
wooden neck band	golden necklace
hairdo unspecified	hair shaven
naked	dressed
low	high
lawless	having law
without honour	having honour

POLITICAL

North	South
Redbad	Charlemagne
Vikings, Danes	Frisians
pagans	Christians
klipskelde	*huslotha*

---

11. H. Nijdam, 'Klinkende munten en klinkende botsplinters in de Oudfriese rechtsteksten: continuïteit, discontinuïteit, intertekstualiteit', *De Vrije Fries* 89 (2009), 45-66.

The 'Free Frisians' and their 'Frisian Freedom' most likely formed the incentive to start writing down the Frisian customary laws. The earliest surviving Old Frisian law manuscripts date from the end of the 13th century, but it is clear that earlier versions existed. The youngest manuscripts date from around 1500.

Exactly when the Frisian law manuscript tradition started is a matter of some debate: some scholars believe that this already happened in the 12th century, according to others not before 1200.[12] The oldest texts may have originated as early as the 11th century. Some very old features, such as the stipulation on a Frisian being captured by Vikings mentioned above, point to this. In which form – orally or written – these texts might have circulated during that period is again a matter of debate.

The Old Frisian law texts have never been properly counted. Their total number runs in the 300s. This includes both small and extensive texts. Sometimes smaller clusters of stipulations later organically cluttered into larger texts. The whole gives the impression of a dynamic law system that was constantly reworked. Also, as mentioned above, not all Frisian law texts have been handed down in the Old Frisian language. In total, there are ca. 150 texts which were written in Old Frisian. They can be found in ca. 20 manuscripts containing various texts each.

Starting around 1400, the region which is now the province of Groningen in the Netherlands saw a language shift from Frisian to Low German under the influence of its capital, also called Groningen, which came to dominate the region during that period. This resulted in a large corpus of ca. 150 manuscripts with Low German translations of Frisian law texts. This language shift also took place in what is now Ostfriesland in Germany. From this region, only a handful of manuscripts with Frisian law in Low German translation have been handed down.[13] Due to the loss of countless original Old Frisian law manuscripts, the Low German translations in many cases are the only version available to modern scholars.

Within this corpus, the two pan-Frisian law texts known as the *Seventeen Statutes* and the *Twenty-four Land Laws* are the oldest. These are the ones which contain references to the Vikings, which means they may date back to the 11th or early 12th century. They can be found in manuscripts from all Frisian regions. Next, there are the compensation tariffs, on which more below. These can also be found in all Frisian manuscripts but there is no pan-Frisian tariff. The so-called *General Compensation Tariff*, however, is a

12. R.H. Bremmer, *Hir is eskriven. Lezen en schrijven in de Friese landen rond 1300* (Hilversum: 2004) ('not before 1200'); D.J. Henstra, 'De eerste optekening van de algemeen-Friese keuren', *It Beaken* 64 (2002), 99-128 ('possibly in the 11th century').
13. C. Borchling, *Die niederdeutschen Rechtsquellen Ostfrieslands. I. Die Rechte der Einzellandschaften* (Aurich: 1908).

text which pertained to the large area between the rivers Lauwers and Weser. For the area west of the Lauwers no single compensation tariff exists, only smaller regional text traditions.

All other Frisian law texts were in use in one or several of the Frisian autonomous *terrae*. The oldest of these with a secure date attached to them stem from the second half of the 13th century. These are the *Langewold Statutes of 1250* and the *Hunsingo Statutes of 1252*.[14]

3. Frisian compensation tariffs

Within the corpus of Old Frisian law the genre known as injury tariffs or compensation tariffs is widely attested. All Old Frisian law manuscripts contain at least one. In one case 25 per cent of the entire manuscript consists of these tariffs.

A short philological overview of the various traditions shows that between the rivers Lauwers and Weser, one text tradition, the *General Compensation Tariff* mentioned above, was valid until the end of the 13th century. The birth of the various independent countries or *terrae* in the 12th and 13th centuries led to regional courts of law and regional law texts. This development is thus reflected both in the oldest dated regional law texts such as the earlier mentioned *Langewold Statutes of 1250* and the *Hunsingo Statutes of 1252* and in the conception of regional compensation tariffs.

These regional tariffs are relatively small and badly structured in the oldest manuscripts, but are fully grown and matured in the youngest Old East Frisian manuscripts, dating from 1400-1450. Some figures: the *General Compensation Tariff* had an average of ca. 130 stipulations. The oldest versions of the regional tariffs contained ca. 70 stipulations, which is less than the two complete tariffs that can be found in the *Lex Frisionum*. These had almost 90 stipulations each. The youngest Old East Frisian tariffs easily make up for this: the first contains ca. 200 paragraphs, the second slightly more than 400, making it the largest Old Frisian tariff.

From the region west of the river Lauwers (the present day province of Friesland in the Netherlands), a slightly different picture emerges. Here all surviving manuscripts stem from the 15th century. They all contain a large number of regional compensation tariffs. Most are rather small: ca. 130 stipulations on average. One tradition – the *Bireknade Bota* 'Calculated Compensations', a quotation from which is given below – probably

---

14. T.S.B. Johnston, *Codex Hummercensis (Groningen, UB, PEIP 12). An Old Frisian Legal Manuscript in Low Saxon Guise* (Leeuwarden: 1998), 215-25 (*Langewold Statutes*); 179-85 (*Hunsingo Statutes*). The *Langewold Statutes* have not been handed down in the Frisian vernacular, but only in a Low German translation.

developed into a general West Frisian tariff in the course of the 15th century and reached a size of ca. 300 paragraphs.

Although these tariffs are so prominent within the Old Frisian text corpus, they were very understudied when I began my research. From a certain perspective this can be understood: one has to see the value in long lists of injuries to the human body and the compensations they required. A small sample is given here in translation:

> Concerning the eyes.
> 58. The loss of the right eye is to be compensated with 14 pounds.
> 59. The loss of the left eye is to be compensated with 13 pounds, and according to the custom 5 marks, not counting the compensation for the violent deed which caused it.
> 60. Damage to the corner of the eye: 6 groats.
> 61. If the eye is partly blinded, the compensation is 1 mark.
> 62. If the eye-ball has come out of the head, then the compensation is 10 pounds. Some composition tariffs have 20 pounds, and it is 32 pounds according to the custom.
> 63. If the eye is entirely motionless in the head, and it is not moist, the plaintiff must claim by oath a measurable wound. He can then claim the same (compensations for) side-effects for his sight as is the case with hearing. Thus the compensation for (the loss of) the three quarter parts of the sight is 2½ pounds each, provided that, as with hearing, a measurable wound has been claimed.[15]

If, however, one realises that this genre is the only one that can both already be found in the *Lex Frisionum* and as abundantly there as in the later Old Frisian law texts, the maths are not that hard to do: these texts must have been very important to the Frisians for a very long period.

4. Why compensation tariffs were so important: human universals and cognitive sciences

How can the continuity of the compensation tariffs in medieval Frisia be explained? Not only do they appear in the *Lex Frisionum* dating from the end of the 8th century, reappear in the Old Frisian vernacular law texts some 500 years later and continue to thrive until the end of the Middle Ages, but the tariffs in the *Lex Frisionum* are also clearly expressions of the same legal tradition as the Old Frisian texts. Since the *Lex Frisionum* was almost

---

15. *Bireknade Bota*, §§ 58-63, ed. and transl. by H. Nijdam in H. Nijdam, 'The Old West Frisian Composition Tariff *Bireknade Bota* (Part 2)', *Us Wurk* 50 (2001), 27-64, at 35-37.

certainly not known to later medieval Frisians, these two independent sources cannot be anything else but the testimonies of a tradition that was passed down orally for centuries.

A continuity like this usually makes historians trained in the second half of the 20th century uncomfortable. During that period in modern history, much energy was put into deconstructing myths, researching invented traditions, and such. Poststructuralism and Postmodernism were reigning.[16] The core of these paradigms is that human minds were viewed as 'blank slates' or lumps of silly putty, totally malleable by the culture the humans carrying these minds were born into. More on this below.

These paradigms were, for a large part, reactions to the Romanticism of the 19th century and the catastrophic way in which this paradigm was abused by the ideologists of Nazi-Germany.[17] Because of these historical events, a number of topics became taboo in academia after 1945. Continuity also falls into this category, because this could mean a continuity of cultural phenomena which reached back into a Germanic past.

Explaining the Old Frisian compensation tariffs – their existence, purpose and continuity – demands a different perspective on the topic, one in which a 'Germanic' continuity is no longer the primary focus. One has to take a step back a few paces, so to say, from the pure textuality and philological approach to these written sources and instead look at what the compensation tariffs were aiming to accomplish within the society that used them. This opens a line of research that leads to more universal themes of violence, revenge, feud and honour.

We will start with revenge. It is one of the two sides of the coin called reciprocity. Humans (as well as numerous other species, among which our primate 'cousins') have a tendency to pay back in kind both violence and sociable deeds.[18] At first glance, taking revenge seems counterproductive. It does indeed have a number of negative effects on a person: it can consume one for years on end, some people sacrifice their very lives in order to take revenge, and revenge very often leads to a level of violence which surpasses the original act by far. Psychologist Nico Frijda, however, also sees profits

---

16. E.G. Slingerland, *What Science Offers the Humanities. Integrating Body and Culture* (Cambridge: 2008).
17. There is much literature on this topic. See for instance: M.H. Kater, *Das "Ahnenerbe" der SS 1935–1945. Ein Beitrag zur Kulturpolitik des Dritten Reiches* (München: 1997).
18. C. Boehm, 'The Natural History of Blood Revenge', in J. Büchert Netterström & B. Poulsen (ed.), *Feud in Medieval and Early Modern Europe* (Aarhus: 2007), 189-203; S. Pinker, *The Better Angels of our Nature. Why Violence Has Declined* (New York: 2011); F. de Waal, *Our Inner Ape. A Leading Primatologist Explains Why We Are Who We Are* (New York: 2005).

in taking revenge. If people have been seriously wronged or injured, they have been brought in a state of feeling powerless, ashamed and hurt. Taking revenge firstly frightens one's wrongdoer off, preventing them from ever attacking again and secondly makes the victim powerful again: they have won back the upper hand. It furthermore restores the victim's pride and takes away their feeling of being ashamed because of having been defeated. It also eases the emotional pain. Lastly, it makes the scores between the two parties even again.[19]

If these principles are transferred to a human kin group, it becomes apparent how taking revenge as a group yields profits from an evolutionary-biological point of view. Furthermore, one of the rules or 'distinctive features' of feuding is that when retaliation is required for a killing between kin groups, another member than the original killer can be targeted.[20] In this way, the kin group turns into a kind of super-individual, constructed by all its members. This phenomenon is called 'social substitutability'.[21] Add to this recipe the concept of honour (and its flip side shame) and the result is a combustible mixture that can cause conflict to flare up for years on end in any pre-modern society. Such conflicts have a destabilising effect on said societies.

Blood money or wergeld has been a brilliant invention to stop endless feuding and retaliation. The essence of compensating a killing or an injury by paying money or other valuables is that it buys off revenge. Its oldest attestation is to be encountered in the laws of the Mesopotamian king Hammurabi, ca. 1750 BC. Anthropologist Christopher Boehm describes it as 'a very prominent peace-making mechanism that has been invented over and over again, all over the world'.[22]

Boehm also states that

> for historians, ethno-historians, and students of the epic, the payment of blood money becomes diagnostic of a type of egalitarian political society that rather strictly limits centralised authority, and in which honour is of high importance culturally.[23]

---

19. N.H. Frijda, *De wetten der emoties* (Amsterdam: 2008).
20. See for these 'rules' or 'distinctive features' of feuding: H. Þorláksson, 'Feud and Feuding in the Early and High Middle Ages', in Büchert Netterström & Poulsen (ed.), *Feud in Medieval and Early Modern Europe*, 69-94; J.L. Byock,'Defining Feud: Talking Points and Iceland's Saga Women', in Büchert Netterström & Poulsen (ed.), *Feud in Medieval and Early Modern Europe*, 95-111.
21. Boehm, 'The Natural History of Blood Revenge', 199.
22. Boehm, 'The Natural History of Blood Revenge', 201.
23. Boehm, 'The Natural History of Blood Revenge', 203.

This description fits medieval Frisia like a glove. After having put the Old Frisian compensation tariffs in a wider comparative setting, it now becomes perfectly clear why they are so prominent within the medieval Frisian corpus of law texts. They were used to prevent or end blood feuds. Medieval Frisia was indeed an example of what William Miller, talking about medieval Iceland, has called an 'economy of honour'.[24] It is, I think, no coincidence that within the myths of the Frisian Freedom, the winning of honour as one of the outcomes of their battle in Rome is so explicitly mentioned.

In short, the compensation tariffs as an expression of a flourishing legal system of blood money and compensating for injuries perfectly fits the type of society medieval Frisia was. The absence of a central government (i.e. the Frisian Freedom, very much comparable to the Icelandic Freestate in which the Icelandic sagas were set) explains both how the text genre flourished in medieval Frisia and its long continuity. The tariffs and the system of compensation remained intact in Frisia for such a long time because Frisia retained its economy of honour throughout the Middle Ages.

Before bringing the insights gained here into the debate on 'Proto-Germanic' law, a few words on paradigms and paradigm shifts. In many disciplines within the humanities, the second half of the 20th century has been dominated by some adaptation of the postmodern paradigm. The following definition by Edward Slingerland is illuminating:

> The core feature of 'postmodernism', in my mind, is a model of humans as fundamentally linguistic-cultural beings, combined with the belief that our experience of the world is therefore mediated by language or culture *all the way down*. On this model, we have no direct cognitive access to reality, and things in the world are meaningful to us only through the filter of linguistically or visually mediated cultural preconceptions. Common corollaries of this stance are strong linguistic-cultural relativism, a suspicion of any sort of universalist truth-claims, and a 'blank slate' view of human nature: we are nothing until inscribed by the discourse into which we are socialized, and therefore nothing significant about the way we think or act is a direct result of our biological endowment.[25]

This article is not the place to discuss science history in-depth. The point here is that 'overphilologising' medieval texts – in this case medieval law texts – only brings researchers that far. Especially when we are dealing with themes such as the ones addressed in this article – violence, the human body, revenge, honour – we have to be aware of the fact that first, we are dealing with phenomena that can be found in human cultures all over the

---

24. W.I. Miller, *Bloodtaking and Peacemaking. Feud, Law, and Society in Saga Iceland* (Chicago & London: 1990).
25. Slingerland, *What science offers the humanities*, 78.

world and second, that all humans share a cognitive hardware, in which much pre-wiring has already taken place at the moment we are born.

The topic of human universals reappeared on the anthropological agenda in 1991, when Donald E. Brown published *Human Universals*, in which he made a convincing case for a reappraisal of the study of universals in human culture. Anthropologists had steered away from this topic for decades, but research into various neighbouring fields, which together can be labelled cognitive or behavioural sciences, had shown that some phenomena can be found among all human cultures. In many cases this was due to the hardware of human cognition. After *Human Universals*, psychologist Steven Pinker wrote *The Blank Slate* (2002), with specific reference to Donald Brown's work. He tackles the topic from a cognitive point of view, with a keen eye for the social and political aspects of embracing the concept of human universals. The latest large monograph on human universals is by the German anthropologist Christoph Antweiler and dates from 2007.[26]

Pinker digested Brown's book into a list of Human Universals, and attached it as an appendix to his book. The following items on that list all are connected to the topic of compensation and law:

- conflict
- conflict, consultation to deal with
- conflict, means of dealing with
- conflict, mediation of
- fairness (equity), concept of
- law (rights and obligations)
- law (rules of membership)
- reciprocity, negative
- reciprocity, positive
- redress of wrongs
- violence, some forms of proscribed[27]

Some of these universals go back so far that humans share them with primates. Frans de Waal, an ethnologist who has written several works on behavioural similarities between primates and humans, describes an illuminating experiment with Capuchin monkeys. Two of these monkeys were placed in adjacent cages so that they had a clear view of each other. First, they had to give back a pebble to the experimenter, in return for which they both received a piece of cucumber. Then, however, one of the monkeys was given a grape in return for the pebble. Since grapes are valued more highly,

---

26. C. Antweiler, *Was ist den Menschen gemeinsam? Über Kultur und Kulturen* (Darmstadt: 2007).
27. Pinker, *The Blank Slate*, 435-39.

the Capuchin who still received cucumber for the same task the other one was now getting grapes for got mad. He furiously threw away several pieces of cucumber in a row and started getting really upset. This was unfair![28]

In recent years, these insights have finally begun to seep through in all parts of the humanities. Even, I dare say, in history, as becomes apparent from a recent review article by Gregory Hanlon on 'The Decline of Violence in the West'.[29] The article starts with summing up what has been going on outside the discipline of history in the last decades and how this affects what historians do:

> Pinker's work [referring a.o. to *The Blank Slate*, HN] employs the findings of two generations of neurologists, animal and human ethnologists and anthropologists who have rediscovered Human Nature. This is a development with huge implications for historians, for it overturns the anti-scientific pretentions of humanists who claim that culture is everywhere unstable, constantly subject to change and transformation.[30]

These words nicely echo the way Slingerland describes the cultural relativity / postmodern stance. Hanlon also takes a step further and coins a term for this new approach:

> The problem here is that we lack, as yet, a convenient label for studying historical behaviour in the light of the behavioural sciences. Calling this approach 'post-cultural' is not to deny that humans transmit their knowledge through education and imitation from one generation to the next, nor does it preclude the idea that the repertoire of knowledge might increase or decrease from one period or context to another. But the difficulty with a culturally-based approach is that it ignores the fact that it really is easier for humans to learn some behaviour rather than others. We may easily imagine a society without social inequality, without bias towards kin or friends, or without social differentiation between the sexes. But, given the reproductive interests of real-life individuals, such societies are, properly speaking, impossible to realise; by

---

28. De Waal, *Our Inner Ape*, 201-03. This experiment can also be viewed on Youtube: http://www.youtube.com/watch?v=gOtlN4pNArk (Accessed 21.12.2013).
29. G. Hanlon, 'The Decline of Violence in the West: From Cultural to Post-Cultural History', *English Historical Review* CXXVIII 531 (2013), 367-400. On historians' backwardness when it comes to picking up new theories, see H. Nijdam, 'Belichaamde eer, wraak en vete. Een historisch- en cognitief-antropologische benadering', *Tijdschrift voor Geschiedenis* 123 (2010), 192-207, especially my comments there (p. 206) on a rather tepid review of Slingerland, *What Science Offers the Humanities*, in that same journal (*Tijdschrift voor Geschiedenis* 122 (2009), 397-98). The gist of this review was that the reviewer could not see how Slingerland's insights might be applied in historians' day-to-day research.
30. Hanlon, 'The Decline of Violence in the West', 368.

Indigenous or Universal?

> dint of repression they might be nudged in that direction for a time, only to spring back to the previous state as soon as the pressure is eased. History is rich in failed social experiments. Anthropology teaches us that the variety of human societies and customs is far from infinite, and that social values are not arbitrary.[31]

To sum up, we are, I think, on the brink of leaving the postmodern paradigm and entering the post-cultural paradigm. This means parting with a paradigm that was like a swamp, i.e. lacking any solid ground, a paradigm in which everything could mean everything and humans and their culture were seen as infinitely malleable. It now has become apparent that this is not the case but instead that when analysing cultural phenomena, there are certain default settings within Human Nature that have to be taken into account. To quote Hanlon one last time:

> Recourse to the wide panoply of behavioural sciences constitutes the most important advance in the discipline of history since its first contact with demography and anthropology in the 1950s and 1960s. Murder and moralistic violence is just one type of behaviour that it can help explain. There are increasingly convincing explanations governing behaviour around display, aesthetic values, hierarchy and governance, economic co-operation and rivalry and environmental management. Someone, soon, should take an inventory of those fields of human behaviour where anthropology, sociology, psychology, human ethology and history converge.[32]

With these insights in mind it might be fruitful to take another look at how successful scholars have been over the centuries in reconstructing Proto-Germanic law, especially in the sphere of compensation. What has been achieved and how should the results be valued, especially in the light of the new post-cultural approach propagated here?

5. Trying and failing to reconstruct Proto-Germanic law

A proper scholarly concept of Proto-Germanic language and culture only started to be outlined after the discovery of the Indo-European language family, at the end of the 18th century.[33] Before that humanist scholars in the

---

31. Hanlon, 'The Decline of Violence in the West', 380.
32. Hanlon, 'The Decline of Violence in the West', 400.
33. D.W. Anthony, *The Horse, the Wheel and Language. How Bronze-Age Riders from the Eurasian Steppes Shaped the Modern World* (Princeton: 2007); R.S.P. Beekes & M.A.C de Vaan, *Comparative Indo-European Linguistics. An Introduction* (Amsterdam & Philadelphia: 2011).

17th and 18th centuries tried but largely failed to make sense of the interrelationships between the Germanic languages.[34]

The whole of the 19th century and the first decades of the 20th can be seen as the heydays of the scholarly search for a Proto-Germanic language and culture. It comprised the combined efforts of a whole range of scholars: historical linguists, historians, archaeologists, legal historians, folklorists. This was the time when the great Jacob Grimm set the standards by writing works such as *Deutsche Grammatik* (1819-1837), *Deutsche Mythologie* (1835), and *Deutsche Rechtsaltertümer* (1828). It is a well-known fact, of course, that the scholars from this age tended to idolize Germanic culture and that this blurred their vision.[35]

In 1970, looking back at what had been achieved during that period, Indo-Europeanist Stephen Schwartz assessed the efforts of legal historians such as Grimm and Wilda in trying to reconstruct Proto-Germanic law.[36] His final judgment was that scholars of this era had not produced a consistent overview of Proto-Germanic legislation. Not down to the knots and bolts of it, that is. He furthermore stated that legal historians had not modernized their methods in the way historical linguists had. His criticism was harsh:

> The study of Germanic legal antiquities was not the only field of scholarship in Europe that received its impetus in the first few decades of the nineteenth century, nor the only field that grew and flourished under the banner of Romanticism. Yet it is probably the only one that still, in large measure, operates according to preconceived and foreordained ideas that shape both a scholarly *modus operandi* and the conclusions that must inevitably be drawn therefrom.[37]

At the end of the article, Schwartz suggested setting up a thorough comparison of all data on Germanic law and a reconstruction of a proto-law on the basis of that information, in a manner parallel to the methods of historical linguistics:

---

34. The Humanist scholar Franciscus Junius (1591-1677) makes a nice example. He studied Gothic, English, Dutch and Frisian. See: R.H. Bremmer (ed.), *Franciscus Junius F. F. and his circle* (Amsterdam: 1998).
35. There is a massive amount of literature on this topic. See for instance: C.B. Krebs, *A Most Dangerous Book. Tacitus's Germania From The Roman Empire to the Third Reich* (New York & London: 2011).
36. S.P. Schwartz, 'Comparative Legal Reconstruction in Germanic', in J. Puhvel (ed.), *Myth and Law among the Indo-Europeans. Studies in Indo-European Comparative Mythology* (Berkeley: 1970), 39-53.
37. Schwartz, 'Comparative Legal Reconstruction in Germanic', 41.

> Up to this point I have stated in what ways I feel that studies of Germanic law have been based upon erroneous premises and have proceeded intuitively rather than systematically, and above all have treated fragments of the legal past, rather than the whole. I recommend abandoning such an approach in favour of using the methodology of comparative and historical linguistics (the 'genetic' approach) to reconstruct a proto-law in the same manner (but obviously with the same limitations and difficulties) that a protolanguage is reconstructed. [...] What we are after is not a miscellaneous grab bag of proto-words, nor the *Geist*, but a series of statements about belief, prohibitions, and social behaviour, to mention but a few. The only way to see if reconstruction of a proto-law will work is to begin to set it up.[38]

In spite of all possible objections to this hortation, Schwartz had a point. A large collection of data and consecutive comparative analysis had not been made at the time the article was written.

In the course of my own research into the Old Frisian compensation tariffs, I encountered the same lacuna Schwartz pointed out. No comparative study had been made in order to say something more on the relative age of the various kinds of stipulations found in the tariffs I was studying. What came closest were studies of the individual legal terms (*Rechtswörter*) in the Germanic languages and their respective age.[39] This can partly be explained by the shift in focus since the end of World War II, which meant turning away from the search for a 'Proto-Germanic' culture (including its law), and opening up to the influences of Roman and Christian culture on European culture. In the field of legal history, this led to the discovery of the influences of Roman law even as early as the *Leges Barbarorum*:

> Anknüpfend an die Entdeckung eines spätantiken 'Vulgarrechts' neben und unter der Hochform des römischen Juristenrechts [...] wurde in der Erforschung der Rechtsquellen des Frühmittelalters einschließlich der 'germanischen' Leges den Spuren und Einflüssen des römischen Rechts erhöhte Aufmerksamkeit gewidmet. Das ging bis zur Infragestellung, ob die germanischen Völkerschaften überhaupt eigene Rechtstraditionen eingebracht, sich nicht vielmehr einer stark vereinfachten provinzialrömischen Rechtstradition bedient hätten.[40]

38. Schwartz, 'Comparative Legal Reconstruction in Germanic', 57.
39. Again, there is a massive literature here. See for instance for Old Frisian / West Germanic: Munske, *Der germanische Rechtswortschatz im Bereich der Missetaten*. For Scandinavian: K. von See, *Altnordische Rechtswörter* (Tübingen: 1964). For the continent especially see the various publications by R. Schmidt-Wiegand.
40. G. Dilcher, 'Leges – Gentes – Regna. Zur Rolle normativer Traditionen germanischen Völkerschaften bei der Ausbildung der mittelalterlichen Rechtskultur: Fragen und Probleme', in G. Dilcher & E.M. Distler (ed.), *Leges – Gentes – Regna. Zur Rolle von germanischen Rechtsgewohnheiten und lateinischer Schrifttradition bei der Ausbildung der frühmittelalterlichen Rechtskultur* (Berlin: 2006), 15-42, at 21.

Looking for 'Germanic' law had thus become out of fashion during the second half of the 20th century.

If we confine ourselves to the field of compensation, it was not until the 2003 article 'The *Leges Barbarorum*: Law and Ethnicity in the Post-Roman West' by Patrick Wormald that an earnest start was made to collect and compare the data in the *Leges*. In his important article, however, Wormald also made some firm statements concerning the 'Germanicity' of the *Leges Barbarorum*:

> [T]here are two good reasons to think that the law brought to light in *Lex Salica* was that of a selfconsciously 'barbarian' culture. In the first place, its keynote is compensation paid to an injured by the injuring party, including the kin of each. The harmonics underlying that note are those of bloodfeud: if payment was not made by the perpetrator and / or his kin to the victim and / or his, then revenge would be taken on any of the former by any of the latter.[41]

Interestingly, Wormald is saying that the injury tariffs form the very core of the *Leges Barbarorum*. He moreover observes that compensation with the threat of revenge and feud behind it, is not Roman: 'whatever its peacekeeping validity, it had not been Roman law's approach to social discord since the time of the Twelve Tables.'[42] The conclusion of his article, then, is that

> Most of these laws were at the outset [...] repositories of ancient traditions, which it is not misleading to call 'Germanic'. They are in fact among the best evidence we have for the stolidity of a Germanic culture.[43]

With Wormald's observations, the concept 'Germanic' had boldly been re-introduced into the field. There appeared to be Germanic law after all and the injury tariffs seemed to form its core. Wormald furthermore attached an appendix to his article, which featured an overview of all injuries mentioned in the various *Leges Barbarorum*, with references to which *Lex* they can be found in and what the compensations amount to.

It was not until recently that this analysis was taken a significant step further. In *The Body Legal in Barbarian Law* (2011), Lisi Oliver collects and compares all injury tariffs in the *Leges Barbarorum*.[44] The result is panoply of all possible injuries and body parts which the collected *Leges*

---

41. P. Wormald, 'The *Leges Barbarorum*: Law and Ethnicity in the Post-Roman West', in H.W. Goetz, J. Jarnut & W. Pohl (ed.), *Regna and Gentes. The Relationship between Late Antique and Early Medieval Peoples and Kingdoms in the Transformation of the Roman World*. (Leiden & Boston: 2003), 21-53, at 30.
42. Wormald, 'The *Leges Barbarorum*', 30
43. Wormald, 'The *Leges Barbarorum*', 46.
44. L. Oliver, *The Body Legal in Barbarian Law* (Toronto, Buffalo & London: 2011).

Barbarorum identify and describe. Oliver uses the human anatomy to structure her work which results in separate chapters on the head (3), the torso, arms and legs (4) and the hands and feet (5).

Although Oliver takes the same point of view on the injury tariffs as Patrick Wormald, i.e. that they are repositories of ancient knowledge, passed down orally for a long period until they were written down, she is not interested in reconstructing a proto-law or, to be more accurate, a proto-tariff. It is even hard to see how this might be brought about, given the enormous variation. Almost the only consistent factors seem to be a) the existence of wergeld and b) that in most (but not all) *Leges*, the hands, eyes and feet are valued at half a wergeld each. Apart from this, all kinds of variation can be found, be it in the relative valuation of the teeth or of the individual fingers, to name but some instances.[45] All things considered Oliver does not get further than finding a rough east-west divide. The bottom line seems to be that all this variation is a confirmation of Wormald's hunch that 'a tariff recognizable as one's own was perhaps itself an ethnic marker'.[46] In other words: each Germanic tribe strived after its own unique tariff as a flag to wave with.

To sum up, it is interesting to see how the injury tariffs have emerged in the 21st century as the aspect of early medieval law which can most rightly be labelled 'Germanic'. At the same time, however, it is impossible to reconstruct some kind of Proto-Germanic tariff. I personally suspect that if any such thing existed, it might have been relatively short. We know of tariffs from African tribes. These consist of some 20 stipulations and address the eyes, ears, nose, hands, feet, testicles, penis, arms, and legs.[47] An important question is when the concept of wergeld arose among the Germanic peoples. Was this already in their proto-phase (linguistically, we would be talking roughly 500 BCE)? For one thing, there is no single term among all Germanic peoples for the concept of wergeld: the oldest words are *wer* / *wergeld* and *leud* / *leuda*, both etymons originally meaning 'man'.[48] This topic needs some new attention in the light of these recent insights.

---

45. Oliver, *The Body Legal in Barbarian Law*, 102-07 (teeth); 154 (fingers).
46. Wormald, 'The *Leges Barbarorum*', 41.
47. Nijdam, *Lichaam, eer en recht*, 60-61.
48. R. Schmidt-Wiegand, 'Wergeld', in H. Beck et al. (ed.), *Reallexikon der Germanischen Altertumskunde* 33 (Berlin & New York: 2006), 457-63.

6. Conclusions

There are two conclusions to be drawn here. The first is that after having approached the topic from two directions, the reconstruction of Proto-Germanic law might now be put back on the research agendas of (legal) historians. Not only do the compensation tariffs in the *Leges Barbarorum* perfectly match the socio-political make-up of the tribal societies they were written for (remember what Christopher Boehm said about blood money being a 'diagnostic of a type of egalitarian political society that rather strictly limits centralised authority, and in which honour is of high importance culturally'). But also, from the viewpoint of Human Universals, it would be foolish to deny the Germanic tribes having had law at all. On top of that, Patrick Wormald and Lisi Oliver have convincingly shown that the tariffs in the *Leges* are indeed repositories of ancient Germanic knowledge on the human body and injuries.

The drawback to all this is that an actual reconstruction of Proto-Germanic law in the domain of the tariffs will not yield a large harvest, as we have seen just now. The amount of variation in the various tariffs is too big to be able to reconstruct a proto-tariff with any kind of certainty. The only more or less common denominators seem to be the wergeld per se and valuing eyes, hands and feet to half a wergeld.

The second conclusion then is that it is much more rewarding to analyse compensation tariffs from a comparative and cognitive perspective. This approach would allow researchers to profit from the wealth of source material on the topic. Questions that need to be asked are e.g.: Why are certain body parts valued the way they are? Is that attributed value because of functional aspects of that body part? Is that functionality universal or cultural? How do the patterns found in the tariffs fit within the larger picture of the culture under study? Which body parts are explicitly connected to each other in the texts? An example of this is the way the hands, eyes and feet are treated in the Old Frisian compensation tariffs. Because they all exacted half a wergeld upon loss, they became a group of their own in the Old Frisian tradition, called 'the six limbs'. These six limbs as a category in turn were used in a variety of ways by the anonymous authors of the Old Frisian tariffs, a.o. as a kind of health check.[49]

An analysis such as this requires that one sets up a well-structured database. First, all medieval European (Germanic) laws can be analysed, including the later Scandinavian laws. But after that the sky is the limit.

---

49. H. Nijdam, 'Compensating Body and Honor: The Old Frisian Compensation Tariffs', in W.J. Turner & S.M. Butler (ed.), *Medicine and Law in the Middle Ages* (Leiden & Boston: 2014), 25-57.

This research project could even be turned into a global project to research how throughout history, humans have dealt with violence and conflict and the injuries that were its result. The new post-cultural paradigm is making this possible, because it provides us with the parameters with which to set up such a project.

SCANDINAVIANS BY THE PAPAL WELL OF GRACE AND JUSTICE AT THE EVE OF REFORMATION

Kirsi Salonen

1. Introduction

This article illustrates how and to what extent the late medieval Scandinavians used the papal courts of law, when they had a juridical issue to solve. The analysis comprises all three medieval Scandinavian countries, Denmark, Norway and Sweden, as well as two important papal offices, the Apostolic Penitentiary[1] and the *Audientia Sacri Palatii*[2], also known as the

---

1. The Apostolic Penitentiary was not a tribunal in the proper sense of the word even though it is often called 'the tribunal of conscience', but one of the offices of the papal curia. The main task of the Penitentiary was that to distribute graces to Christians who either had broken against the regulations of canon law or wished to do so, for a good reason. The Penitentiary documentation includes such legal issues as illegitimate children, illegal marriages, problems with priestly ordination as well as various crimes like homicide, assault, apostasy and sacrilege. In this large spectrum of various matters, the Penitentiary could give absolutions, dispensations, special licenses or official declarations (mainly of innocence in cases of homicide) to the petitioners who turned to its authority. Concerning the powers and history of the Penitentiary, see E. Göller, *Die päpstliche Pönitentiarie von ihrem Ursprung bis zu ihrer Umgestalltung unter Pius V.* 1-2 (Rome: 1907, 1911); L. Schmugge, P. Hersperger & B. Wiggenhauser, *Die Supplikenregister der päpstlichen Pönitentiarie aus der Zeit Pius' II. (1458-1464)* (Tübingen: 1996); K. Salonen *The Penitentiary as a Well of Grace in the Late Middle ages. The Example of the Province of Uppsala 1448-1527* (Helsinki: 2001); K. Salonen & L. Schmugge, *A Sip from the "Well of Grace". Medieval texts from the Apostolic Penitentiary* (Washington D.C.: 2009).

(Sacra Romana) Rota. The time period of this article begins in the 1450s and 1460s, from when the first records of these offices have been preserved, and ends in the 1530s, when the Reformation in Scandinavia cut off the relationships to the papacy.[3]

Both of these papal offices were very busy in the late Middle Ages. Their officials handled each year hundreds if not thousands of cases and their clientele was truly international originating from all over Christendom – a territory ranging from the present-day Portugal to Finland and from Crete to Iceland. Most of the cases handled in these offices originated from the densely populated territories close to the Apostolic See in Rome, such as Italy, Germany, France and Spain, but also Scandinavians turned to them when they had juridical issues to solve.[4]

This article discusses the cases brought to these offices from the Scandinavian territory. The attention is first directed towards the Scandinavian petitions handled by the officials of the Penitentiary[5] and then to the Scandi-

2. The *Audientia Sacri Palatii* was the highest papal tribunal. It is usually not known by this official name but rather by its unofficial name *Sacra Romana Rota* – or only *Rota*. The Rota could act both as a tribunal of first instance for people of the diocese of Rome and the Papal States and as a tribunal of appeal for Christians from the whole territory of the Latin West. The Rota handled mostly litigations related to benefice issues (i.e. who had the right to possess a certain ecclesiastical benefice), but it had the powers to deal with juridical issues concerning marriages and property as well as other kinds of things. Concerning the history of the Rota, see N. Hilling, *Die römische Rota und das Bistum Hildesheim am Ausgang des Mittelalters (1464-1513). Hildesheimische Prozessakten aus dem Archiv der Rota zu Rom* (Münster: 1908); P. Ingesman, *Provisioner og processer. Den romerske Rota og dens behandling af danske sager i middelalderen* (Århus: 2003); S. Killermann, *Die Rota Romana. Wesen und Wirken des päpstlichen Gerichtshofes im Wandel der Zeit* (Frankfurt am Main: 2009); K. Salonen, *Kirkollisen oikeudenkäytön päälähteillä. Sacra Romana Rotan toiminta ja sen oikeudellinen tausta myöhäiskeskiajalla ja uuden ajan alun taitteessa* (Helsinki: 2012).
3. The sources of the Apostolic Penitentiary are preserved (apart from two earlier register volumes) systematically from the year 1448/9 onwards, while the source material in the Rota archives is preserved only from the year 1464 onwards. About the preservation of the Penitentiary sources, see Salonen, *The Penitentiary*, 425-26; Salonen & Schmugge, *A Sip*, 3-9. About the preservation of the Rota sources, see H. Hoberg, *Inventario dell'Archivio della Sacra Romana Rota (sec. XIV-XIX)* (Città del Vaticano: 1994).
4. Concerning the statistics of the provenance of the clients of the Penitentiary, see Salonen & Schmugge, *A Sip*, 27, 48-49, 55-57, 60-61, 63-64, 67-68. Regarding the provenance of Rota cases, see Salonen, *Kirkollisen oikeudenkäytön päälähteillä*, 122-45.
5. Regarding the Norwegian Penitentiary material, I rely mainly on the documentation edited in T. Jørgensen & G. Saletnich, *Synder og Pavemakt. Botsbrev fra Den Norske*

navian processes handled by the Rota auditors.[6] Due to the relatively large number of medieval Scandinavian material this article cannot, unfortunately, go deeply into detail, but it will offer the first comparative glimpses of the use of the papal offices by the Scandinavians.

2. Scandinavians in the Penitentiary material

The archival material of the Apostolic Penitentiary from the late Middle Ages (ca. 1450–1520s) consists of well over 200,000 entries in the copy books of the office. The clients of the Penitentiary originated from all parts of the Latin West, which indicates that the issues of canon law were known and understood everywhere in the territory of Christendom. Scandinavia was no exception to this, even though the Penitentiary handled significantly less petitions from the Scandinavian dioceses than from the more central Christian territories.[7]

The late medieval copy books of the Penitentiary contain copies of almost 1,400 petitioners coming from the three Nordic countries, Denmark, Norway and Sweden. Even though 1,400 documents form a respectable number of sources, the Scandinavian petitions represent only a very small part of all petitions directed to the Penitentiary, less than one percent.[8]

Kirkeprovins og Suderøyene til Pavestolen 1438-1531 (Stavanger: 2004) but which I later have completed. The analysis concerning the Swedish Penitentiary material is based on the results in Salonen, *The Penitentiary* and S. Risberg & K. Salonen (ed.), *Auctoritate Papae. The Church Province of Uppsala and the Apostolic Penitentiary 1410-1526. Diplomatarium Suecanum, Appendix. Acta Pontificum Suecica II. Acta Poenitentiariae* (Stockholm: 2008). The details concerning the Danish Penitentiary material are based on a survey made by Per Ingesman, which I later have completed.

6. The analysis regarding the Danish Rota material is entirely based on tables in Ingesman, *Provisioner og processer* (appendix 4, 750-80), while the analysis of the Swedish cases is based on Salonen, *Kirkollisen oikeudenkäytön päälähteillä* and that of the Norwegian cases is based on my (unpublished) survey in the Rota archives.
7. Concerning the provenance of different kinds of Penitentiary petitions between the years 1455 and 1492, see Salonen & Schmugge, *A Sip*, 17-68.
8. 1,400 petitions out of the estimation of 200,000 cases make 0.7 percent.

Table 1. Number of Penitentiary petitions from the Scandinavian church provinces

Province	Cases	%
Denmark	780	57 %
Norway	144	10 %
Sweden	451	33 %
Crowne	2	0 %
Total	1,377	100 %

Source: APA, *Reg. Matrim. et Div.* 1-83; ASV, *Arm.* XXII, vols 54B, 61; Risberg & Salonen (ed.), *Auctoritate Papae*.

The three Scandinavian kingdoms, represented by the ecclesiastical provinces of Lund, Nidaros and Uppsala, were not equally represented among the Penitentiary sources. As the numbers in table 1 demonstrate, more than half of the Scandinavian petitions directed to the Penitentiary were of Danish origin, while the cases from Sweden and especially from Norway were less numerous. There were as many as 780 petitions from the province of Lund, 144 petitions from the province of Nidaros and 451 petitions from the province of Uppsala. In addition to these, the Penitentiary material includes two petitions made by the Union Queen Dorothea. Since she does not mention any Scandinavian diocese as her 'home diocese' but just states that she was the Queen of Denmark, Sweden and Norway (*Regina Dacie, Swecie et Norwegie*), her petitions have been classified here as their own category of origin. Queen Dorothea – or most probably her representative, since she was not personally present in Rome – turned to the Penitentiary on 23 February 1461 and petitioned for a 'Butterbrief', e.g. for a license to consume meat, eggs and dairy products during Lent. In her second petition, dated on the same day, she asked for a license to choose herself any confessor she wanted.[9]

If we turn back from the Queen to the numbers in table 1, we can see how the Penitentiary material demonstrates that the Danes were much more

---

9. The petitions are edited in Risberg & Salonen (ed.), *Auctoritate Papae*, documents nos. 93 and 94 (dated in Rome, 23.2.1461). Both of the documents are very short and formulaic, so they do not reveal anything special about the Union Queen, but it seems that she has made the petition – especially for the license to eat forbidden products during Lent – in a real need. The first hint towards that is the wording in her petition that she needed the license since she 'was burdened by a decease' (*quadam infirmitate opressa*). Another hint is the date of the petition. Her request has been handled and approved by the Cardinal Penitentiary Filippo Calandrini on 23.2.1461. Her license was requested in the right moment since the Easter was in that year on 5.4. and consequently the Lent began already on 25.2., only two days after Dorothea had received her license.

active than the other Scandinavians in turning to the papal curia with their issues of canon law. The number of petitions from the Swedish church province (451) is significantly smaller than the number of Danish cases, but still far larger than the number of petitions from the Norwegian church province (144). Regarding the Norwegian numbers we have to take into account even the fact that they include, until the year 1472, also cases from the Hebrides and Orkney isles, which until then belonged administratively – thus not *de facto* – to the province of Nidaros. In fact, there are only 85 petitions to the Penitentiary from the dioceses in the Norwegian mainland.[10]

This result is significant in the sense that the numbers give clear evidence of the fact that the Christians from the Danish dioceses were much more active in using the services of the papal curia when they had an issue of conscience and/or canon law to solve. This general trend is also well in line with the number of other papal documentation from the same time period. It is well known that the number of other kinds of papal letters directed to persons in the province of Lund is also higher than the number of letters directed to persons in the provinces of Uppsala or Nidaros.[11]

If we take a closer look at the provenance of the Penitentiary petitions and go into the diocesan level, we can notice certain significant differences too. Each Scandinavian diocese had its own characteristics that affected the number of petitions directed to the Penitentiary from these dioceses. It has been argued at a general level that the number of inhabitants and important ecclesiastical institutions, like monasteries, should have had their effect on the need to turn to the Penitentiary; the more inhabitants or ecclesiastical institutions there were in a territory, the bigger should have been the need to use the services of the papal offices.[12]

How was the need to turn to the papal authority within the Scandinavian dioceses? In the following tables 2a, 2b and 2c are given the number of petitions from each Danish, Norwegian and Swedish diocese to the Apostolic Penitentiary. It is not reasonable to take a closer look at the case of each

---

10. More about the medieval situation of the Norwegian dioceses outside the mainland in S. Imsen (ed.), *'Ecclesia Nidrosiensis' and 'Noregs veldi'. The role of the Church in the making of Norwegian domination in the Norse World. Trondheim Studies in History* (Trondheim: 2012).
11. The Scandinavian relationships to the papal curia have not been studied for the late medieval period, so it is impossible to give any direct numbers concerning the papal letters to the different provinces, but already a comparison of the number of the documents edited in Acta Pontificum Danica or Diplomatarium Norwegicum or listed in the Huvudkartotek of the Diplomatarium Suecanum (http://riksarkivet.se/sdhk) demonstrates that the ratio is the same: the Danish documents are in majority. See also Peter Ståhl's article in this book.
12. Salonen, *The Penitentiary*, 414-15.

diocese in this occasion, since the provenance of both the Swedish and Norwegian Penitentiary petitions has already been discussed.[13] Therefore the following discussion is limited to general trends. The half numbers in the tables refer to petitions in which there have been two petitioners originating from two different dioceses. In these cases half a digit has been given to both dioceses.

Table 2a. Penitentiary petitions from the Danish church province of Lund

Diocese	Cases	%
Lund	72.5	9 %
Aarhus	87.0	11 %
Börglum/ Aalborg	43.5	6 %
Odense	125.0	16 %
Ribe	67.5	9 %
Roskilde	190.0	24 %
Schleswig	140.0	18 %
Viborg	46.5	6 %
S.d.	4.0	1 %
Other	4.0	1 %
Total	780.0	100 %

Source: APA, *Reg. Matrim. et Div.* 1-83; ASV, *Arm.* XXII, vols 54B, 61.

Table 2b. Penitentiary petitions from the Norwegian province of Nidaros

Diocese	Cases	%
Nidaros	34.0	24 %
Bergen	10.0	7 %
Hamar	6.0	4 %
Hebrids	44.0	31 %
Orkney	5.0	3 %
Oslo	26.0	18 %
Skálholt	10.0	7 %
Stavanger	9.0	6 %
Total	144.0	100 %

Source: APA, *Reg. Matrim. et Div.* 1-83; ASV, *Arm.* XXII, vol. 61; Jørgensen & Saletnich (ed.), *Synder og Pavemakt*.

13. I have done similar analysis on the petitions from different Swedish dioceses in Salonen, *The Penitentiary*, 370-92, 415. Regarding the analysis of the Norwegian cases, see Jørgensen & Saletnich (ed.), *Synder og Pavemakt*, 31-34.

Table 2c. Penitentiary petitions from the Swedish province of Uppsala

Diocese	Cases	%
Uppsala	113.5	25 %
Linköping	72.0	16 %
Skara	45.0	10 %
Strängnäs	42.5	9 %
Turku	126.5	28 %
Västerås	37.0	8 %
Växjö	8.5	2 %
Other	6.0	1 %
Total	451.0	100 %

Source: APA, *Reg. Matrim. et Div.* 1-83; ASV, *Arm.* XXII, vol. 61; Risberg & Salonen (ed.), *Auctoritate Papae.*

The numbers in the tables show that there were petitions from each Scandinavian diocese to the Apostolic Penitentiary. This means that the powers of the Penitentiary were known everywhere in Scandinavia and that the Christians up in the North did not hesitate to turn to its authority in case of necessity. The tables show, too, that the number of petitions from different dioceses varies significantly. On the one hand there is the Danish diocese of Roskilde with 190 petitions to the Penitentiary, while on the other hand there are dioceses with only a few petitions, like the diocese of Hamar from the Norwegian province of Nidaros with only six supplications. The number of petitions from the diocese of Roskilde is surprisingly high, twice the number of petitions from the dioceses in the Norwegian mainland and Iceland.[14] Such differences are a clear demonstration of the fact that there were different kinds of needs to the use of the Penitentiary in different dioceses and territories, and the case of Roskilde clearly underlines the special significance of that diocese.

The case of Roskilde brings forward also an interesting curiosity regarding the Danish church province, which we also meet in other Scandinavian provinces, namely that the number of petitions from none of the archbishop's dioceses dominate the material of that province. In Denmark, there are only 72.5 cases from the archdiocese of Lund, while the number of petitions from the diocese of Roskilde is 190, from the diocese of Schleswig 140, from the diocese of Odense 125 and from the diocese of Aarhus 87. A similar trend can be observed in the Swedish church province as well: there are 126.5 petitions from the diocese of Turku, which exceeds, though only

---

14. Dioceses of Nidaros, Bergen, Hamar, Oslo and Stavanger in present-day Norway as well as that of Skálholt in present-day Iceland.

slightly, the number of petitions from the archbishopric of Uppsala that number to 113.5. Also in Norway, the 44 petitions from the Hebrides exceed the number of petitions from the archbishop's diocese of Nidaros, but otherwise the number of petitions from the Norwegian dioceses remains below the number of petitions from the archbishop's diocese of Nidaros.

It is difficult to try to explain this phenomenon. One would expect that the ecclesiastical centre of each province would have produced the largest number of petitions, but this has clearly not been the case, especially in Denmark so strongly dominated by the petitions from other dioceses than the archdiocese of Lund. In the Swedish context, the 'over-representation' of the petitions from the diocese of Turku was partly explained by the fact that papal representatives, who visited Sweden, occasionally had the powers to deal with similar kinds of cases as the Penitentiary did, and consequently the Christians preferred to turn to these persons instead of travelling to Rome to settle their problems. But since the papal representatives very seldom, if ever, visited the Finnish territory, the Christians of the diocese of Turku had to turn to the papacy to get their issues settled, which resulted in an elevated number of petitions to the Penitentiary if compared to the number of inhabitants in the diocese.[15]

Another plausible explanation for the phenomenon is that the archbishops of each province possessed larger powers to deal with different kinds of issues than their suffragan bishops and therefore the Christians from other dioceses than the archbishops' dioceses have turned to the Penitentiary more often. There is, however, no clear evidence of that, unlike with the presence of the papal representatives in Scandinavia. But such a phenomenon can be observed particularly in the English petitions to the Penitentiary, where the supplications from the archbishop's diocese of Canterbury are almost absent due to the extensive powers of the archbishop to deal locally with many different kinds of matters.[16]

Concluding, it can be said that all parts of Scandinavia were represented in the Penitentiary material, however so that there were more petitions from the more central parts of each Kingdom and less material from the more remote parts. Since the same trend can be observed also in the Penitentiary material as a whole,[17] the Scandinavian pattern seems to fit perfectly to the international trend.

15. Salonen, *The Penitentiary*, 370-76.
16. P.D. Clarke & P.R.N. Zutshi (ed.), *Supplications from England and Wales in the Registers of the Apostolic Penitentiary, 1410-1503* 1 (Suffolk: 2013), passim.
17. K. Salonen, 'The Penitentiary under Pope Pius II. The Supplications and Their Provenance', in G. Jaritz, T. Jørgensen & K. Salonen (ed.), *The Long Arm of Papal Authority. Late Medieval Christian Peripheries and Their Communication with the Holy See* (Budapest: 2005 – 2nd edn), 11-21.

Then to the next point of this essay: What kinds of cases were brought from Scandinavia to the Penitentiary? This detail can be studied at a general level by examining how many cases of different petition categories there are from each Scandinavian province. Such an analysis can easily be based on the internal division of the Penitentiary records. The copy books of the Penitentiary are internally divided into six main groups: *de matrimonialibus* (regarding marriages = Matr.), *de diversis formis* (various types of cases = DF), *de declaratoriis* (declaratory cases = Decl.), *de illegitimiis*[18] (regarding illegitimacy = Illeg.), *de promotis et promovendis* (regarding priestly ordinations and the quality of priest candidates = Prom.), as well as *de confessionalibus* (licenses for choosing one's confessor = Conf.).[19] Table 3 shows, how many petitions of each group were brought to the Penitentiary from each of the three Scandinavian provinces.

Table 3. Number of different kinds of Penitentiary petitions from the Scandinavian church provinces

Province	Matr.	DF	Decl.	Illeg.	Prom.	Conf.	Other	Total	%
Lund	80	234	96	283	23	63	1	780	57 %
Nidaros	19	37	10	61	3	11	3	144	10 %
Uppsala	68	127	67	120	10	59	2	453	33 %
Total	167	398	173	464	36	133	6	1377	100 %
Scand. %	12 %	29 %	13 %	34 %	3 %	10 %	0 %	100 %	
Whole %	(37 %)	(20 %)	(4 %)	(19 %)	(8 %)	(12 %)	(-)	(100 %)	

Source: APA, *Reg. Matrim. et Div.* 1-83; ASV, *Arm.* XXII, vols 54B, 61; Jørgensen & Saletnich (ed.), *Synder og Pavemakt*; Risberg & Salonen (ed.), *Auctoritate Papae*.

First of all it can be noticed that petitions related to illegitimacy (464 cases) and different types of cases registered in the *de diversis formis* category (398 cases) form the biggest petition groups within the Scandinavian material. The numbers in table 3 also show that there are no significant differences regarding the proportions of various types of petitions from the three different Nordic provinces. However, some variation between the different provinces can be observed.

If we look at the numbers and proportions of different petition groups in different countries, we can notice that there seems to be proportionally too

18. In the earlier Penitentiary volumes the petitions concerning illegitimacy are divided into two separate categories, *de defectu natalium* and *de uberiori*, but the later volumes contain only one category, *de illegitimiis*.
19. Concerning the various types of petitions in the different categories, see Schmugge, Hersperger & Wiggenhauser, *Die Supplikenregister*, 68-217; Salonen, *The Penitentiary*, 103-210; Salonen & Schmugge, *A Sip*, 17-68.

few marriage cases and confessional letters from the province of Lund, while the number of such petitions is larger in the material from the province of Uppsala. At the same time illegitimacy cases are proportionally over-represented in the material from the Danish and Norwegian provinces and under-represented in the material from the Swedish province. These differences are, nevertheless, not big and it must be legitimate to conclude that the cases from the three Nordic provinces follow more or less the same pattern.

If we compare the proportions of different petition categories in the Scandinavian material to the proportions in the whole material (the per cent numbers in the whole material are indicated in table 3 lowest row), we can observe some interesting differences. There are much fewer petitions related to marriages in the Scandinavian material than in the whole material (12 % vs. 37 %). This difference seems to be so big that it must be significant, especially because the number of marriage petitions is low in all three Scandinavian provinces. I have elsewhere explained the under-representation of marriage petitions in the Swedish material by the fact that according to Swedish secular legislation, marriage was not considered as an ecclesiastical issue but rather as a secular one. In order to ensure the inheritance rights of one's offspring, it was important to contract a marriage according to the regulations of secular law, where the church played only a minor role, if any. The same explanation could also be applied to the other Scandinavian countries, where the marriage practices were much more secular than for example in Italian dioceses, where the marriage regulations of Roman and consequently canon law were applied more rigorously, and consequently the need for dispensations and absolutions in order to ensure the rights of offspring was much larger.[20]

The comparison of the proportions of different petition categories also shows opposite trends in certain types of cases. For example, the Scandinavian average for the illegitimacy petitions is as high as 34 % against the general proportion of 19 %. This means that illegitimacy was a larger issue in the North than in the South. Interestingly, the Scandinavian average corresponds very well with the German proportions. Schmugge has suggested that the large German proportion of petitions related to illegitimacy is on one hand a sign of a larger number of illegitimate children in the German society and on the other hand a sign that illegitimate children had good chances in striving for an ecclesiastical career in the German diocese.[21] We could assume that the Scandinavian situation was similar to the German one. The small proportion of illegitimate children in the Italian material

20. Salonen, *The Penitentiary*, 264-67.
21. L. Schmugge, *Kirche, Kinder, Karrieren. Päpstliche Dispense von der unehelichen Geburt im Spätmittelalter* (Zürich: 1995).

might also reflect the above-mentioned trend of strict control of marriages in southern Europe.

The Scandinavians are also over-represented in the *de diversis formis* (29 % vs. 20 %) as well as in the *de declaratoriis* (13 % vs. 4 %) petitions, but in these categories the Scandinavian proportions are not so much above the international average. Since these two petition categories generally contain cases of relative severity, it becomes evident – as it has already been pointed out regarding the Swedish Penitentiary material – that the Scandinavians did not turn to the Penitentiary for small matters, but rather in cases when this was absolutely necessary. Therefore the proportion of severe crimes, like homicide, assault and apostasy, is much more present in the Scandinavian material than, for example, in the material from the southern parts of Christendom. This is simply due to the fact that it was not reasonable to leave for an expensive petition journey to Rome from the North if the matter was not of a certain importance.[22]

Judging from what was discussed above we can conclude that even though the Scandinavian trend within the Penitentiary documentation seems to follow the general trend in many respects, the numbers also clearly demonstrate that there were slightly different issues at stake in Scandinavia than elsewhere in Christendom.

3. Scandinavians in the Rota material

The late medieval archival material of the *Sacra Romana Rota* is also immense, yet much worse preserved than the Penitentiary material.[23] According to the surviving records of the highest papal tribunal we can say without a doubt that the Rota must have handled thousands of litigation processes each year, and the preserved sources give testimony of tens of thousands of processes. The clients of the Rota – just like those of the Penitentiary – originate from all parts of the Latin West, which means that Christians from all over Christendom knew about the existence of the papal tribunal and could use it if necessary – also the Scandinavians.[24]

This study is based on the documentation concerning Scandinavian Rota processes in the late medieval manuals of the Rota notaries, nowadays kept

---

22. Salonen, *The Penitentiary*, 412.
23. According to the (though not necessarily totally correct) estimations of Hilling, only 1/6 or 1/7 of the Rota manuals have survived to our days. Hilling, *Die römische Rota*, 17-18. See also Salonen, *Kirkollisen oikeudenkäytön päälähteillä*, 24-25.
24. About the provenance of the clients of the Rota, see Salonen, *Kirkollisen oikeudenkäytön päälähteillä*, 122-45.

in the Vatican Secret Archives.[25] These manuals contain information of 85 litigation processes related to the Scandinavian dioceses, which is a relatively small number of cases when compared to the total amount of processes handled by the Rota. If the proportion of Scandinavian cases among the Penitentiary material was less than one percent, the proportion within the Rota material is even smaller.[26]

Table 4. Number of Rota processes from the Scandinavian church provinces

Province	Cases	%
Denmark	73	86 %
Norway	0	0 %
Sweden	12	14 %
Total	85	100 %

Sources: ASV, *S. R. Rota, Manualia Actorum* 1-151, 153.

As the numbers in table 4 demonstrate, the Scandinavians did not use the services of the Rota equally, but most of the litigations, 73 in total, concerned the province of Lund.[27] There are records of only 12 litigation processes from the Swedish church province[28] and no records at all regarding the province of Nidaros.[29] On the basis of this we can conclude that the Rota material points exactly to the same direction as the Peniten-

25. There is information about Rota processes (also about processes that cannot be traced in the preserved Rota manuals) in other papal copy books. Since the amounts of other papal copybooks number to several thousands, they have not been included in this essay. This essay is based on the thorough study of the survived ca. 160 Rota manuals (of which each includes several hundreds of folios and which do not contain any indexes). ASV, *S. R. Rota, Manualia Actorum* 1-151, 153.
26. Due to the very badly survived Rota documentation, it is impossible to estimate the total number of processes handled by the tribunal. But in any case that amounts to tens of thousands for the period of the whole later Middle Ages, since the amounts of processes handled in the Rota during the years 1466, 1486, 1506 and 1526 amounted to ca. 3,500 processes – even though only a small part of the manuals have survived. If we compare the proportion of Scandinavian Rota cases to that of the Penitentiary cases (0.7% of all cases), 85 cases is a very small number (0.7% out of ca. 12,200 cases). Therefore, the share of Scandinavian processes in the Rota must be much smaller than the share of Scandinavian cases in the Penitentiary.
27. See Ingesman, *Provisioner og processer*, 750-80.
28. See Salonen, *Kirkollisen oikeudenkäytön päälähteillä*, 297-315.
29. The lack of survived documentation in the Rota archives, on which the analysis of this essay is based, does not mean that there were no Norwegian Rota processes in the Middle Ages. But I have excluded all other medieval source material from this article for the sake of proportionality in work load.

tiary material. It demonstrates that the Danes were much more active than their fellow Scandinavians in using the services of the papal curia when they had legal issues to solve. The numbers in table 4 confirm, too, the impresssion that the Swedes were more active users of the papal justice than the Norwegians.

Then – following the same scheme of analyzing the material as above with the Penitentiary documentation – it is time to take a closer look at the Scandinavian Rota processes and to see what was their provenance. The provenance of the Scandinavian Rota processes is expressed at a diocesan level in tables 5a and 5b.

Table 5a. Rota processes from the Danish province of Lund

Diocese	Cases	%
Lund	0.5	1 %
Aarhus	1.5	2 %
Börglum/ Aalborg	5.0	7 %
Odense	4.5	6 %
Ribe	9.0	12 %
Roskilde	8.5	12 %
Schleswig	35.0	48 %
Viberg	9.0	12 %
Total	73.0	100 %

Source: Ingesman, *Provisioner og processer*, 750-80.

Table 5b. Rota processes from the Swedish province of Uppsala

Diocese	Cases	%
Uppsala	2	17 %
Linköping	5	42 %
Skara	0	0 %
Strängnäs	1	8 %
Turku	3	25 %
Västerås	1	8 %
Växjö	0	0 %
Total	12	100 %

Source: ASV, *S. R. Rota, Manualia Actorum* 1-151, 153;
Salonen, *Kirkollisen oikeudenkäytön päälähteillä*, 297-315.

Due to the small number of processes from all Scandinavian countries, no big differences can be observed. We can see that there are processes from all Danish dioceses, but that there is only half a process concerning the

195

archbishop's diocese of Lund and also relatively few cases from the other Danish dioceses – with the big exception of the diocese of Schleswig, from where half of the Danish cases originate.[30] The situation of the Swedish dioceses with only 12 processes is much less varying. Linköping is represented by 5 processes, Turku with 3, Uppsala with 2 and Strängnäs and Västerås with 1 each, while no processes originate from Skara or Växjö.[31] They are thus in line with the Norwegian dioceses with no cases at all.

If we want to compare these numbers to those concerning the Penitentiary, we can see that the difference is quite remarkable. Suddenly the cases from Schleswig dominate the Danish material and those from Linköping the Swedish ones. But since 12 cases are too few for a reliable analysis there is no reason to draw further conclusions regarding the Swedish situation. The only general conclusion we can draw is that the number of cases from different dioceses handled on the one hand in the Penitentiary and on the other hand in the Rota do not correspond with each other. But again we can see the same trend that the more central dioceses are better represented than the more remote and smaller ones.

Then we will proceed to the next point: For what kinds of litigations did the Scandinavians turn to the Rota? In principle, the processes handled by the Rota may be classified in four main categories: Benefice litigations, marriage litigations, property litigations as well as 'other litigations' which includes all the rest.[32] Table 6 shows, how many different types of litigations there are in the Scandinavian Rota material in different categories.

Table 6. Number of different kinds of litigations in the Rota from the Scandinavian church provinces

Province	Benefice	Marriage	Property	Other	Total	%
Lund	65	0	4	4	73	86 %
Nidaros	0	0	0	0	0	0 %
Uppsala	8	0	1	3	12	14 %
Total	73	0	5	7	85	100 %
Scand. %	86 %	0 %	6 %	8 %	100 %	
Whole %	(80 %)	(1 %)	(14 %)	(5 %)	(100 %)	

Source: ASV, *S. R. Rota*, *Manualia Actorum* 1-151, 153;
Ingesman, *Provisioner og processer*, 750-80.

30. I have discussed the speciality of the diocese of Schleswig in the Danish Rota material in K. Salonen, "'Danish' and 'German' Schleswig – the testimony of late medieval Vatican sources', in M. Brengsbo & K.V. Jensen (ed.), *Schleswig Holstein – contested region(s) through history* (Odense: forthcoming).
31. Salonen *Kirkollisen oikeudenkäytön päälähteillä*, 301-03.
32. About the different litigation categories in the Rota material, Salonen, *Kirkollisen oikeudenkäytön päälähteillä*, 98-122.

The numbers in table 6 demonstrate clearly that the benefice litigations were in a very clear majority among the Scandinavian litigations: 65 processes from Denmark and eight from Sweden. The number of other types of processes is much smaller, but the Scandinavian material includes a few property issues as well as a few processes classified in the 'other' category. Instead, there are no marriage litigations in the Scandinavian Rota material. Since the comparison between Danish and Swedish proportions would be problematic due to the small number of Swedish processes, it is not wise to draw any comparative conclusions.

Instead, it is possible to compare the proportions of different litigation types in the Scandinavian material to the proportions in the whole material (per cent numbers below in table 6). As can be seen, the Scandinavian 'trend' corresponds relatively well with the general trend. The benefice issues were without a doubt the biggest litigation group both in the whole and in the Scandinavian material, while the property and other issues form smaller groups and the marriage cases are the least represented in both materials. This means that it is possible to conclude that unlike with the Penitentiary documentation, the Scandinavian needs for turning to the authority of the Rota seem to have been very similar to the needs from elsewhere in the Latin West.

4. Conclusions

Then to conclusions: In this last table 7 are given the numbers and proportions of the Penitentiary and Rota cases from the three Scandinavian provinces. What can be seen here?

Table 7. Scandinavian Penitentiary cases and Rota processes

Province	Penitentiary	%	Rota	%
Denmark	780	57 %	73	86 %
Norway	144	10 %	0	0 %
Sweden	451	33 %	12	14 %
Crowne	2	0 %	0	0 %
Total	1,377	100 %	85	100 %

Source: APA, *Reg. Matrim. et Div.* 1-83; ASV, *Arm.* XXII, vols 54B, 61; ASV, *S. R. Rota, Manualia Actorum* 1-151, 153; Ingesman, *Provisioner og processer*, 750-80.

First of all, we can notice that the number of Scandinavian Penitentiary cases is much larger than the number of Scandinavian Rota processes: almost 1,400 Penitentiary petitions against less than one hundred Rota processes. It was also pointed out that the proportion of Scandinavian cases in the Penitentiary material was higher than the proportion of Scandinavian processes in the Rota material. However, the differences between the Penitentiary material and the Rota material cannot be compared directly since the powers of the two papal offices were so different from each other. But these numbers demonstrate clearly that the Apostolic Penitentiary was well known by the Scandinavians and if they needed absolution or dispensation from a violation of canon law, they did not hesitate to turn to the Penitentiary and ask for that. At the same time, the small number of Scandinavian Rota processes indicates that the existence of Rota was known in Scandinavia but that only a very few persons wanted – or dared – to turn to a papal tribunal in their juridical issues. It is my impression that this took place only when the litigants really needed to do so.

Another general impression we can discover on the basis of these numbers is that the Danes have used the services of the papal curia much more often than the Christians from the other Scandinavian provinces. Similarly these numbers tell that the Norwegians were among the Scandinavians the least active in using the papal curia. This can be explained at a simple level by the fact that the number of inhabitants in Norway was the smallest of the three Scandinavian provinces.

SCANDINAVIA CONSULTS 'ROME', CA.1104-1202: CONTEXTS AND CONSEQUENCES

Anne J. Duggan

1. Introduction

The essential background to the establishment of regular relations between Scandinavia and the papacy was the creation, in the course of the 12th century, of the three ecclesiastical provinces (Lund, Nidaros/Trondheim and Uppsala), one each for the emerging kingdoms of Denmark, Norway and Sweden, and the initiative came from Scandinavia. Danish kings had been seeking independence from the archbishops of Hamburg-Bremen through the reigns of Svein Estridsen (1047-1074/6),[1] Harald III (1074/6-1080),[2] and Cnut IV the Holy (1080-1086).[3] Svein began (ca. 1060) the structural reorganization of the kingdom into seven dioceses (Ribe, Viborg, Aarhus, Roskilde, Dalby, Lund and Jutland [Jylland]) and Bishop Henry of Orkney (Cnut the Great's former treasurer) received Lund, instead of Egino, the candidate presented and consecrated by the archbishop of Hamburg-Bremen.[4] Although Henry's appointment was an augury for the future, he soon died (1066), unlamented it seems, and Egino (1067/71-1072) received

---

1. A. Forte, R. Oram & F. Pedersen, *Viking Empires* (Cambridge: 2005), 359-62; T. Nyberg, *Monasticism in North-Western Europe 800–1200* (Aldershot: 2000), 39-44, 47-49.
2. Forte, Oram & Pedersen, *Viking Empires*, 362-64; Nyberg, *Monasticism*, 54.
3. Forte, Oram & Pedersen, *Viking Empires*, 364-68; Nyberg, *Monasticism*, 54-61.
4. Forte, Oram & Pedersen, *Viking Empires*, 359-60; Nyberg, *Monasticism*, 44.

the now combined diocese of Lund and Dalby (1067/71).[5] Equally significantly, the new cathedrals of Lund and Roskilde were dedicated, not to the Virgin, in imitation of Hamburg, but to the Holy Trinity, following the example of Winchester, where Cnut the Great had been buried in 1035. Lund's primacy over all Scandinavia was obtained by Erik Ejegod Svendsen (1095-1103) during a pilgrimage to Rome in 1103,[6] and the newly elevated archbishop, Asser, already bishop since 1089,[7] received the pallium from the papal envoy Alberic in 1104.[8] Despite the elaborate story surrounding the transmission of the head of Pope St Lucius to Denmark, it was probably Erik Ejegod who obtained it for the diocese of Roskilde, whose patron Lucius became. Simultaneously, Erik intensified connexions with England: installing Evesham monks at Odense and appointing an English canon from Lund (Hubald) as the new bishop of Roskilde.

Although the archbishops of Hamburg-Bremen vigorously opposed this diminution of their jurisdiction, the popes consistently defended Lund's independent metropolitan status, except for five years (1133-1138) during the Anacletan schism (1130 - January 1138), when Innocent II (1130-1143) acceded to the appeal of Archbishop Adalbero of Hamburg and the 'prayers' of Lothar III (*charissimi filii nostri Lotharii regis precibus inclinati*),[9] whom he was about to crown as emperor in 1133.[10] Political pressure there certainly was, but Innocent's *volte face* could be justified by the Danish archbishop's own default, for Asser had failed to answer any of the summonses to defend his position.[11] There is, nevertheless, considerable

---

5. H. Kluger (ed.), *Series episcoporum ecclesiae catholicae occidentalis ab initio usque ad annum MCXCVII, Series* 6/ii, *Lundensis* (Stuttgart: 1992), 35-37; Nyberg, *Monasticism*, 4, 46-48.
6. Forte, Oram & Pedersen, *Viking Empires*, 369-70; Kluger (ed.), *Series episcoporum*, 6/ii, *Lundensis*, 2, 17. Paschal's privilege is lost, but the event is recorded in an Icelandic panegyric in honour of King Erik the Good: E.A. Kock, *Den norsk-isländska skaldediktningen*, 2 vols (Lund: 1946-1949), i, 204; Nyberg, *Monasticism*, 55-58, 100 (he died in Cyprus).
7. Bishop of Lund 1089-1103; archbishop of Lund 1103-1137: Nyberg, *Monasticism*, 77.
8. Kluger (ed.) *Series episcoporum*, 6/ii, *Lundensis*, 17-18.
9. King 1125-1133; Emperor 1133-1137.
10. *PL*, clxxix, 180-81, no. 137, at 180. For the short mandate to Asser, see *Diplomatarium Danicum*, 1/ii (Copenhagen: 1963), 114-15, no. 59 (27.5.1133) and *PL*, clxxix, 182, no. 140, whose incipit should read *Quemadmodum juris praecepta*: A. Winroth, 'Innocent II, Gratian, and Abbé Migne', *BMCL* 28 (2008), 145-51.
11. Innocent's privilege for Adalbero referred to many summonses to Asser and the bishops of 'Dacia', from Popes Calixtus II (1119-1124), Honorius II (1124-1130) and himself, either to return to their obedience or to present their arguments to the Apostolic See, but they neither came nor sent replies: *PL*, clxxix, 180-81, no. 137 (27.5.1133), at 180: 'Frequenter autem et a predictis predecessoribus nostris Calixte et

doubt about whether Innocent's mandates reached their Scandinavian recipients,[12] for Asser continued to act with full metropolitan authority through the period.[13] Innocent restored Lund's status in 1138 (when 'Anacletus II' and Lothar III were both dead), in favour of the new archbishop, Eskil Christiansen, already bishop of Roskilde, when he sent the pallium to Lund by the hands of Eskil's chaplain Hermann (from Klosterrath).[14] That was followed by the dispatch of a legate, Cardinal Theodwin,[15] who, with Eskil, held the first provincial council of the new province at Lund in August 1139,[16] attended by five Danish bishops (Roskilde, Viborg, Børglum, Ribe, Schleswig), one each from Norway (Bergen) and Sweden (Linköping), and Bishop Orm from the Faroe islands.

That confirmation of Lund's status was the first step in the establishment of three metropolitan churches: Lund (1103/4), initially for Denmark and the whole of Scandinavia; Nidaros/Trondheim for Norway (1153) and

Honorio, atque a nobis, eis mandatum est ut aut ad tuam et Hammenburgensis Ecclesiae redirent obedientiam, aut si quam super hoc justam se confiderent rationem habere, ad sedem apostolicam uenirent ostendere preparati. Ipsi uero apostolicis contemnentes obedire mandatis, nec uenerunt, nec responsales miserunt'.

12. *Diplomatarium Danicum*, 1/ii (Copenhagen: 1963), nos. 57-61; *PL*, clxxix, 180-82, nos. 137-41. Since no Danish envoys were present, the mandates would have been given to Adalbero for transmission to the North and may have 'withered on the wine'. For important new light on the complex early history of the archbishopric of Hamburg-Bremen, see E. Knibbs, *Ansgar, Rimbert and the Forged Foundations of Hamburg-Bremen* (Farnham: 2011), esp. 209-23

13. Kluger (ed.), *Series episcoporum*, 6/ii, *Lundensis*, 18-19.

14. Bishop of Roskilde (1134-1137), archbishop of Lund (1137/8-1177): Kluger (ed.), *Series episcoporum*, 6/ii, *Lundensis*, 20-28, at 20-21 (with full bibliography); *Dansk Biografisk Leksikon* (1980 – 3rd edn), iv, 256-59; *Dictionnaire d'histoire et de géographie ecclésiastiques* 15 (1963), 884-85. For a full treatment, see Nyberg, *Monasticism, passim*; for Hermann, later unsuccessful bishop of Slesvig, from which he had to resign (1145) before dying (1150) in Lund, see Nyberg, *Monasticism*, 117, 159-60.

15. Theodwin, a German Benedictine, former abbot of Gorze (1126-1134) and a key player in the recognition of Pope Innocent, was inserted into the top echelon of the curia as cardinal bishop of S. Rufina and Porto (1134-1150), where he became the expert on German affairs and later played a significant role in the election of King Conrad III (1138-1152): B. Zenker, *Die Mitglieder des Kardinalkollegiums von 1130 bis 1159* (Diss. Würzburg: 1964), 26-28. Theodwin's legation to Denmark was unknown to Zenker; cf. Nyberg, *Monasticism*, 157.

16. *Diplomatarium Danicum*, 1/ii, 146-50, no. 77, to the brethren of St Knud in Odense, 8. 8.1139, witnessed by Theodwin, Eskil, and 8 bishops. W. Seegrün, *Das Papsttum und Skandinavien, bis zur Vollendung der nordischen Kirchenorganisation (1164)* (Neumünster: 1967), 141-42; Kluger (ed.), *Series episcoporum*, 6/ii, *Lundensis*, 21; Nyberg, *Monasticism*, 157.

Uppsala for Sweden (1164). The initiative for the elevation of Uppsala came from Archbishop Eskil of Lund, supported by the Swedish king (Karl Sverkersson, 1161-1167),[17] and Lund's primacy over the Swedish province was carefully preserved from the beginning. It was Eskil who consecrated the French Cistercian Stephen (one of the colonizers of Alvastra Abbey) as the first archbishop of Uppsala in the presence of Pope Alexander III, at Sens, on Sunday, 2 August, 1164,[18] in a ceremony which Innocent III recalled thirty-four years later (1198) in his great privilege for Eskil's successor, Absalon.[19] All three provinces remained independent from Hamburg-Bremen.

An immediate consequence of these defining events was that Scandinavia turned increasingly to France for higher learning. Eskil of Lund had been educated in Hildesheim, but Absalon[20] and Anders Sunesen (1201-1228)[21] were educated in Paris, under the guidance of the Augustinian canons regular at Ste-Geneviève, where the canonist Stephen 'of Tournai' was abbot (1176-1192) before his elevation to Tournai.[22] Øystein (1157/61-1188), Eirik (1189-1205) and Tore (1206-1214) of Nidaros, and Peter of Uppsala (1188-1197) were also educated in Paris, and Stephen of Uppsala (1164-1185) was a product of Clairvaux.[23] Paris exposed them to the educational advances of the time, introducing them to the study of canon law, only recently compiled for teaching by Master Gratian at Bologna. The general

---

17. *Precibus et interventu charissimi filii nostri Caroli illustris regis Suevorum et Gothorum episcoporum*: PL, cc, 301-03, nos 260-61, at 302-03.
18. Three days later (Sens, 5.8.[1164]), Alexander III issued the requisite letters which established the province, with four bishoprics (Skara, Linköping, Strängnäs and Aarhus), subject to the primacy of Lund: PL, cc, 301-03, nos 260-61.
19. PL, ccxiv, 395-96, no. i. 419, *In eminenti apostolice sedis specula* (23.11.1198), at 396: below, at n. 145. Two years later, in Paris, before 7.9.1166, Eskil consecrated Ralph (1166-1171) and Svein/Svend (1166-1191) to Ribe and Aarhus, respectively.
20. Kluger (ed.), *Series episcoporum*, 6/ii, *Lundensis*, 89-93 (Roskilde) and 28-33 (Lund). Absalon was in Paris between 1146 and 1155 (*ibid.* 90); cf. K. Friis-Jensen & I. Skovgaard-Petersen (ed.), *Archbishop Absalon of Lund and his World* (Roskilde: 2000).
21. T.K. Nielsen, 'The Missionary Man: Archbishop Anders Sunesen and the Baltic Crusade, 1206–21', in A.V. Murrey (ed.), *Crusade and Conversion on the Baltic Frontier 1150–1500* (Aldershot: 2001), 95-117.
22. C. Vulliez, 'Études sur la correspondence et la carrière d'Étienne d'Orléans dit de Tournai (d. 1203)', in J. Jongère (ed.), *L'Abbaye parisienne de Saint-Victor au moyen âge* (Paris & Turnhout: 1991), 195-231, at 196, 224-25.
23. He had been one of the French Cistercian colonizers of Alvastra Abbey and bishop-elect from 1158/60: Nyberg, *Monasticism*, 215-17.

reception of the vulgate form of Gratian's *Decretum* (1141 x 45)[24] accelerated the standardization and professionalization of ecclesiastical jurisdiction across Europe. Rights and privileges were expressed and defended in the language of that law, legal cases had to be conducted according to due process defined in handbooks (*ordines judiciarium*),[25] and a new learned élite was created, trained in the knowledge, application and practice of the written *ius canonum,* which derived much of its language and technical procedure from Justinianic Roman law.[26]

24. Anders Winroth revolutionized the study of Gratian by arguing that there were two recensions by two different authors, of which the first appeared ca. 1140 (after the Second Lateran Council, 1139), and the second, possibly as late as 1158: A. Winroth, *The Making of Gratian's Decretum* (Cambridge: 2000); cf. K. Pennington's review in *Speculum* 78 (2003), 293-97. There followed a burst of research, which shows no signs of abating, proposing alternative interpretations. The 'two recension' theory was broadly accepted by P. Landau, 'Gratian and the *Decretum Gratiani*', in W. Hartmann & K. Pennington (ed.), *The History of Medieval Canon Law in the Classical Period, 1140–1234. From Gratian to the Decretals of Pope Gregory IX* (Washington D.C.: 2008), 22-54, but it was challenged by the concept of evolution by stages, embraced by Spanish scholars (C. Larrainzar, 'La formación del Decreto de Graciano por etapas', *ZRG Kan. Abt.* 118/87 [2001], 67-83; idem, 'La investigación actuel sobre el Decreto de Graciano', *ZRG Kan. Abt.* 121/90 [2004], 27-59; J.M. Viejo-Ximénez, 'La composizione del decreto di Graziano', in S.A. Szuromi [ed.], *Medieval Canon Law Collections and European Ius Commune [Középkori kánonjogi gyűjtemények és az európai ius commune]* [Budapest: 2006], 97-169); K. Pennington, 'The "Bang": Roman Law in the Early Twelfth Century', *Rivista Internazionale di Diritto Comune*, 18 (2007), 43-70, at 45-6 and 53, proposed three stages: an early version in the late 1120s; an intermediate version in the 1130s; and the much expanded Vulgate (Winroth's 'Recension II'), *c.*1141-45. For the current state of this rapidly developing research, in which the language of 'recensions' is abandoned in favour of evolving pre-Vulgate and Vulgate stages, see K. Pennington, 'The Biography of Gratian, the Father of Canon Law', forthcoming in the *Villanova Law Review* (2014).
25. L. Fowler-Magerl, *Ordines Iudiciarii* and *Libelli de Ordine iudiciorum* (Turnhout: 1994); K.W. Nörr, 'Ordo iudiciorum und ordo iudiciarium', *Studia Gratiana* 11 (1967), 327-43; K.W. Nörr, 'Die römische Kurie und die Anfang der Prozessliteratur', *ZRG Kan. Abt.* 59 (1973), 151-74.
26. A.J. Duggan, 'Master of the Decretals: A Reassessment of Alexander III's Contribution to the Development of Canon Law', in P.D. Clarke & A.J. Duggan (ed.), *Pope Alexander III (1159–81). The Art of Survival* (Farnham: 2012), 365-417, at 366-67; A.J. Duggan, '*De consultationibus tuis*: the role of episcopal consultation in the shaping of canon law in the twelfth century', in B.C. Brasington & K.G. Cushing (ed.), *Bishops, Texts and the Use of Canon Law in the Earlier Middle Ages: Studies in Honour of Martin Brett* (Aldershot: 2008), 191-214, at 194-98; P. Legendre, *La pénétration du droit romain dans le droit canonique classique de Gratien à Innocent IV* (1140–1254) (Paris: 1964).

Thereafter, three imperatives drew the Scandinavian provinces closer to the papacy. First was the need to protect their independent status; then the need of prelates to define and protect their own authority, and a corresponding drive to organize their provinces and bring them into conformity with the standards obtaining in the rest of the Latin Church. For this they required up-to-the minute statements or decisions direct from the pope as the highest authority in the Church, and his authority was regularly called in to supplement and support their own. In this they were not peculiar. Archbishops Richard of Canterbury in 1174 and 1175[27] and Walter of Rouen in 1185,[28] for example, obtained batches of papal letters to confirm and reinforce their own authority.

Local separatism was also being broken down by the introduction of new or reformed religious Orders: the Cistercians, enthusiastically promoted by Bernard of Clairvaux, for example, and the Augustinian canons regular, organized in smaller congregations, like the order of Prémontré, actively encouraged by local archbishops, bishops and kings.[29]

They all had similar characteristics: they were international, followed their own distinctive rules, with uniform liturgies and biblical texts, and even standardized ground plans for the layout of their houses. To any new location, they brought a ready-made blueprint for the efficient running of the monastery. Equally important, they maintained contact with their houses across Europe and exchanged personnel, information and strategies. As well

27. A.J. Duggan, 'Making Law or Not? The Function of Papal Decretals in the Twelfth Century', in P. Erdő and S.A. Szuromi (ed.), *Proceedings of the Thirteenth International Congress of Medieval Canon Law, Esztergom 2008* (Città del Vaticano: 2010), 41-70, at 42 and esp. 44, where the archbishop obtained nine letters designed to supplement his own council of Westminster (1175).

28. Six mandates obtained from Lucius III in Verona, on or around 16.10.1185: (1) *Ad audientiam*, JL –: S. Chodorow & C. Duggan (ed. & rev.), *Decretales ineditae saeculi XII* (Città del Vaticano: 1982), 34-35, no. 19; (2) *Ad hoc sumus*, JL 15208; (3) *Ad hoc te credimus*, JL – : Chodorow & Duggan (ed. & rev.), *Decretales ineditae*, 33-34, no. 18; (4) *Cum in archiepiscopatu (Littere cum serico)*, JL 15208: J. Ramackers (ed.), *Papsturkunden in Frankreich*, ii, *Normandie* (Göttingen: 1937), 346-47, no. 252; (5) *Improba pestis falsitatis*, JL 15207: C. Duggan, "*Improba pestis falsitatis*'. Forgeries and the Problem of Forgery in Twelfth-Century Decretal Letters (with special reference to English cases)', in H. Fuhrmann (ed.), *Fälschungen im Mittelalter*, ii: *Gefälschte Rechtstexte. Der bestrafte Fälscher* (Hannover: 1988), 319-61, at 325, 345-46, no. 17 (repr. with the same pagination in C. Duggan, *Decretals and the Creation of 'New Law' in the Twelfth Century. Judges, Judgements, Equity and Law* (Aldershot: 1998), no. VIII; (6) *Quoniam sepe (littere cum serico)*, JL 15284; *PL*, cci, 1325-26, no. 202.

29. For a full treatment of this subject, see Nyberg's excellent *Monasticism in North-Western Europe*; cf. B.P. McGuire, *The Cistercians in Denmark* (Kalamazoo: 1982).

as their books and customs, however, they came with the practice of independent management of their own affairs, including the right to elect their own superiors[30] and the right to have disputes judged in ecclesiastical courts according to canonical process. Like the bishops, they also sought confirmation of their privileges and properties from the pope and could appeal to him if their rights were infringed. There was thus a regular transmission of envoys to the papal Curia, increasing in frequency as the twelfth century progressed.

2. Papal legates

Moreover, the papacy remained directly involved in the shaping of the new provinces. A legate (Theodwin) had presided at the council of Lund in 1139 and Cardinal Nicholas Breakspear was sent in 1152, presumably after some unrecorded approach from interested parties, to create two new metropolitan sees, one for Norway and the other for Sweden. Having chosen Nidaros/Trondheim as the seat of the Norwegian province,[31] he held a council at Nidaros (1153?) and issued decrees. These are lost, but may be reflected in King Håkon IV Håkonsson's law code of 1224.[32] Following that, Nicholas travelled to Sweden, where, although conditions were not conducive to appointing an archbishop, he held a council, probably at Linköping, and again issued decrees. Their text also is lost, but something

---

30. It is significant that Eskil of Lund's privilege for the cathedral monastery of S. Knud at Odense (1171) confirmed the monks' right to choose their abbot and to have the first voice in the election of the bishop, on the basis of canon law and papal precepts (*secundum canonicam eciam legem et apostolica precepta*): Kruger (ed.), *Series episcoporum*, 6/ii, *Lundensis*, 26; C.A. Christensen, H. Nielsen & L. Weibull (ed.), *Diplomatarium Danicum*, 1/iii.1 (Copenhagen: 1976), 21-24, no. 19, at 23.
31. Confirmed in Anastasius IV's privilege for Archbishop Jón Birgirsson, issued ca. November 1154, which listed the bishoprics and territories subject to the jurisdiction of Nidaros: C.R. Unger & H.J. Huitfeldt (ed.), *Diplomatarium Norvegicum*, 8, *Oldbreve* (Christiania: 1871), 1-4, no. 1; *PL*, clxxxviii, 1080-84, no. 84. The version in *PL* derives ultimately from a notarized copy made at Nidaros on 29.6.1629, which lists (col. 1083) a sequence of similar privileges from six popes, all with their seals: 'Adriani quarti, Clementis tertii, Innocentii tertii, Gregorii noni, Innocentii quarti et Clementis quarti cum impendentibus sigillis omni prorsus suspicione carentes […]'.
32. Håkon IV (1217-1263); A.O. Johnsen, *Studier vedrørende Kardinal Nicolaus Brekespears legasjon til Norden* (Oslo: 1945), ch. 6; Seegrün, *Das Papsttum*, 150-58, has been called 'over-confident in its reconstruction' (A. Bergquist, 'The Papal Legate: Nicholas Breakspear's Scandinavian Mission', in B. Bolton & A.J. Duggan (ed.), *Adrian IV. The English Pope (1154–1159), Studies and Texts* (Aldershot: 2003), 41-48, at 44, n. 17).

of their content can be gathered from the letters that Pope Anastasius IV (1153-1154) sent to Sweden after Nicholas's return to Rome. The letters, addressed respectively to the Swedish bishops and to King Sverker I[33] and the nobles, were issued on 28 November 1154, just five days before his own death (3 December 1154).[34]

To the bishops of Sweden (*episcopis Suecie*),[35] Anastasius expressed his joy at the extension of the Church to the ends of the earth (*in fines orbis terrarum*) and the excellent reception accorded to Cardinal Nicholas as the ambassador of the Apostolic See. Sending his blessing, he urged them to observe the instructions issued by the cardinal (presumably the canons first issued at Nidaros and re-issued at Linköping) and to be assiduous in instructing the people:

> 'Remember', he wrote, 'that you have been appointed watchmen to the house of Israel, the trumpet is in your mouth and you should not silence it; tell God's people their iniquity lest if you do not declare his iniquity to the impious and he dies in his sin, his blood will be required at your hand',

a play on the terrible threat in Ezekiel,[36] and they must make their own lives conform to their teaching.[37] All that was normal instruction for new bishops in new lands; but then, no doubt reflecting Nicholas's report of difficulties in Sweden, he made a significant modification to the operation of *Si quis suadente*, canon 15 of the Second Lateran Council of 1139,[38] which had

---

33. Ruler of Östergötland from 1125; king of the Swedes, etc. 1130-1156.
34. *PL*, clxxxviii, 1084-87, nos 86-87.
35. *PL*, clxxxviii, 1084-86, no. 86: *Gaudemus fratres* (28.11.1154).
36. *PL*, clxxxviii, 1085: 'Attendite quoniam speculatores dati estis domui Israel, tuba sit in gutture uestro et non detis silentium ei; annuntiate populo Dei scelera eorum, ne si forte non annuntiaueritis impio iniquitatem suam, ipse quidem moriatur in peccato suo, sanguis autem ejus de manibus uestris requiratur', For 'non annuntiaueris [...] requiratur', cf. Ezek. 3:18.
37. *PL*, clxxxviii, 1085: 'Contemptibilis quidem habetur sermo doctoris, cum predicationi ejus exemplum bone uite non concordat'.
38. Transmitted in Gratian, C.17 q.4 c.29. The Lateran decree was reissued by Eugenius III at Reims in 1148 (c.14), when Eugenius appears to have given a milder interpretation: K. Christensen, 'The "lost" gloss on Si quis suadente (C.17 q.4 c.29): John of Salisbury and the canonical tradition in the twelfth century', *BMCL* 18 (1988), 1-11. Cf. R.H. Helmholz, '*Si quis* suadente (C.17 q.4 c.29)', in P. Linehan (ed.), *Proceedings of the Seventh International Congress of Medieval Canon Law, Cambridge, 23–27 July 1984* (Città del Vaticano: 1988), 426-38.

decreed automatic excommunication for anyone who laid violent hands on a religious person:[39]

> Although it was established in the General Council that anyone who laid violent hands on a cleric should remain excommunicate until he/she comes to the Apostolic See to make satisfaction, because of the great remoteness of the territories, we are minded to moderate that constitution, so that only he/she [...] who hands over a cleric, monk or *conversus* to death or cuts off a limb should be sent for satisfaction to the Apostolic See.

Others, guilty of lesser assaults, could be absolved by the bishops, after imposing appropriate penance, as long as they had taken an oath to obey the bishops' mandates.[40] And, finally, he required them to collect and transmit to the Apostolic See the annual census (Peter's Pence), which the kingdom and people had established.

The letter to King Sverker and the nobility (*proceribus*) begins in similar fashion,[41] urges perseverance in the Christian faith, which will be achieved if they 'always keep in mind the apostolic teaching and the preaching of our brother (Cardinal Nicholas), strive to be doers of the word, not merely hearers, and persist in loyalty to the holy Roman Church'. More specifically, Anastasius instructed them 'to observe our said brother's decrees concerning the freedom of your churches, the non-bearing of arms and other matters relating to the salvation of the people'.[42]

The contents of the decrees issued at Nidaros and Linköping remain unknown, but the reference to 'the General Council', in the letter to the bishops, points directly to the Second Lateran Council, which the recipients were expected to know something about, and the phrase 'freedom of your churches' in the letter to the king and nobility suggests that the Lateran decrees against lay abuse of ecclesiastical persons and property and all forms of trafficking in sacred things (simony),[43] as well as *Si quis suadente*

---

39. *PL*, clxxxviii, 1085-86, 'licet in generali concilio sit constitutum ut quicunque in clericum uiolentas manus injecerit, tamdiu excommunicationi subjaceat donec ad sedem apostolicam satisfacturus accedat; pro longa tamen remotione terrarum eamdem constitutionem duximus temperandam, ut uidelicet his tantum qui forte [...] neci tradiderit clericum, monachum vel conuersum, vel aliquod ei membrum inciderit, satisfacturus ad sedem transmittatur apostolicam.'
40. *PL*, clxxxviii, 1085: 'Alii autem a uobis competenti satisfactione ipsis indicta, ab excommunicationis nexibus absoluantur, prestito tamen primitus iuramento, quod mandato uestro debeant obedire.'
41. *PL*, clxxxviii, 1086-87, no. 87, *Inter cetera*, (28.11.1154).
42. *PL*, clxxxviii, 1087: 'prefati fratris nostri statuta de libertate ecclesiarum uestrarum, armis non portandis et aliis ad salutem populi spectantibus firmiter obseruetis'.
43. Lateran II, cc. 1, 2, 5, 10, 24, 25, 26, 16.

Anne J. Duggan

(c.15), were re-promulgated, with the addition of what was by then the general prohibition of clerics and monks bearing arms; and, if later tradition is to be believed, a relaxation of the consanguinity rules allowed marriages in the sixth and seventh degree.[44] Something similar had happened ten or so years earlier (1143) at Valladolid. There, at a great gathering attended by prelates from León, Castile and Portugal, as well as Alfonso VII (1126/7-1157), self-styled 'Emperor of all the Spains',[45] Cardinal Guido of Pisa[46] had reissued sixteen of the Lateran decrees, together with two additional canons.[47] In the light of the Valladolid evidence, one should look for the ghost of Lateran II behind the legatine decrees in Scandinavia. Anastasius IV's modification of *Si quis suadente* in consideration of the remoteness of the region is the first such relaxation of the general law in the light of local conditions, a modification which anticipated the much fuller treatment of the subject in Celestine III's important consultation for Archbishop Eirik of Nidaros almost forty years later in 1191-1192.[48]

3. The province of Nidaros

The first archbishop of Nidaros was already bishop of the diocese when he received the dignity of archbishop from Cardinal Nicholas, but when his successor, Øystein Christianson, was appointed by King Inge Haraldsson (1136-1161)[49] in 1157, he deferred his consecration until he could receive it from the hands of the pope. Then, having opted for Alexander III as the legitimate pope in the schism in 1159,[50] he travelled to Rome for papal

44. Bergquist, 'The Papal Legate', 44-45; T.K. Nielsen, 'Pope Innocent III and Denmark, Sweden, and Norway', *Analecta Romana Instituti Danici* 28 (2001), 1-32, at 29-30, n. 96.
45. King of Galicia from 1111 and of León and Castile from 1126/7 to 1157.
46. Guido of Pisa, cardinal deacon of SS. Cosma e Damiano 1132-1149, Chancellor 1146-1149: Zenker, *Die Mitglieder des Kardinalkollegiums*, 146-48; J.M. Brixius, *Die Mitglieder des Kardinalkollegiums von 1130–1181* (Berlin: 1912), 43, 89 n. 61.
47. C. Erdmann (ed.), *Papsturkunden in Portugal* (Berlin: 1927; repr.: 1970), 198-203, no. 40: Lat. II, 1–2 = Val. 1–2; Lat. II, 3 = Val. 3 + 4; Lat. II, 5–6 = Val. 5–6; Lat. II, 7 = Val. 7 + 8; Lat. II, 8 = Val. 9; Lat. II, 10 = Val. 10-12; Lat. II, 15 = Val. 14; cc.21-22 = Val. 15-16; c.24 = Val. 17; cc. 25(*in.*) + 16 = Val. 18; c.25(*ex.*) = Val. 19; c.11 = Val. 20; c.18 = Val. 21; c.15(*ex.*) = Val. 23. The additions are: Val. 22 and 24.
48. A.J. Duggan, '*Manu sollicitudinis*: Celestine III and Canon Law', in J. Doran & D.J. Smith (ed.), *Pope Celestine III (1191–1198). Diplomat and Pastor* (Farnham: 2008), 188-235, at 199-203 and 231-35.
49. Surviving son of the assassinated King Harald Magnusson Gilli (1130-1136).
50. For the Scandinavian reaction, see Seegrün, *Das Papsttum*, 178-99, although one should beware of interpreting papal letters through the lens of 'Gregorianism'.

consecration in 1161, following which he set about establishing due order in his extended province. His first action was an attempt to stabilize the kingdom by supporting and crowning the young king Magnus Erlingsson in 1163/4, in the presence of a papal envoy, Master Stephen of Orvieto, subdeacon of the Roman Church. Stephen's presence cannot have been coincidental. Rather, it suggests that Øystein had sought papal approval for the intended coronation, and it is significant that the young king's oath contained a commitment to the holy Roman Church and Pope Alexander and his catholic successors, as well as a promise to observe 'what the Lord Pope Adrian decreed when he was legate in the realm of Norway, relating to Peter's Pence and the affairs of kingdom and Church'; and he also promised to do justice to all *secundum patrias leges et secundum sanctorum canonum statuta.*[51]

Possibly associated with the coronation was the issue of the so-called *Canones nidrosienses*, fifteen decrees relating to church order and law issued, many believe, at an ecclesiastical council in or around 1164.[52] Walther Holtzmann demonstrated their marked dependence on Gratian in 1953.[53] He showed that all but two (cc. 10 and 11) of the fifteen canons contained echoes of authorities in the *Decretum*, and some were scarcely more than mosaics of citations expertly woven together. This aspect was

---

51. W. Holtzmann, 'Krone und Kirche in Norwegen im 12. Jahrhundert (Englische analekten III)', *Deutches Archiv* 2 (1938), 341-400, at 376-77.
52. This date has been much discussed. V. Skånland, *Det eldste norske provinsialstatutt* (Oslo: 1969), favoured the 1170s, whereas O. Sandaaker, 'Canones Nidrosienses i intermesso eller opptakt?', *Historisk Tidsskrift (Oslo)* 77 (1998), 181-96, argued for 1183-1188, after Øystein's repatriation. I am very grateful to Professor Sverre Bagge of Bergen, both for advice on current Norwegian scholarship on this matter. S. Bagge, 'Den heroiske tid – kirkereform og kirkekamp 1153–1214', in S. Imsen (ed.), *Ecclesia Nidrosiensis 1153–1537. Søkelys på Nidaroskirkens og Nidarosprovinsens historie* (Trondheim: 2003), 51-80, at 55 supports a date of 1163/4 or slightly later. In challenging Sandaaker's much later dating, he cites the English manuscript evidence, which he links with Øystein's English exile from 1180 to 1183, for which see A.J. Duggan, 'The English Exile of Archbishop Øystein of Nidaros (1180–83)', in L. Napran & E. van Houts (ed.), *Exile in the Middle Ages: Selected Proceedings from the International Medieval Congress, University of Leeds 8–11 July 2002* (Turnhout: 2004), 109-30, at 123. Although I have allowed the possibility that they were issued by Nicholas Breakspear in 1152/3, as argued by O. Kolsrud in 'Kardinal-legaten Nicolaus av Albano i Noreg 1152', *Historisk Tidsskrift* 33 (1945), 485-512, I am now inclined to favour the later date.
53. Holtzmann, 'Krone und Kirche in Norwegen', 376-82; W. Holtzmann, 'Die Benutzung Gratians in der päpstlichen Kanzlei im 12. Jahrhundert', *Studia Gratiana* 1 (1953), 325-49, esp. 347-48.

recently discussed by Anders Winroth in respect of cc. 2-6.[54] He commented on the evident juridical skill of the compiler and concluded, not unreasonably, that Master Stephen compiled the canons, in consultation with Archbishop Øystein, al-though the presence in Øystein's household five years later (1169) of two *magistri* with Anglo/Norman names allows the possibility that the necessary legal skill was already available closer to home.[55] One short example may be cited for illustration. Canon 14 (in Holtzmann's numeration)[56] combines parts of two chapters from Gratian. The first segment, ordaining that churches may not be deprived of their tithes if clerics or lay persons of either sex assign their own houses or properties to somewhere else (*alicubi*), contains most of Causa 16 q.1 c.42;[57] the second, which declares that monks and clerics who profess the common life should not be compelled to pay tithes from the fruit of their own labour or from their own provisions, paraphrases the core of Causa16 q.1 c.47.[58]

No *auctoritates* were cited in the uniquely surviving English manuscript, but spaces were left between the canons for later insertion by the rubricator.[59] These would have named the authority as transmitted in Gratian: 'in Maguntiensi Concilio' (Mainz, 922) for the first and 'Pascalis II' (1099-1118) for the second. The *canones* are evidence that a version of Gratian's Recension II was available for systematic use in Norway in 1163/4, possibly brought by Master Stephen, although transmission by other hands is not impossible.[60]

Although laced with the language of Gratian, some of the Nidaros/Bergen decrees, like the clauses on lay abuses and lay investiture, were in the spirit of Lateran II.[61] The decree that priests must not wear the cloaks, 'called *schut* in Norwegian', is a particular application of Lateran II's requirement

---

54. A. Winroth, 'Decretum Gratiani and Eystein's Canones Nidrosienses', in T. Iversen (ed.), *Archbishop Eystein as Legislator. The European Connection* (Trondheim: 2011), 73-86, at 76-84.
55. Below, at n. 67.
56. He counts the oath sworn by King Magnus as the first canon.
57. 'Laici uel clerici et persone utriusque sexus, si proprietatis sue [loca uel r]es alicubi delegauerint, decimationis prouentum priori ecclesie legitime assignatam inde abstrahere nullam habent penitus potestatem.'
58. 'Monachi autem uel clerici communem uitam professi de laboribus et propriis nutrimentis suis episcopis uel quibuslibet personis decimas reddere minime compellantur.'
59. Duggan, 'English Exile of Archbishop Øystein', 123.
60. Gratian's *Decretum* was being cited in letters of Theobald of Canterbury in 1160: *The Letters of John of Salisbury*, i: *The Early Letters*, ed. and trans. W.J. Millor and H.E. Butler, Nelson's Medieval Texts (London: 1955; reissued, Oxford: 1986), 226-37, no. 131, at 231.
61. *Can. Nidrosienses*, 2 (cf. Lat. II: 5, 10), 4 (cf. Lat. I: 25).

of appropriate dress for clerics,[62] as is the instruction that cathedral canons must elect a new bishop within three months of the death of his predecessor, and if they are not unanimous, the metropolitan must choose the better man, on grounds of merit and education.[63]

Others, however, concern local problems not directly treated by Lateran II: priests should not undertake secular business, but could, if driven by poverty, engage in an occupation (*artificio*) that did not discredit their office (12); bishops, priests and others 'fighting in the Church should be distinct from those fighting in the world' and should not bear arms or attend royal expeditions except to give counsel (3); the rules of celibacy were eased (7-9); priests may not refuse to baptize children of unknown parentage (10); marriages may not be dissolved at will (11); bishops may not ordain 'alien' clergy[64] without letters or permission from their own bishops (13); churches should not lose tithes when properties are transferred to others (14); clerics may not be tried by the ordeal of hot iron (*candensis ferri*): if there is insufficient evidence, then seven reputable priests should swear to their innocence (purgation) (15).[65] One clause, however, stands somewhat apart. Clause 5 decreed that the archbishop himself was to be elected by his suffragans in consultation with the clergy and people of the cathedral city, following which he should go to the supreme pontiff for consecration, accompanied by his archdeacons and senior clergy.

Professor Winroth considered this an absurd example of 'armchair legislation', drafted by a 'Roman bureaucrat' wholly out of touch with the realities of the situation in the Norwegian Church and the dangers of long-distance travel from Nidaros, pointing out, for example, that the legate himself was shipwrecked off the Yorkshire coast as he travelled back in 1163/4.[66] But the instruction was more likely to have come from Øystein himself. After all, he had made the long journey to Rome for his own consecration only two or three years earlier in 1161. It is not known who travelled

62. *Can. Nidrosienses*, 16 (cf. Lat. II: 4).
63. *Can. Nidrosienses*, 6 (cf. Lat. II: 28).
64. Meaning from outside their own dioceses.
65. This was a standard canonical solution to the problem of evidence, traceable to a decree of the Visigothic Council of Agde (506), transmitted in Gratian, *Decretum*, C.2 q.5 c.12: 'Si legitimi accusatores crimina sacerdotis probare non potuerint, et ipse negauerit, cum septem sociis suis eius ordinis (si ualet) a crimine semetipsum expurget.' A similar directive had been given by Innocent II in a case relating to Bishop Altmann of Trento (1138 x 1142): Gratian, *Decretum*, C.2 q.5 c.17; *Liber Extra* (X), 5.34.5 (§§ab), in A. Friedberg (ed.), *Corpus iuris canonici II, Decretalium collectiones* (Graz: 1959 – repr.), cols 870-71.
66. Winroth, 'Decretum Gratiani and Eystein's Canones Nidrosienses', 85. I suggested in 2004 that Stephen fell victim to the notorious Redcar rocks (where Oystein's ship foundered in 1180): Duggan, 'English Exile of Archbishop Øystein', 114.

with him, but he would not have travelled alone. Consecration by the hands of the pope conferred a special dignity on the recipient, and it was one that others were seeking. Archbishop Richard of Canterbury, for example, travelled to Anagni in 1174. Moreover, such visits were a perfect opportunity for successive archbishops to establish a personal relationship with the pope and cardinals.

Five years later, in late 1169, possibly spurred by the murder of Bishop Thorstein of Oslo, Øystein sent Godfrey ('Godefridus') and Walter, two of his *magistri*, to present a series of very specific questions (*consultationes*) to the Curia.[67] The result was a dossier of up to eleven letters, which together comprised what I have recently called 'a blueprint for the organization of his province'.[68] Among the *responsa* were definitions of his own rights of discipline,[69] guidance on questions relating to liturgical practice[70] and the use of the pallium,[71] as well as condemnation of trial by ordeal of hot iron (*per igniti ferri examinationem*)[72] and secular control of ecclesiastical offices.[73] Particular emphasis was placed on the binding quality of Christian marriage as a commitment for life, in which neither partner was free to marry during the lifetime of the other.[74]

67. A.J. Duggan, 'The Decretals of Archbishop Øystein of Trondheim (Nidaros)', in U.-R. Blumenthal, K. Pennington & A.A. Larson (ed.), *Proceedings of the Twelfth International Congress of Medieval Canon Law, Washington D.C., 1–7 August 2004* (Città del Vaticano: 2008), 491-529, Appendix, no. 7 (Chodorow & Duggan (ed. & rev.), *Decretales ineditae*, 152-53, no. 87); cf. Holtzmann, 'Krone und Kirche', 391-92, no. 7.
68. A.J. Duggan, 'Eystein, Thomas Becket, and the Wider Christian World', in K. Bjørlykke et al. (ed.), *Eystein Erlendsson – erkebiskop, politiker og kirkebygger* (Trondheim: 2012), 24-41, at 36.
69. Duggan, 'Decretals of Archbishop Øystein', 504-05 and Appendix, nos. 8(f) and 10(a-c); Holtzmann, 'Krone und Kirche', 383-95, nos. 8(§1) and 10(§§1-3).
70. Duggan, 'Decretals of Archbishop Øystein', 505 and Appendix, nos. 2(§§d, f), 5, 6(§§a, c-e), 8(§§c-d), 12(§a): Holtzmann, 'Krone und Kirche', 383-95, nos. 2(§§4, 6), 6(§§1, 3-5), 8(§§3-4), 12(§1). Even in the thirteenth century, problems relating to the use of liquids other than water in baptism gave rise to concern: see M. Kauftold, 'Eine norwegische Biertaufe: Probleme liturgische Normierung im 13. Jahrhundert', *Zeitschrift der Savigny-Stiftung für Rechtsgeschichte, kanonistische Abteilung* 83 (1997), 362-76.
71. Duggan, 'Decretals of Archbishop Øystein', 503 and Appendix, no. 8(§c); Holtzmann, 'Krone und Kirche', 383-95, no. 8(§3).
72. Duggan, 'Decretals of Archbishop Øystein', 505 and Appendix, no. 8(§a); Holtzmann, 'Krone und Kirche', 383-95, no. 8(§1).
73. Duggan, 'Decretals of Archbishop Øystein', 504 and Appendix, no. 9; Holtzmann, 'Krone und Kirche', 383-95, no. 9.
74. Duggan, 'Decretals of Archbishop Øystein', 505-06 and Appendix, no. 12(§b); omitted by Holtzmann, 'Krone und Kirche'.

Simultaneously, however, the letters acknowledged local needs. Øystein was authorized to grant indulgences to pilgrims visiting St Olav's shrine in Nidaros[75] and to moderate the general law in the light of the difficult conditions in the province. One important concession, for example, allowed Øystein to relax the consanguinity rules for the inhabitants of an island 'twelve days and more (*xii dietas et amplius*)' distant from Norway, almost certainly meaning Greenland. They were to be allowed to marry within the fifth, sixth and seventh degrees of consanguinity, until such time as the Almighty removes the pressing need (*donec omnipotens dominus tantam ab eis aufert necessitate*)'.[76] This was in fact an interesting anticipation of the crucially important determination of the Fourth Lateran Council in 1215 (c.50), which reduced the prohibition to the fourth degree.[77] Other concessions allowed him to arrange the celebration of religious feasts, which should be celebrated *de vespera in vesperam*, according to the length of the days (*sicut magnitudo dierum exigit celebrari*),[78] and to relax the ban on servile labour on Sundays and feast days, except the most solemn, so that the people could catch herring (*alecia*) if a shoal came close to the shore on those days (*si alecia terre se inclinaverint*), and to substitute fish or other food when fasting on bread and water was imposed as a penance.[79] In this instance, what one may call the 'herring privilege' was adopted into the vernacular Frostathing Law in 1274, where it was described as an act of papal clemency bestowed in response to petitions from King Magnus, his father Erling Skakke and Archbishop Øystein.[80] These responses were supplemented in a later letter from 1173, giving advice on the celebration of

---

75. Duggan, 'Decretals of Archbishop Oystein', 509 and Appendix, no. 11(§b); Holtzmann, 'Krone und Kirche', 383-95, no. 11(§2).
76. Chodorow & Duggan (ed. & rev.), *Decretales ineditae*, 1149-51, no. 86, at 149; Duggan, 'Decretals of Archbishop Oystein', Appendix, no. 1; Holtzmann, 'Krone und Kirche', 383-95, no. 1.
77. On the background to this, A.J. Duggan, '"Our letters have not usually made law (*legem facere*) on such matters" (Alexander III, 1169): a new look at the formation of the canon law of marriage in the twelfth century', in J. Goering, A. Thier & S. Dusil (ed.), *Proceedings of the Fourteenth International Congress of Medieval Canon Law, Toronto, 5–11 August 2012* (Città del Vaticano: forthcoming).
78. From *Licet tam ueteris*: *X* 2.9.2.
79. *X* 2.9.3 + 5.38.6, with mistaken address to 'the archbishop of Tribur'!: Duggan, 'Decretals of Archbishop Oystein', Appendix, no. 5 (§§a and b); Holtzmann, 'Krone und Kirche', 383-95, no. 5(§§1and 2).
80. Noted by P. Landau, 'Canon Law in the Periphery of Europe: the example of Archbishop Eystein', in Iversen (ed.), *Eystein as Legislator*, 70-71, citing R. Meissner, *Norwegisches Recht. Das Rechtsbuch des Frostathings, Germanenrecht* 4 (Weimar: 1939), 32.

the feast of St Matthias in leap years, which was recorded in the *Ordo Nidrosiensis*.⁸¹

Øystein's decretals demonstrate the operation of an effective partnership between a Norwegian archbishop and the pope (Alexander III) in the consolidation of the archbishop's authority and the establishment of regular order and discipline in the Norwegian Church, very much tailored to the needs of the region; and that partnership was continued under his successor.

When Eirik Ivarsson, archbishop of Nidaros (1189-1205), was forced into exile (in Lund) in 1191 because of his refusal to crown King Sverre and disagreements about ecclesiastical rights and immunities, he turned to Celestine III, who issued a comprehensive memorandum on the rights of the Norwegian Church from St Peter's on 15 June 1194 (*Ea cura et diligentia*), witnessed by twenty-three cardinals, including Lothario, cardinal deacon of SS. Sergio e Baccho, the later Innocent III.⁸² Eiric and the church of Nidaros were taken under the protection of St Peter and the pope, all their rights, properties and immunities were confirmed, followed by specific confirmations, including the right to appoint suitable persons to chapels founded or endowed by royal generosity, 'as in the other churches and chapels of your province', without [the kings'] assent or presentation, according to the renunciation of rights of patronage made by public instrument and privilege',⁸³ and a declaration that elections of bishops and abbots should be entirely free (*nulla uis, nulla potentia, nulla auctoritas vel consensus regis seu principis interueniat*) and only the man who the electors agree is more fitting in learning and habits (*moribus*) should obtain the office.⁸⁴ The clergy of the kingdom of Norway should enjoy due liberty, and, when they possess no *regalia*, no bishop, abbot, or cleric should take up arms or go on expedition, or be compelled to supply anything for this purpose, unless so grave a need occurs in which the diocesan bishop and the wiser and more

---

81. L. Gjerløw (ed.), *Ordo Nidrosiensis ecclesiae* (Oslo: 1968), 87-88; Duggan, 'Decretals of Archbishop Oystein', 506 and Appendix, no. 12 (a); omitted by Holtzmann, 'Krone und Kirche'.
82. *PL*, ccvi, 1039-42, no. 162; *Dip. Nor.*, ii, no. 3; see Nielsen's excellent summary in T.K. Nielsen, 'Celestine III and the North', in Doran & Smith (ed.), *Pope Celestine III*, 159-78, at 172-76.
83. *PL*, ccvi, 1040: 'Licitum quoque sit tibi et successoribus tuis in capellis, a regia libertate fundatis uel dotatis, sicut in aliis ecclesiis uel capellis prouinciae tuae, idoneas instituere sine ipsorum assensu uel presentatione personas, secundum renuntiationem, quam de iure patronatus per publica instrumenta et per priuilegia sua constat eosdem reges fecisse.'
84. *PL*, ccvi, 1040.

discreet ecclesiastics agree that it should be permitted. And a great deal more.[85]

Pilgrims to St Olav's shrine were to be protected; clerics must not submit to secular judgment; consecrated churches should not be destroyed or moved without approval of the diocesan bishop; no king or prince may change the written laws of the country (*patria*) without the consent of the bishops and the advice of the learned (*sapientum*), or change the monetary penalties whether for clerics or for laymen to the detriment of the churches, or exact homage from any bishop or abbot without regalia. And when the bishops who had remained in Norway crowned Sverre (19 June 1194), Celestine solemnly excommunicated them in St Peter's,[86] and Nicholas of Oslo (1195), Njål of Stavanger (1197) and Mårten of Hamar (1199) duly sought reconciliation with Eirik. Meanwhile, Eirik excommunicated Sverre, and Innocent III finally interdicted the kingdom (6 October 1198).[87] Sverre's son then made peace with the archbishop, enabling him to release the dying Sverre and his followers from the excommunication and interdict.

4. The province of Lund

Simultaneously, in Denmark, papal authority was invoked to legitimize new ventures such as the approval of the transformation of the Benedictine Veng into a Cistercian monastery (1165), an action which demonstrates that King Valdemar I (1157-1181) had returned to Alexander's obedience by that time.[88] This was followed four years later (4 November 1169) by the grant to Absalon of Roskilde[89] of jurisdiction over the recently converted Wends

---

85. *PL*, ccvi, 1040: 'ne aliquis episcopus, abbas seu clericus, cum ipsi regalia non habeant, arma sumere uel in expeditionem ire, uel ad hoc quidquam de suo impendere compellantur; nisi forte necessitas tam grauis immineat, quod id a dioecesano episcopo et sapientioribus et discretioribus uiris ecclesiasticis communicato consilio fieri permittatur.'
86. 18.11.1194, as recorded in William of Aebelholt's letter to Celestine III: *PL*, ccix, 675, no. ii.2.
87. Unger & Huitfeldt (ed.), *Diplomatarium Norwegicum* vi, 7; Eirik Vandvik: *Latinske dokument til norsk historie fram til år 1204* (Oslo: 1959), no. 36.
88. *PL*, cc, 428-30 nos 415-16, addressed respectively to King Valdemar and Bishops Absalon of Roskilde and Tuco (*Tuconi*) of Børglum and bishops-elect Ralph of Ribe and Svein of Åarhus, approving the proposed change and urging the recall of Archbishop Eskil.
89. Absalon was bp of Roskilde 1157/8-92 and abp of Lund 1177/8-1201: *Series episcoporum*, 6/ii, *Lundensis*, ed. Kluger, 89-93 (Roskilde) and 28-33 (Lund); cf. *Archbishop Absalon of Lund and his World*, ed. K. Friis-Jensen and I. Skovgaard-Petersen (Roskilde: 2000).

on Rügen Island[90] and, more important for the consolidation of the dynasty, the authorization of the canonization of Valdemar's murdered father, Knud Lavard (d. 1131). The Rügen letter was issued in response to letters from King Valdemar and others, the intervention (*interventu*) of Eskil of Lund and the bishops and people of the realm, and at the earnest supplication (*instantia*) of Archbishop Stephen of Uppsala, Abbot Briennus [from Kalvø],[91] Master John, the king's envoy,[92] and Master Walter, Absalon's clerk.[93] The word *instantia* suggests that all four (Stephen, Briennus, John, and Walter) were at the papal Curia together.

That such was indeed the case, is confirmed by the canonization letter, issued just four days later (8 November). Addressed to Archbishop Eskil, legate of the Apostolic See, 'and all the bishops, abbots, priors, and other prelates in Denmark', Knud's canonization was granted in response to written petitions (from the king, archbishops, and bishops) and the scrupulous account of the 'archbishop of Uppsala and those who came with him', who were prepared to testify on oath that miracles had been performed at Knud's tomb (in Ringsted Abbey, now Skt Bendts Kirke), which had been the centre of a local cult for some time, specifying 25 June (1170) as the date for the elevation of Knud's relics, no doubt in accordance with the king's specific request.[94]

It is noteworthy also, that Valdemar and Absalon were represented by *magistri*, members of the learned élite, perhaps with legal learning. Their

90. Rügen Island is now linked by a bridge to Stralsund in Germany.
91. The recently-colonized Cistercian house (1168), from which the important monastery of *Carus locus/Cara Insula* (Øm) was later founded (1172): Nyberg, *Monasticism*, 112, 188-93, 248, figg. 12.1-2. See Alexander III's letter to King Valdemar: PL, cc, 650-52 no. 693, on the complaint of Abbot Briennus.
92. Possibly the later archbishop of Uppsala: below, n. 132.
93. PL, cc, 607-08 no. 632 (Benevento, 4 Nov. 1169), *Cum Christianae fidei*, at 608: 'interuentu quoque uenerabilium fratrum nostrorum E. Lundensis archiepiscopi apostolicae sedis legati et episcoporum et principum regni et instantia uenerabilis fratris nostri Upsalensis archiepiscopi et dilectorum filiorum nostrorum Brianensis [recte Brienni] abbatis, Joannis magistri nuntii ejusdem regis et magistri Galteri clerici tui nihilominus inclinati'. Could this Master John be the later Archbishop Jöns of Uppsala (1185-57) who obtained a solemn confirmation of his rights from Lucius III in 1185: below, at n. 133.
94. PL, cc, 608-09 no. 633 (Benevento, 8 Nov. 1169), *Ex litteris charissimi*, at 608: 'Ex litteris charissimi in Christo filii nostri W. illustris Danorum regis, necnon ex scriptis uestris *atque ex diligenti narratione uenerabilis fratris nostri Upsalensis archiepiscopi et illorum qui secum uenerunt'*. Stephen's leading rôle was noted in St Knud's liturgy, which also records that Valdemar consulted Archbishop Eskil about the translation: *The Offices and Masses of St. Knud Lavard*, 2 vols, ed. J. Bergsagel (Copenhagen and Ottawa: 2010), ii, 36.

names suggest English, Norman, or French origins, and it was they who negotiated the precise legal form of the privilege which granted Absalon the *curam et administrationem illius insule* [...] *quantum ad spiritualia*, and added weight to the promotion of St Knud, whose translation formed the setting for the coronation of Valdemar's seven-year-old son as co-ruler (Cnud VI, co-ruler 1170-1182; sole king 1182-1202). St Knud's elevation not only created a royal and national saint for Denmark, but contributed significantly to the establishment of the Valdemarian dynasty.

5. The province of Uppsala

Such direct consultation of the papacy was becoming commonplace. In the same year that Øystein secured his dossier (1169), Stephen, the first archbishop of Uppsala, took advantage of his membership of the royal Danish embassy, discussed above, to obtain a mandate addressed to his 'parishioners', forbidding them to accuse him or any other ecclesiastical prelate before laymen or to draw them before secular judgment (*nec eum aut alium quemlibet ecclesie prelatum coram laicis accusare, seu ad seculare iudicium trahere presumatis*), since the archbishop's person was subject only to the judgment (*examini*) of the Roman pontiff.[95] This was followed, two or three years later, by an even more important embassy, led by Fulk, the newly created missionary bishop to Estonia.[96] In 1171 or 1172 he obtained the famous 'September letters', a dossier of nine instruments issued from Tusculum and addressed to various Scandinavian recipients.[97]

---

95. *Suggestum est nobis*, PL, cc, 609-10, no. 634 (Benevento, 8.11.1169). The mandate, complete with bull suspended by a hempen cord, still survives: Stockholm, Riksarkivet, Orig. perg. (1167) 8/11. I am very grateful to Peter Ståhl of the National Archives in Stockholm for providing a fine image of the original.
96. On him, see L. Falkenstein, 'Die Sirmondsche Sammlung der 56 Litterae Alexanders III', in R. Hiestand (ed.), *Hundert Jahre Papsturkundenforschung. Bilanz – Methoden – Perspektiven* (Göttingen: 2003), 302-03, who also corrects the mistaken belief that he was a Cistercian: he was, of course, a Benedictine, trained under Peter of Celle at Montier-la-Celle.
97. Tiina Kala is seriously mistaken in writing that Alexander was at that time in exile in the south of France and that 'Eskil was not on best terms with the Danish king [...] so the appointment of Fulco could have been an expression of their mutual political support' ('The Incorporation of the Northern Baltic Lands', in *Crusade and Conversion on the Baltic Frontier*, 3). Alexander had withdrawn from France in September 1165; Valdemar I had renounced the schism and recognized Alexander III after the death of the anti-pope 'Victor IV' (d. 20.4.1164) and had recalled Eskil (ca. late 1167). The two papal letters (*PL*, cc, 428-30, nos 425-26: 1165) had urged Eskil's recall; cf. Nyberg, *Monasticism*, 190-92, 248.

Three related to his own mission, but the other six, which mostly concerned the enhancement of episcopal authority, responded to consultations respecttively from the archbishop of Uppsala and the bishops of Linköping and Strängnäs.[98]

Fulk's letters reflect the collaboration between Eskil of Lund and Peter of Celle, then abbot of St-Rémi in Reims,[99] to secure Pope Alexander's support for a mission to Estonia.[100] The first, *Lex divina*,[101] to Øystein of Nidaros and A(mund), former bishop of Stavanger (???-1171),[102] requested and admonished them (*rogamus attentius et monemus*) to allow the monk Nicholas, said to be Estonian (*de gente illa*), to accompany Bishop Fulk on his mission; the second,[103] a general letter addressed to the kings, princes and all Christ's faithful in the realms of the Danes, Norwegians, *Guetemorum* and Goths (*regibus et principibus, et aliis Christi fidelibus, per regna Danorum, Norvegensium, Guetomorum, et Gothorum constitutis*), encouraged armed intervention and granted all who participated an indulgence of one year, similar to that granted to those who visited the tomb of the Lord in Jerusalem (*sicut his qui sepulcrum Dominicum uisitant, concedere consueuimus*), and a full indulgence to those who died in the enterprise, subject in both cases to prior confession of sins and acceptance of penance. The third, to all God's faithful in Denmark (*Ad universos Dei*

---

98. *PL*, cc, nos 977, 980, 983 (Fulk); nos 975, 976, 979 (Uppsala); nos 974, 984 (Linköping); no. 973 (Strängnäs). The letters survived, not in Scandinavia, but in a now lost manuscript assembled in the monastery of St-Rémi in Reims, first published by J. Sirmond in 1613 (J. Sirmond (ed.), *Petri Abbatis Cellensis qui post deinde S. Remigii Remensis Abbas, et Episcopus fuit Carnotensis, Epistolarum libri IX* [...] [Paris: 1613]): cf. Falkenstein, 'Die Sirmondsche Sammlung', 267-334, esp. 277-78, nos 19-27 and 299-304; cf. J. Haseldine (ed. and trans.), *The Letters of Peter of Celle* (Oxford: 2001), 340-47, nos 76-77, 398-401, 399 n. 1, 422-27, nos 104-05, 686-89, no. 181, 719-20; L. Weibull, 'Påven Alexander III: septemberbrev til Norden', *Scandia* 13 (1940), 90-98.
99. Abbot of Montier-la-Celle ca. 1145-1162, abbot of St-Rémi 1162-1181 and bishop of Chartres 1181-late 1183: *Letters of Peter of Celle*, xxxi-xxxii.
100. For the broader context, see I. Fonnesberg-Schmidt, *The Popes and the Baltic Crusades, 1147–1254* (Leiden: 2007), 56-65.
101. *PL*, cc, 852-53, no. 977 (JL 12115), *Lex divina*, Tusculum, 9.9.[1171/2].
102. The bishopric had been established in ca. 1112 by Reginald (Reinald), an English Benedictine from Winchester, and was dedicated to St Swithun. Reginald was hanged in 1135 by King Harald Gille.
103. *PL*, cc, 860-61, no. 980 (JL 12118); *Diplomatarium Danicum*, 1/iii.1, no. 27: *Non parum animus*, 11.9.1171/2; cf. I. Fonnesberg-Schmidt, 'Alexander III and the Crusades', in Clarke & Duggan (ed.), *Pope Alexander III*, 341-64, at 355-59, esp. 356-57.

fideles per Daciam constitutos), urged them to give material support to Bishop Fulk.[104]

Two of the three letters to Stephen of Uppsala are similar in purpose to those impetrated by Øystein's clerks two or three years earlier.[105] They are essentially reinforcements of the archbishop's authority, underlining his right to deal effectively with the particular problems of a semi-Christianized society and a defiant clergy.

The first, addressed to Stephen and his suffragans,[106] is virtually a penitential code, condemning infanticide, incest, bestiality,[107] consanguinity and the killing of small children in various circumstances. Those who kill their own children, or counsel or consent to it, or kill their parents/close relatives (*parricidas*), or have illicit relations with their mother, daughter, first cousin (*consobrina*), or niece (*nepta*), or unite with beasts of burden (*jumentis*)[108] should be compelled to go to the Apostolic See, unless they are too old or too poor. Those who, while sleeping, inadvertently suffocate a child, should do penance for three years if the child was baptized, but five years if it was not; but if the parents were absent when the death occurred, or the child was in the charge of another, they were blameless, unless they had entrusted the child to a mad woman (*furiosa*). Passing from the misdeeds of the lay population, the letter condemned priests who used dried-up dregs and crumbs of bread dipped in wine to celebrate Mass: only bread and wine mixed with water could be used in the sacrifice of the body and blood of Christ. Finally, marriages should not be celebrated clandestinely and without the blessing of a priest, or between persons related within seven degrees of consanguinity, nor can they be dissolved except canonically with the consent of the bishop. Stephen and his suffragans, however, were directed not to separate those joined in the fifth or fourth degree, although they must forbid them in the future.

The second (*Constituti a Domino*), also addressed to Stephen and his suffragans in Sweden and Götaland (*Gothia*), is one of the longest letters

---

104. *PL*, cc, 863, no. 983 (JL 12120): *Omnes qui pie*, Tusculum, 17.9.
105. Above, at nn. 67-81. The third letter, *PL*, cc, 851-52, no. 976 (JL 12114), *Grauis admodum*, Tusculum, 9.9.1171/2, to Stephen and Jarl Guthorm (Guthermus), instructed them not to help the Finns, because they had abandoned the Christian faith and abused preachers.
106. *PL*, cc, 849-52, no. 975 (JL 12113): Tusculum, 9.9.1171/2.
107. Honorius III referred to bestiality (*brutis animalibus [...] se nefarie commiscendo*) in a *responsum* to the archbishop of Lund in 1227: *Svenskt Diplomatarium* online, 248-49, no. 242, cited by Mia Korpiola, 'Animal Passions: Bestiality and the Law in Medieval and Reformation Sweden', forthcoming in the *festschrift* for Mario Ascheri.
108. Cf. Levit. 18:23; 20:15.

sent to Scandinavian recipients in the twelfth century.[109] It opens with a fierce denunciation of the *abusio* [...] *et insolentia laicorum*, concentrating on the practice of lay appointment, everywhere attended by various forms of simony (*omnia simoniace, siue per pecuniam, siue per priuatam gratiam, uel odium agentes*). Through this practice, priests are appointed without proof of ordination, so that runaway monks, sometimes murderers, assumed the priestly office, while others bribe the influential to supplant the incumbent priest. In addition, clerics in litigation with laymen find themselves forced to submit to the judgment of laymen (*laicorum judicia*) and prosecute or defend according to their *instituta siue leges*. Not only minor clerics, but bishops themselves (*uos ipsi*) can be summoned to the ordeal of hot iron (*ad igniti ferri examen*) or some other execrable trial (*exsecrabile judicium*).[110] Further, clerics are regularly beaten or killed with impunity.

After a call to arms, the letter lays out a tariff of penalties, citing authorities from Gratian ('Recension II') for nearly every sentence – a feature to which Marcel Pacaut drew attention nearly seventy years ago in 1954.[111] I count twenty-four references, and a more diligent search may find more. Clerics who accept a church or investiture from a layman, whether freely or for a price, are to be excommunicated; a priest who buys a church is to be deprived and degraded. Clergy from another diocese should not be accepted without letters from their own bishop (citing the fifth-century council of Chalcedon); clergy should not be drawn before secular tribunals; trial by boiling water or hot iron or single combat is not permitted; tithes should be faithfully paid and if necessary compelled by threat of anathema, after three admonitions; gifts made to churches cannot be taken back; those who lay violent hand on clerics, except in self-defence, incur excommunication, which can be raised only by the Roman pontiff or by his mandate. In conclusion he orders the recipients to accept and observe (*acquiescite [...] observate*) all the above.

The broad contents of these two letters might well be compared with the Øystein's decretals and with the *canones nidrosienses*, as well as with the Northumbrian priests' law, drawn up in Old English by Wulfstan of York between 1008 and 1023.[112] Like the *canones*, the second letter, especially,

---

109. *PL*, cc, 854-60, no. 979 (JL 12117): *Constituti a Domino*, Tusculum, 10.9.1171/2.
110. This paragraph is an interesting antecedent of Lateran Council III, c.14, par. *Praeterea quia*: *Oecumenical Councils*, 218-19.
111. M. Pacaut, *Alexandre III. Étude sur la conception du pouvoir pontifical dans sa pensée et dans son oeuvre* (Paris: 1954), 313-17.
112. *Councils and Synods*, 1/i, 449-68, esp. the penalties: for receiving or buying another priest's church, unless he has committed a serious crime [2:1]-[2.2]; for disobedience to the bishop [3]-[4]; for taking an ecclesiastical case to a layman [5]; for wrongly receiving ordination outside the diocese [12]; for consecrating the host in a wooden

was heavily laden with direct quotations from Gratian. Should one infer that the Curia expected there to be copies of the *Decretum* available in Sweden, or the opposite? The French-educated Cistercian archbishop of Uppsala might well have been expected to have the book, or a good abbreviation, in his possession, but that cannot have been assumed for the whole of his province. I am inclined to think that the second letter was drafted at Stephen's request for circulation among the senior clergy of the province, for whom it provided a succinct summary of essential rules, supported by authorities drawn from the generally received book of canon law (Gratian) and underwritten by the authority of the pope. The same was being done elsewhere in the Latin West. As I argued recently in respect of Normandy, citing a canon from a venerable *codex* was much less effective than a short letter from a living authority. Prelates found it helpful to have new statements addressed directly to themselves and expressed as forcefully as the papal chancery could devise. When faced with defiance or dumb resistance, they could cite the authority, not only of their own office, but also that of the Apostolic See.[113] Holding up a letter from the living pope, with the leaden *bulla* suspended from it, carried more weight than the ancient canons. Not only could it be read at synods, but it could be copied and circulated to all the bishops.

Three further letters demonstrate the drawing of papal authority into local affairs. The two to Conon (Kol) of Linköping (1171/2?-1185) concerned his irregular appointment. In the first (*Ex dispensatione*),[114] Alexander approved the resignation of his predecessor Stenar (11??-1171/2),[115] who had freely resigned his episcopal dignity into the hands of Archbishop Eskil and the *regalia* in the presence of the king (Knut Eriksson) and magnates of the realm (*pontificalem dignitatem in manu venerabilis fratris nostri Eskili Londensis archiepiscopi, apostolicae sedis legati, et regalia coram rege et primatibus regni libere et spontanee resignante*), even though such

        chalice [15]; for celebrating Mass without wine [17]; for wrongfully driving a priest from his church [22]; for wounding a priest [23]; for slaying a priest or deacon [24]; for refusing to submit to the bishop's ordinance [45]; and for indulging in heathen practices (sacrifice or divination) or practising witchcraft [48]; as well as rules for marriage [61]-[62], [64], [65].
113. A.J. Duggan, 'Canon Law in Normandy, *c*.1100–1234' in Y. Mausen & G. Davy (ed.), *Normandie, terre des traditions juridiques* (forthcoming).
114. *PL*, cc, 849, no. 974 (JL 12112): *Ex dispensatione commisse nobis*, Tusculum, 8.9.1171/2.
115. Stenar transferred to Växjö in Denmark. Twenty years later (1191), Colon (Kol) of Linköping appealed against him to Celestine III. Celestine ordered Stenar to restore Linköping's rights and delegated the trial of the border dispute to the legate Cinthius, CD of S. Lorenzo in Lucina, Peter of Uppsala and Jerulf of Scara: *PL*, ccvi, 906-07, nos. 39 and 40, Lateran, 28.12.[1191].

resignation was not permitted without the authority of the Roman pontiff, and confirmed Conon's election by the clergy and people, with the assent of the archbishop, king and local Jarl (*de assensu predictorum archiepiscopi et regis, atque ducis terre, te in patrem et episcopum suum unanimiter et concorditer elegerunt*).[116]

Two aspects of this exchange are significant: that Conon should have sought papal confirmation in the form of a bull, *cum (filo) serico*;[117] that the bull reinforced the canonical requirement that bishops' resignations required papal approval[118] and should be of their own volition and freely made (*libere et spontanee*); that elections should be free, with the approval of archbishop and king. Equally important, however, was the clear distinction between the spiritual authority of the episcopal dignity subject to the archbishop and the secular rights (*regalia*) held under royal and ducal authority. This short authorization (257 words) was accompanied by an equally short mandate to the clergy and laity of Linköping.[119] They were ordered to show the same obedience and respect to Bishop (Kol) as they had to the renowned Gisle, his predecessor of happy memory (ca. 1139-1160s).[120] More specifically, they were to obey his admonitions and mandates in the things of God and in matters relating to their own salvation and answer fully to his judgments (*et plenarie respondeatis*); and the pope would confirm any sentence reasonably imposed on the contumacious.[121]

---

116. For a recent discussion of the possible political manoeuverings behind the resignation of Stenar and the election of Kol, see P. Line, *Kingship and State Formation in Sweden 1130–1290* (Leiden: 2007), 97-98.
117. Meaning that the *bulla* would have been suspended by a red and yellow silken cord. The solemn character of the letter is indicated by the final formula, 'Decernimus ergo ut nulli omnino hominum hanc paginam nostre confirmationis infringere liceat, uel ei aliquatenus contraire. Si quis autem hoc attentare presumpserit, indignationem omnipotentis Dei et beatorum Petri et Pauli apostolorum ejus se nouerit incursurum.' Generally used to adorn *privilegia*, the silken cord indicated the enhanced authority of the letter: see L. Falkenstein, *La papauté et les abbayes françaises au xie et xiie siècles. Exemption et protection apostolique* (Paris: 1997), xxvii, 15-16.
118. Alexander had refused Bishop Henry of Winchester's request between 1162 and 1164, for example: A.J. Duggan (ed. and trans.), *The Correspondence of Archbishop Thomas Becket* (Oxford: 2000), i, no. 6.
119. *PL*, cc, 863-64 no. 984 (JL 12122): *Decet uniuersitatem uestram*, Tusculum, 17.9.(1171/2).
120. For Gisle's collaboration with Archbishop Eskil in the implantation of religious houses in the province, see Nyberg, *Monasticism*, 127, 129, 131, 140, 143, 157, 158, 165, 174, 178, 206.
121. *PL*, cc, 864, 'Si qui autem uestrum, ei contumaces uel rebelles exstiterint, sententiam quam idem episcopus propter hoc in eos rationabiliter tulerit, auctore Domino, ratam et firmam habebimus.'

The last of the batch, addressed to William of Strängnäs, was also issued *cum serico*.[122] Its principal purpose was to place the church of Strängnäs under the protection of St Peter and the pope and to confirm in writing, to the bishop and to his church, all the properties lawfully possessed by grant of the king, Archbishop Eskil (of Lund) and his own metropolitan (Uppsala). But the letter of grace opened with an assertion of the pope's obligation to love his fellow bishops, especially those placed in the midst of a perverse race (*pravae nationis*)[123] and to bestow the grace and favour of the Apostolic See upon them.

Nor were the secular authorities excluded from this flurry of diplomatic activity, for Knut Ericsson, king of Sweden (1167-1195/6), sent a letter, carried by a priest, Richard (whose name suggests English or Norman origins), and an un-named associate,[124] accompanied by a gift. Its purpose was probably to secure papal recognition of his status, for Knut was poised to establish his authority over all Sweden, having recently won the struggle against three relatives of Karl Sverkerson (1161-1167),[125] whom he had defeated and killed in 1167. His approach evoked *Aeterna et incommutabilis*, issued by Alexander III from Tusculum on 6 July 1172.[126] Addressed to 'K(nut), king of the Swedes and Goths (*Suevorum et Gothorum regi*), the bishops and the noble Jarl, the *responsum* opened with a declaration of the primacy of the Roman Church, then set out a series of basic Christian principles: that marriage was established by the Creator and defined more precisely by Christ, who taught that a man might not dismiss his wife, except for fornication, and if he did and married another, he would be considered an adulterer, and his wife also (citing Matt. 19:9); that neither could marry a relative of a dead spouse, for that was the *crimen incestus*; that those who attack bishops, priests, monks and other religious persons who teach the word of God, or seize them or invade their property persecute Christ himself and commit sacrilege; that it is a great crime and sacrilege to seize or convert to their own use anything given to such persons for the redemption of their sins or the salvation of their souls;[127] that the Old and

---

122. *PL*, cc, 848-49, no. 973 (JL 12111): *Fratres et coepiscopos nostros*, Tusculum, 7.9.1171/2.
123. For the difficulties in Sweden, see Nyberg, *Monasticism*, 127.
124. *PL*, cc, 1261: 'Richardum presbyterum et alium socium suum latores presentium'.
125. Karl's brother (Johan Sverkerson) and nephews (Kol and Bukeslev, Johan's sons).
126. *PL*, cc, 1259-61, no. 1447: *Aeterna et incommutabilis*, Tusculum, 6.7.[1172].
127. *PL*, cc, 1260: 'ualde enim iniquum est, et ingens sacrilegium est quecunque pro remedio peccatorum uel pro salute aut requie animarum unusquisque ecclesie aut religioso loco contulerit uel certe reliquit, ab iis maxime quibus seruare conuenit, id est Christianis et Dominum timentibus hominibus, et presertim a principibus et magnatibus regionum, preripi, uel auferri, aut in domesticos et proprios usus transferre,

New Testaments teach that tithes should be paid. On the other hand, 'We have been told that some among you disinherit their children and give all their goods to the Church': this is not permitted.[128] It is not permitted to marry the wives of men taken into captivity by pagans or others;[129] nor may the man who died in a drunken stupor be honoured as a saint: indeed, no one may be publicly venerated without the permission of the Roman pontiff.[130] Finally, he relaxed the terms of the 'Martinmas Lent' (before 11 November), instructing that only the Friday fast should be observed, in honour of Christ's Cross.[131]

    cum laicis quantumlibet religiosis de ecclesiasticis facultatibus aliquid disponendi nulla prorsus sit attributa facultas.'

128. *PL*, cc, 1260: 'Ad hec nuntiatum nobis est quod sunt aliqui inter uos qui, exheredatis legitimis filiis, bona sua omnia ecclesiis derelinquunt, quod quidem nullo iure permittitur; sed qui habet filios duos, si uult, alterum faciat Christum, dimidiam ecclesie relinquendo. Qui habet tres, faciat tertium Christum, et sic in ceteris, quoniam ecclesia, exheredatis filiis, recipere totum non debet, quod nimirum fratres, uel sorores, fratribus uel sororibus pretermissis, facere possunt, ut sine filiis decedentes, totum ecclesiis derelinquant.'

129. *PL*, cc, 1261: 'Viris autem in captiuitate a paganis uel Christianis deductis, non licet eorum uxoribus, aliis, illis uiuentibus, copulari. Quod si copulate fuerint, uiris prioribus quandocunque de captiuitate redeuntibus sine ulla questione reddantur, alioquin adulterii crimine quandiu cum secundis fuerint, postquam priores uiros uiuere nouerint, maculantur.'

130. *PL*, cc, 1261: 'Denique quiddam audiuimus, quod magno nobis fuit horrori, quod quidam inter uos sunt qui diabolica fraude decepti, hominem quemdam in potatione et ebrietate occisum quasi sanctum, more infidelium, uenerantur, cum uix etiam pro talibus in suis ebrietatibus interemptis orare permittat ecclesia. Dicit enim Apostolus quoniam ebriosi regnum Dei non possidebunt 1 Cor. 6:10). [Unde a potationibus et ebrietatibus, si regnum Dei habere desideratis, uos continere oportet, et] hominem illum de cetero colere in periculum animarum uestrarum nullatenus presumatis. Cum etiamsi signa et miracula per eum plurima fierent, non liceret uobis pro sancto absque auctoritate Romanae Ecclesiae eum publice uenerari.' This section, without *Unde [...] oportet et*, was transmitted into the canonical tradition, reaching *X* 3.45.1. The drunken saint may have been Knud Magnussen, murdered in 1157: Line, *Kingship and State Formation*, 99-100, 371-73.

131. *PL*, cc, 1261: 'Si autem ea que dicta sunt, custodire, auctore Domino, uolueritis, et in aliis uirtutum operibus ambulare, nos de Christi misericordia et auctoritate, et potestate beatorum Petri et Pauli apostolorum eius confidentes, quadragesimam quae est ante festum sancti Michaelis [*recte* Martini?] uobis remittimus, excepta sexta feria, quam pro reuerentia crucis Christi in ieiuniis et aliis bonis operibus debetis attentius uenerari.'

In similar fashion, fourteen or so years later in 1185, the new Archbishop Jöns (Johannes) of Uppsala (1185-1187)[132] obtained an important statement of his rights from Alexander's successor, Lucius III (1181-1185), supported by papal protection (*sub beati Petri et nostra protectione suscipimus*). Issued in the form of a solemn privilege witnessed by fifteen cardinals, it listed the properties and rights of the see.[133] More importantly, it forbade, under threat of anathema, that anyone should seize the goods of the church during a vacancy, or disturb it, or impede the canonical election of an archbishop.[134] Moreover, presumably at Jöns's request, the pope inserted a clause underscoring the bishop's disciplinary authority in his own province. Lucius solemnly forbade anyone to admit to communion or ecclesiastical office any persons interdicted or excommunicated by Jöns, without his knowledge and consent, or to act contrary to his canonically promulgated sentence (*contra sententiam tuam canonice promulgatam*). Only at the point of death could the excommunication be lifted by someone other than the archbishop, following the form of the Church, after satisfaction had been made (*nisi [...] periculum mortis immineat [...] per alium secundum formam Ecclesiae, satisfactione premissa, oporteat ligatum absolvi*).[135]

In the light of this series of consultations, it is not surprising that, seven years later (1192), King Knut Ericsson consulted Celestine III on the delicate matter of resuming marital life with his wife, despite her having assumed the religious habit many years previously and more recently taken a vow of continence when she thought she was dying. The papal response, *C[h]arissimus in Christo*, addressed to Archbishop Peter of Uppsala (ca. 1188-1197) and the abbots and suffragan bishops,[136] is typical of Celestine's adept handling of tricky situations, paying careful attention to the specific circumstances of the case as supplied by the king's written petition carried by an unnamed *nuntius*. When he and his dear wife (*cara uxor*) were both very young, they had bound themselves (*mutua fide voto*) to contract a

---

132. Line, *Kingship and State Formation*, 333. I wonder whether this Jöns is the Master John who represented Valdemar I at the papal Curia in 1169: above, n. 92.
133. *PL*, cci, 1373-74, no. 245: *Ex injuncto nobis*, Verona, 5.11.1185. The original still survives in Stockholm, Riksarkivet, Orig. perg. 1185 5/11. I am very grateful to Peter Ståhl of the Riksarkivet for providing fine images of the original.
134. *PL*, cci, 1373-74: 'uacante ecclesia tua, res ejus diripere, aut eam quomodolibet perturbare uel archiepiscopi electionem canonicam impedire.'
135. Nicholas, bishop elect of Oslo, similarly received responses and confirmations. From Clement III, *Perpendimus* (1190-1191), JL 16552: Holtzmann, 'Krone und Kirche', 395-96, no. 12. From Celestine III, *Transmissam* (1192), JL 16572: V. Skånland, 'Supplerende og kritiske bemerkninger til Eirik Vandvik: Latinske dokument til norsk historie fram til år 1204', *Historisk Tidsskrift* 41 (1961-1962), 129-46, at 141-42.
136. *PL*, ccvi, 909-10, no. 50 (from Liljegren (ed.), *Diplomatarium Suecanum*, i, 682); *X* 3.32.11.

lawful marriage (*contrahendi legitimi matrimonii*), but when he had been defeated by his enemies and feared for her safety, she took the religious habit in a convent, without any intention of remaining there permanently. Following his victory, he had publicly married his wife (1167) (*solemniter duxisset cum grandi exsultatione uxorem*) and they had sons, one of whom had been chosen as his successor. More recently, suffering from grave illness and thinking herself close to death, she had taken a vow of continence, which the king had approved, *pro tempore*. Now, however, to stifle the slanders and reproaches of his rivals (*ad reprimendas aemulorum suorum detractationes et obloquie*), he requested papal permission to resume married life.

Celestine referred the matter to the archbishop of Uppsala, in association with the bishops and abbots of the kingdom, directing that if they found that she had entered the convent under the circumstances described, and especially since she had later publicly married the king, they were to declare that the convent (*monasterium*) had no hold over her: for that action cannot annul a contracted marriage, although it may perhaps impede the making of a contract (*Non enim factum illud contractum matrimonii potest dirimere, etsi forte posset matrimonium contrahendum impedire*). If they found that she had made the continence vow, and her husband had agreed to respect it without himself taking the vow, they should instruct the wife to cohabit with her husband and both should treat one another with marital affection. If, however, they found that the king had vowed perpetual continence, they were to judge in accordance with canon law. Nevertheless, since the king is a friend (*amator*) of the Christian religion, fights against pagans and claims that he needs the support of his wife's relatives, Celestine wrote, 'we wish to accede to the king's petition and make provision against the king's overthrow (*oppressio*)'. If the recipients had already allowed an indulgence, the pope confirms it; but if they had already issued sentences, the king must obey and they must impose silence on the slanders of his enemies on the matter of the king's marriage.[137]

This really is a remarkable case. It demonstrates the extent to which the canon law relating to Christian marriage had reached the highest level in the Swedish kingdom, not only in the posing of the king's question, but also in the very precise legal terminology in which the *responsum* was written, paraphrasing the terms of the lost petition. At the same time, the referral of

---

137. The final paragraph, 'Si vero aliter [...] exequaris', survives only in the copy in the *Collectio Seguntina* (Siqüenza): W. Holtzmann, 'La "Collectio Seguntina" et les décrétales de Clément III et de Célestin III', *Revue d'histoire ecclésiastique* 50 (1955), 400-53, at 447, no. 95; cf. Nielsen, 'Celestine III and the North', 177; C.M. Rousseau, 'A Prudent Shepherd and a Pastoral Judge: Celestine III and Marriage', in Doran & Smith (ed.), *Pope Celestine III*, 287-304, at 296, 298-99.

the case to Peter of Uppsala and his suffragans, and the recognition that adjustments might already have been made, or might have to be made, in the interests of preserving the king's position, reinforced the authority of the Swedish Church.

6. Conclusions

From the final years of the eleventh century onwards, the Scandinavian provinces were drawn more and more closely into the religious, administrative and legal structure of Latin Christendom. Institutions and individuals, including kings and bishops, could appeal directly to the papal Curia for advice, support, or judgment. The letter-collection of the French-born William of Aebelholt, abbot of the Augustinian St Thomas of Paraclete (Aebelholt),[138] testifies not only to a regular exchange of *consultationes* and *responsa* with the papal Curia, especially under Celestine III (1191-1198) and Innocent III (from 1198 until William's death in 1202), but also his own learned discussions of canonical problems with correspondents in France and the Curia, all of which display a mastery of current canon law and its intricacies.[139]

This was the context of the famous Ingeborg case. When in 1193 the northern French bishops dissolved the marriage of the Danish princess Ingeborg (ca. 1176 - ca. 1237) to Philip II, the young girl cried out, 'Mala Francia. Roma! Roma!', thus launching her appeal to the papal court. On her side were not only her brothers, Kings Cnut VI (1182-1202) and

---

138. Educated in Paris, canon regular at Ste-Geneviève (Paris), William was recruited by Absalon, then Bishop of Roskilde, to reform the house of secular canons of St Thomas at Eskilsø (1165). His three companions did not survive for long, but William transformed the house into a monastery of Augustinian canons regular dedicated to the Paraclete (Holy Spirit) and moved it to Aebelholt (1176), where he died in 1202. Archbishop Anders Sunesen (Lund) petitioned Honorius III for his canonization, which was achieved in 1224, after the papal legate, Gregory de Crescentius, sent a favourable report.
139. *PL*, ccix, 635-728; *Diplomatarium Danicum*, 1/iii.2 (Copenhagen: 1977). For recent studies, see I. Boserup, 'A French-Danish Letter Collection and Some Danish Diplomataria: Historical and Literary Remarks on the Epistulae of Abbot William of Æbelholt', in E. Petersen (ed.), *Living Words and Luminous Pictures: Medieval Book Culture in Denmark: Essays* (Copenhagen: 1999), 78-95; N. Damsholt, 'Abbot William of Æbelholt: A Foreigner in Denmark', in L. Bisgaard et al. (ed.), *Medieval Spirituality in Scandinavia and Europe* (Odense: 2001), 3-19: A. Perron, 'Fugitives from the Cloister: Law and Order in William of Æbelholt's Denmark', in H. Vogt & M. Münster-Swendsen (ed.), *Law and Learning in the Middle Ages* (Copenhagen: 2006), 123-36.

Valdemar II (1202-1241), but the royal chancellor Anders Sunesen (later archbishop of Lund, 1201-1228)[140] and his two younger relatives, Peder of Roskilde and Absalon of Lund,[141] all three French educated; and they were advised by Bishop Stephen of Tournai (1192-1203), formerly abbot of Ste-Geneviève (1176-1192) (and a Bologna-trained early commentator on Gratian's *Decretum*)[142] and the erudite William of Aebelholt, who composed letters in the names of Ingeborg and her brother, Cnut VI, as well as himself, in her defence.[143] The adamant resistance of Philip II prolonged the case for twelve years, during which Popes Celestine III and Innocent III resisted the legal devices of Philip's lawyers, even to the extent of proclaiming an interdict on France in 1200. Ingeborg's marriage was pronounced valid, although Philip refused to treat her as his wife. She was finally released from captivity in 1213 and after Philip's death in 1226, she received her dower and was honoured as a widowed queen of France.[144] Meanwhile, Archbishop Absalon secured full confirmation of Lund's primacy over Uppsala from Innocent III in 1198, in an extraordinary privilege (*In eminenti*) which reviewed the history of the foundation of the three Scandinavian provinces and the sequence of papal privileges that underpinned it.[145]

The Ingeborg case was perhaps the most spectacular example of 'Scandinavia' (Denmark) 'consulting Rome', or rather, appealing to its jurisdiction, but it exemplifies much of the dynamic of the previous century. For the most part, the initiatives came from persons or institutions (kings, queens, bishops, archbishops, abbots, religious corporations, etc.), but the practice established precedents, and participation in the sophisticated legal processes required personnel trained in the learned law based on Gratian, conciliar decrees and papal decretals, among whom one may tentatively place the

---

140. Above, n. 21.
141. Above, n. 19. Absalon's letter to Celestine III, challenging Philip II's claims of affinity, survives in William of Aebelholt's Letter Collection: *PL*, ccix, 635-728, at 683-85, ii. 22.
142. J.F. von Schulte (ed.), *Die Summa des Stephan von Doornick über das Decretum Gratiani* (Giessen: 1891); H. Kalb, *Studien zur Summa Stephans von Tournai: Ein Beitrag zur kanonistischen Wissenschaftsgeschichte des späten 12. Jahrhunderts* (Innsbruck: 1983); above, n. 22.
143. William's Letter-collection (*PL*, ccix), i, nos 30-33, etc.
144. The Ingeborg case is neatly summarized in two recent chapters: Nielsen, 'Celestine III and the North', 159-78; and P. Montaubin, 'Celestine III and France', in Doran & Smith (ed.), *Pope Celestine III*, 113-28, at 123. In the dispute about the dating of crucial documents, Nielsen argues persuasively that the whole process under Celestine III was completed in 1195.
145. *PL*, ccxiv, 395-96 no. i. 419, 23.11.1198, at 396.

magistri who have made fleeting appearances above.[146] The long-term consequence of this engagement for the development of Scandinavian vernacular law remains to be worked out.

146. Masters Godfrey and Walter, serving Archbishop Oystein of Nidaros in 1169; Masters John and Walter, representing King Valdemar I (Denmark) and Archbishop Absalon of Lund; and possibly the unnamed *nuncius* of King Knut Ericsson (Denmark): above, at nn. 67, 92, 93, and before n. 136. For the survival and preservation of papal letters received in Scandinavia, see A. Winroth, 'Papal letters to Scandinavia and their Preservation', in A.J. Kosto & A. Winroth (ed.), *Charters, Cartularies and Archives. The Preservation and Transmission of Documents in the Medieval West. Proceedings of a Colloquium of the Commission Internationale de Diplomatique* (Princeton and New York, 16–18 November 1999) (Toronto: 2002), 175-85. Winroth counts about 200 letters before 1198, of which ten are original: five from Sweden, three from Denmark and two from Norway.

PAPAL LETTERS RELATING TO MEDIEVAL SCANDINAVIA – A SURVEY FROM THE 11TH CENTURY TO THE BEGINNING OF THE WESTERN SCHISM

Peter Ståhl

1. Introduction

The aim of this paper is to provide an overall account of the papal letters addressed to recipients in Denmark, Norway and Sweden in the Middle Ages. Right at the beginning, I have to state that it has not been possible to include Iceland, nor has it been possible to include the entire Middle Ages. I have chosen to concentrate on the earlier period, during which canon law was gradually introduced and spread in the Western Church. My presentation will end around 1380, shortly after the outbreak of the Western Schism, when the Catholic Church was temporarily divided between two papal obediences, that of Rome and that of Avignon.

2. The earliest papal letters to Scandinavia

The first time a pope addressed a person in Scandinavia in a written document, as far as we know, was in 864. In a letter, Pope Nicholas I thanks the Danish King Horic II for gifts which had been sent to him.[1] This very

---

1. Edition in J.M. Lappenberg (ed.), *Hamburgisches Urkundenbuch* I, (Hamburg: 1907), no. 15, et al.; Summary in P. Jaffé (ed.), *Regesta pontificum Romanorum ab condita ecclesia ad annum post Christum natum MCXCVIII* (Leipzig: 1885-1888), no. 2761 (2087); Danish summary in C.A. Christensen & H. Nielsen (ed.), *Diplomatarium*

early sign of direct contact between the pope and Scandinavia was of course long before Christianity had prevailed in Denmark, let alone in the rest of the Nordic countries. Obviously, there was a mutual interest from both sides in maintaining contact during the 9th and 10th centuries. The Scandinavian kings found the Christian Church useful for maintaining their power over their people, and this was essential for the final success of the Christian Church in the three countries, as has been shown in earlier and more recent research.[2]

The next time a pope wrote to Scandinavia was almost two hundred years later. Pope Leo IX, who reigned between 1048 and 1054, sent a bull of excommunication addressed to the archbishops and their suffragans in France and Denmark, where he condemns the malefactors who plunder the Christian churches of their goods and treasures.[3] The authenticity of this document has been very much disputed over the centuries, but the Danish scholar Niels Skyum-Nielsen was finally able to prove that this most probably is an authentic bull.[4] The wording has survived thanks to a copy in a letter issued much later, in 1336, which has been transmitted in the *Registrum ecclesie Lundensis*, MS A 11 at the Swedish National Archives (Riks-arkivet), Stockholm.[5] This indicates that the bull of Leo IX, which was issued before Lund became an archbishopric and even before the famous donation by King Knud of 1085, was either preserved as an original

---

Danicum I:1 (Copenhagen: 1975), no. 118 (hereafter: *DD*). The protocol begins as follows: *Nicolaus episcopus seruus seruorum Dei Horico regi Danorum* (...). Cf. A. Winroth, 'Behovet av Scandinavia Pontificia', in *Ny väg till medeltidsbreven. Från ett medeltidssymposium i Svenska Riksarkivet 26-28 november 1999* (Stockholm: 2002), 89.

2. See esp. A. Winroth, *The Conversion of Scandinavia. Vikings, Merchants, and Missionaries in the Remaking of Northern Europe* (New Haven: 2012), 163; S. Brink, 'Early Ecclesiastical Organization of Scandinavia, especially Sweden', in K. Salonen, K.V. Jensen & T. Jørgensen (ed.), *Medieval Christianity in the North. New Studies* (Turnhout: 2013), 23-39. Important contributions to the field are also found in B. Sawyer, P. Sawyer & I. Wood (ed.), *The Christianization of Scandinavia. Report of a Symposium held at Kungälv, Sweden, 4-9 August 1985* (Alingsås: 1987).

3. The salutation of the bull: *Leo episcopus seruus seruorum Dei dilectissimis filiis et fratribus archiepiscopis et suffraganeis eorum, abbatibus et monachis in Francia, Dacia et vbique in locis fidelium commorantibus salutem in Domino*. For edition, see note 5 below.

4. N. Skyum-Nielsen, 'Den ældste pavebulle til Danmark', in *Runer og rids. Festskrift til Lis Jacobsen 29. januar 1952* (Copenhagen: 1952), 167-73.

5. 12.10.1336; edition in J.G. Liljegren et al. (ed.), *Diplomatarium Suecanum* (Stockholm: 1829-), no. 3257 (hereafter: *DS*).

or at least existed as a copy at the archiepiscopal archives of Lund in the first half of the 14th century.[6]

The earliest papal letter addressed to Norway is from the 1060s, issued by Alexander II (1061-1073). The recipient is King Harald (Sigurdsson) who died in 1066.[7] In this bull we are confronted with the conflict between the archbishop of Hamburg-Bremen and the Norwegian king concerning the management of the Christian church in Norway. Should the Norwegian church and bishops be ruled by the archbishop of Hamburg-Bremen or should they be independent from German influence? Well, at this early stage the pope was still supporting the archbishop of Hamburg. This was before the great conflict between the papacy and the German Emperor in the late 11th century – a conflict which eventually was going to favour the independence of the three Nordic countries from the archbishops of Hamburg-Bremen. In this letter, the pope expresses himself in a rather straightforward way, beginning by saying that the king and his people are still unsteady and shaky in their Christian faith. Alexander would like to visit them in order to give divine admonitions, but he is not able to do so because of the great distance. He has instead delegated this responsibility to Archbishop Adalbert of Hamburg. The archbishop, on the other hand, had complained that the bishops of Norway were either not ordained or, if they were, they had been ordained in England or France by giving money, i.e. by simony. Alexander urges the king and his people to submit themselves to the archbishop of Hamburg.[8]

Now, let us have a look at the earliest papal letters addressed to Sweden. There are two letters issued by Gregory VII in the early 1080s, which are closely connected to each other. Both of these letters have been very much discussed by scholars.[9] The first one was issued on 4 October 1080, to King

---

6. The donation of King Knud is discussed in S. Skansjö & H. Sundström (ed.), *Gåvobrevet 1085. Föredrag och diskussioner vid Symposium kring Knut den heliges gåvobrev 1085 och den tidiga medeltidens nordiska samhälle* (Lund: 1988).

7. Edition in G. Storm et al. (ed.), *Diplomatarium Norvegicum* XVII (Christiania: 1902-1913), no. 1 (hereafter: *DN*). Jaffé (ed.), *Regesta*, no. 4471 (3375). The salutation: *Alexander episcopus servus servorum Dei Haroldo regi Nordmannorum salutem et apostolicam benedictionem.* Cf. W. Seegrün, *Das Papsttum und Skandinavien bis zur Vollendung der nordischen Kirchenorganisation (1164)* (Neumünster: 1967), 72-73.

8. The text of Alexander II's bull to king Harald has been transmitted in Scholion 69 of the *Gesta Hammaburgensis ecclesiae pontificum* by Adam of Bremen, edited by B. Schmeidler (Hannover & Leipzig: 1917), 160-61.

9. The most intense discussion is to be found in two articles by Heinrich Holze and Carl F. Hallencreutz from 1990 and 1992; see H. Holze, 'Från rikskyrka till påvekyrka. Gregorius VII:s regimen universale i hans brev till Skandinavien (Von der Reichskirche zur Papstkirche. Das regimen universale Gregors VII. in seinen Briefen

Inge (Stenkilsson).[10] The pope asks the king to send a bishop or another man of the clergy to the Apostolic See. He hopes that this man representing the Swedes can inform the pope about the habits of his people and, furthermore, that this man can learn the rules of the Apostolic Church and report to his fellow countrymen.

The second letter, probably from the year 1081, is addressed to *Wisigothorum gloriosis regibus I. et A. et populis*.[11] These titles are indeed interesting and I will comment on them further on. In the beginning of the letter, the pope joyfully reports that a bishop from the country of the recipients has informed the pope about the conversion of the people to the Christian faith. This would indicate that the pope's request in the first letter had been fulfilled, and that the king had actually sent a bishop to Rome. It has been suggested that the bishop was Rodulvard of Skara who was apparently closely associated with King Inge. Could it have been Rodulvard who actually inspired the papal chancery to use the expression *Wisigothorum gloriosis regibus* in the *inscriptio* as a learned association between the people of Västergötland in south-west Sweden and the Visigoths who sacked Rome in 410 and eventually settled in Spain and other parts of Europe?[12] The connection between the (Visi)goths and the Swedes (*Sueones*) had in fact already been suggested by Adam of Bremen in his first book of the *Gesta Hammaburgensis ecclesiae pontificum*.[13]

Just a short commentary on the two initials of the kings, I. and A. These have generally been interpreted as indicating the two kings Inge and Halsten.[14] There is support for this interpretation in the *Hervarar saga* (also known as *Heiðreks saga*), where it says that Inge and Halsten ruled jointly. The problem is that we have different versions of the protocol. In the transmission of the text we also find a version without the letter *A*. The

---

nach Skandinavien', *Kyrkohistorisk årsskrift* (1990), 21-34; C.F. Hallencreutz, 'När Sverige blev europeiskt', *Kyrkohistorisk årsskrift* (1992), 163-73.

10. *DS*, no. 24; O.S. Rydberg (ed.), *Sverges Traktater* I:1 (Stockholm: 1877), no. 27; Jaffé (ed.), *Regesta*, no. 5185 (3907). Salutation: *Gregorius episcopus servus servorum Dei I... glorioso Sueonum regi salutem et apostolicam benedictionem.*
11. Text according to the edition in Rydberg (ed.), *Sverges Traktater* I:1, no. 28; Jaffé (ed.), *Regesta*, no. 5221 (3936). For an edition based on another manuscript, see *DS*, no. 25.
12. On Bishop Rodulvard of Skara see Seegrün, *Das Papsttum und Skandinavien*, 95; Hallencreutz, 'När Sverige blev europeiskt', 167. Hallencreutz has a deep discussion on the expression *Wisigothorum gloriosis regibus* and the association with (Väster)götland. Cf. also P. Sawyer, *När Sverige blev Sverige* (Alingsås: 1991), 24-25.
13. Adam Bremensis, *Gesta Hammaburgensis ecclesiae pontificum* I, ch. 26 (ed. Schmeidler 1917, 32).
14. See for instance Sawyer, *När Sverige blev Sverige*, 36-37; J.A. Hellström, *Vägar till Sveriges kristnande* (Stockholm: 1996), 241-44.

Swedish scholar Carl F. Hallencreutz has suggested that Gregory VII's letter was perhaps addressed to King Inge and *all future kings*. Maybe we have not heard the last word in this discussion.[15]

3. The establishment of national archdioceses

The next step in this development was when the three Scandinavian archdioceses, Lund, Nidaros and Uppsala, were founded. The Danish King Erik Ejegod managed to move the archiepiscopal see of the three Scandinavian countries from Hamburg-Bremen to Lund around 1103. We do not know of any extant papal document concerning the establishment of Lund as an archbishopric.[16] In any case, when pope Paschal II issues a letter to the bishops of Denmark regarding the paying of Peter's pence (*DD* I:2, no. 30), the archbishop of Lund is mentioned. This letter has no year indicated, but it is most probably from 1104. The famous Danish author Saxo Grammaticus is an important source concerning the establishment of Lund as an archdiocese, maybe more so than the extant letters from the period.[17]

We are better informed concerning Nidaros. In 1152 the English Cardinal Nicholas Breakspear of Albano arrived in Norway in order to establish Nidaros as a new archbishopric. The establishment was made during a general meeting at the beginning of 1153.[18] In the following year, after the cardinal's return to Rome, Pope Anastasius IV issued the privilege of the Norwegian church province. In the document, addressed to Archbishop Jon (Birgisson) and his future successors, all the suffragans of Nidaros are properly numbered.[19]

There was a plan that Cardinal Nicholas, during his stay in Scandinavia, should also establish an archdiocese in Sweden. In fact, on his way from Rome, he had brought two pallia, one for Norway and one for the future

---

15. Bertil Nilsson comes to the conclusion, and rightly so, that we will never be sure of the interpretation of the initials; B. Nilsson, *Sveriges kyrkohistoria I. Missionstid och tidig medeltid* (Stockholm: 1998), 88.
16. Rydberg (ed.), *Sverges Traktater* I:1, no. 29 with a comprehensive discussion on the lost document concerning the establishment of Lund as archbishopric; Seegrün, *Das Papsttum und Skandinavien*, 120-21.
17. Saxo Grammaticus, *Gesta Danorum* XII, ch. 6.
18. A.O. Johnsen, *Studier vedrørende kardinal Nicolaus Brekespears legasjon til Norden* (Oslo: 1945), 96-97; Seegrün, *Das Papsttum und Skandinavien*, 150; K. Helle, *Norge blir en stat 1130-1319. Handbok i Norges historie* 3 (Oslo: 1974), 45-53.
19. 30.11.1154; *DN* VIII, no. 1; *DD* I:2, no. 115; Jaffé (ed.), *Regesta*, no. 9941 (6816); Seegrün, *Das Papsttum und Skandinavien*, 163-66. Protocol: *Anastasius episcopus seruus seruorum Dei venerabili fratri Johanni Trwdensi archiepiscopo eiusque successoribus canonice substituendis in perpetuum.*

Swedish archbishop.[20] But his success in Norway could not be repeated in Sweden, due to the political situation at the time. Saxo Grammaticus tells us that the Swedes (*svear*) and the Goths (*götar*) could not agree, neither on the location of the see, nor on which person should be appointed as archbishop. These problems could not be solved until 1164. In this year Pope Alexander III issued two bulls, one addressed to Archbishop Stephan of Uppsala and his successors and one addressed to the bishops of Sweden.[21]

Now to the question of how the earliest papal letters have been transmitted. All the bulls up to the 1160s are transmitted in early copies or copybooks. The main series of the Vatican Registers begins with the papacy of Innocence III in 1198, but there are also registers from the age of Gregory VII (1073-1085).[22] The earliest extant original bulls in Scandinavian archives are from the 1160s. There are ten extant original bulls altogether from the period before 1200, five in Sweden, three in Denmark and two in Norway.[23]

4. Quantity of papal letters up to 1380

The establishment of Uppsala as an archiepiscopal see could be considered as the end of a long process of Christianization of the three Scandinavian countries. They were all a part of the Western Church and from now on there was a massive explosion of papal letters of all kinds.

---

20. Saxo Grammaticus, *Gesta Danorum* XIV, ch. 11; Johnsen, *Studier vedrørende kardinal Nicolaus Brekespears legasjon til Norden*, 357, 361.
21. (5.8.1164); *DS*, no. 49-50; *DD* I:2, no. 153-54; Jaffé, *Regesta*, no. 11047-11048 (7386-7387).
22. L.E. Boyle, O.P., *A Survey of the Vatican Archives and of its Medieval Holdings* (Toronto: 1972), 103-04; P. Ingesman, 'Danmark og pavestolen i senmiddelalderen. Problemer og muligheder i det pavelige kildemateriale – med særlig henblik på perioden 1474-1526', in P. Ingesman & J.V. Jensen (ed.), *Danmark i senmiddelalderen* (Aarhus: 1994), 299-300; T. Frenz, *Papsturkunden des Mittelalters und der Neuzeit* (Stuttgart: 2000 – 2nd edn), 59-66.
23. Winroth, 'Behovet av Scandinavia Pontificia', 90-94. The earliest original bull in Scandinavia is preserved at the Swedish National Archives, Stockholm (ed. *DS*, no. 62; Rydberg (ed.), *Sverges Traktater* I:1, no. 45). The letter is issued by Alexander III (1159-1181) 8.11.[1167-1169]. No year indicated, probably from 1167-1169. The addressees are the parishioners of the church of Uppsala.

Table 1. Number of papal letters to Scandinavian recipients 864-1380

	864-1199	1200-1299	1300-1380
Denmark	90	720	623
Norway	40	322	383
Sweden	32	376	528
Total	162	1418	1534

Only letters which are explicitly issued by the popes and addressed to Scandinavian recipients are included in the statistics above.[24] The following letters are not included: Material from the Apostolic Chamber, accounts etc., as well as letters concerning Denmark, Norway or Sweden addressed to recipients in other European countries.

Denmark is by far the country which received most papal letters. Before 1200 around 90 letters were addressed to Denmark and between 1200 and 1299 there are more than 700. As far as the 14th century is concerned a great deal of research has been carried out by Per Ingesman.[25] However, since Per Ingesman's statistics concern all papal material, also accounts from the Apostolic Chamber and material not explicitly addressed to recipients in Denmark – e.g. letters where Denmark or Danes are only mentioned – it is not possible to use these statistics directly in this context.[26] Ingesman points out that some years in the 14th century produced an extra-large amount of papal letters regarding Denmark: 1320, 1355, 1364 and 1372.[27]

As for Norway the search functions online of both the *Regesta Norvegica* and the *Diplomatarium Norvegicum* offer good facilities. They bring us the following statistics. Before 1200 there are 40 letters issued by the pope to Norwegian recipients. The letters concerning Norway or Norwegians to external recipients are of course not included, among these the letter to Archbishop Ebo of Reims from 822-823 (*Regesta Norvegica*, no. 1). From 1200 to 1299 there are 322 letters and from the period 1300 to 1380 there are 383.

It goes without saying that the statistics for Sweden do not include the papal letters to Lund, since this diocese belonged to Denmark in the Middle

---

24. The main sources are as follows. Denmark: *DD*; L. Moltesen, A. Krarup & J. Lindbæk (ed.), *Acta pontificum Danica I-II* (Copenhagen: 1904-1907); A. Krarup (ed.), *Bullarium Danicum* (Copenhagen: 1931-1932); Norway: Regesta Norvegica (digital resource online); Sweden: SDHK (Svenskt Diplomatariums huvudkartotek, digital resource online).
25. Per Ingesman has especially focused on papal letters from the 15th and early 16th centuries. Ingesman, 'Danmark og pavestolen i senmiddelalderen', 292-316.
26. Cf. Ingesman, 'Danmark og pavestolen i senmiddelalderen', 295, note 13.
27. Ingesman, 'Danmark og pavestolen i senmiddelalderen', 307.

Ages. In any case, it is worth noting that Sweden has more extant original papal letters from the Middle Ages than any other Scandinavian country. For the period examined here, up to 1380, there are 125 originals. They are preserved mainly at the Swedish National Archives in Stockholm. This institution also holds eight original bulls from the period regarding Lund. These documents were transported to Stockholm – together with other archival materials from Lund Cathedral and other ecclesiastical institutions in the diocese of Lund – in the late 17th century after the Swedish takeover of the province of Scania.

We have reason to believe that the number of papal letters addressed to Scandinavia in the Middle Ages was in fact even larger than what we know today. Many papal documents were lost back in the Middle Ages and later, during and after the Reformation. In addition to this, a great deal of letters issued by the popes were never copied in the Vatican Registers.[28]

5. Recipients and various categories of letters

Who were the recipients of these papal letters? As has been noted already, the political leaders of the people, i.e. the kings, were the first to receive papal letters. Next in line chronologically were the bishops, followed by abbots, priors and monasteries. This pattern is common for all three countries. It should also be stated that a papal bull was in most cases the result of a petition to the curia made by one or several individuals or by an ecclesiastical institution.

Formally, the letters can be divided into three major categories:

1. Privileges
2. Litterae (apostolicae)
3. Bulls

The papal privilege, in the technical sense of the word, should always have a formula displaying the eternal character of the document, normally *in perpetuum*, at the end of the protocol. At the end of the context we should find the word *Amen*, in the most solemn form threefold. After the *datatio* in the eschatocol we find the *Rota* (Fig. 1) followed by the names of the pope and the cardinals.[29] The *Rota* ('wheel') is made of two concentric circles

---

28. Boyle, *A Survey of the Vatican Archives*, 105; Ingesman, 'Danmark og pavestolen i senmiddelalderen', 299-300.
29. H. Bresslau, *Handbuch der Urkundenlehre für Deutschland und Italien* I (Leipzig: 1912 – 2nd edn), 80; T. Frenz, *Papsturkunden des Mittelalters und der Neuzeit*, 19-23.

divided into four parts by a cross. On the inside, *Sanctus Petrus, Sanctus Paulus* and the name of the pope are written. In the space between the two circles the device or the motto of the actual pope is indicated.

The majority of the papal letters are written in the form of *Litterae apostolicae* (or just *litterae*).[30] In the protocol we find the apostolic salutetion: *salutem et apostolicam benedictionem*. In connection with the material of the cord attaching the seal, the letters were called either *Litterae cum filo canapis* ('letter with a cord of hemp') or *Litterae cum filo serico* ('letter with a cord of silk'). The hemp was used for mandates and commissions *(litterae iustitiae)*, while the silk was used for letters of grace *(litterae gratiae)*.

Fig. 1: Detail of Rota. Lucius III, November 5th, 1185. Ed. *DS*, no. 96 (Swedish National Archives, Stockholm)

30. Frenz, *Papsturkunden des Mittelalters und der Neuzeit*, 23-27.

Peter Ståhl

Fig. 2: Papal seal, front. Gregory IX, January 23rd, 1229. Ed. *DS*, no. 248
(Swedish National Archives, Stockholm)

The word *bulla*, which originally designated the round metal seal, was soon used for the document itself in a general sense. However, during the papacy of Innocence IV (1243-1254) a new kind of papal letter called *bulla* was created.[31] This was a mix of the earlier categories, privilege and *litterae*. In the protocol we find the formula *ad perpetuam rei memoriam* instead of the apostolic salutation and the address *(inscriptio)* is missing.

There are papal seals made of lead from as early as the 7th century, but the usual type was used from the papacy of Paschal II (1099-1118) throughout the Middle Ages and later.[32] On the front (Fig. 2), it shows the name, title and number of the pope. On the back (Fig. 3), the effigies of St. Paul and St.

31. Frenz, *Papsturkunden des Mittelalters und der Neuzeit*, 27-29.
32. Frenz, *Papsturkunden des Mittelalters und der Neuzeit*, 54-56.

Peter are found (St. Paul to the left and St. Peter to the right) with the following text: S·PA·S·PE.

Fig. 3: Papal seal, back. Gregory IX, January 23rd, 1229. Ed. *DS*, no. 248
(Swedish National Archives, Stockholm)

A very common type of letter was the letter of indulgence. The keywords of the Latin formula in the dispositive part are as follows:

> Cupientes ... ut cathedralis ecclesia Vpsalensis ... frequentetur, omnibus ... qui ad eandem ecclesiam in die ... accesserint ... unum annum et quadraginta dies de iniunctis eis penitencijs ... relaxamus.[33]
> *Desiring ... that the cathedral of Uppsala should be visited ... we exempt everyone ..., who visits the cathedral (on specific feasts), from one year and forty days of penance.*

During the Avignon papacy in the 14th century, we can observe a massive increase in other types of letters such as licences and provisions. As for the cases handled by the Penitentiary there was an even larger variety, but they belong mainly to a later period and are not dealt with in this paper.[34] The provisions for higher offices of the Church reach a peak towards the end of the period under examination here, between 1350-1377.

The provisions concerning bishops were based on former reservations by the pope. In this system the election of the chapter was first cancelled by the pope, even if the chapter's candidate was finally provided with the office. In order to see how this worked in reality, we are going to examine the formulas in the provision of Henrik Gödekesson as bishop of Växjö in 1377. The original bull is missing and we know the content of this provision only from a copy in the Avignon Registers.[35] The key formulas in Latin are presented here with a brief translation.

Salutatio
Dilecto filio Henrico electo Vexionensi salutem et cetera...
Greeting to the beloved son Henrik, elected bishop of Växjö etc.

---

33. Letter of indulgence issued by Boniface VIII, 28.10.1295 (*DS*, no. 1145).
34. For the Penitentiary material concerning Norway see T. Jørgensen & G. Saletnich (eds.), *Letters to the Pope. Norwegian Relations to the Holy See in the Late Middle Ages* (Stavanger: 1999); T. Jørgensen & G. Saletnich (ed.), *Synder og pavemakt. Botsbrev fra Den Norske Kirkeprovins og Suderøyene til Pavestolen 1438-1531. Diplomatarium Poenitentiariae Norvegicum* (Stavanger: 2004). As for Sweden see K. Salonen, *The Penitentiary as a Well of Grace in the Late Middle Ages. The Example of the Province of Uppsala 1448-1527* (Saarijärvi: 2001) and S. Risberg & K. Salonen (ed.), *Auctoritate Papae. The Church Province of Uppsala and the Apostolic Penitentiary 1410-1526. Diplomatarium Suecanum Appendix. Acta Pontificum Suecica II. Acta Poenitentiariae* (Stockholm: 2008).
35. ASV, *Reg. Aven.* 202, fol. 26v-27v. Gregory XI, 11.3.1377 (*DS*, no. 9444 a).

Narratio
Dudum siquidem... prouisionem eiusdem ecclesie ordinacioni et disposicioni nostre ... duximus specialiter reseruandam, decernentes extunc irritum et inane, si secus super hijs... contingeret attemptari.
Formerly ... we considered... that the provision of this church should be specially reserved for our disposition, and we decided it to be null and void if any attempt would be made otherwise concerning this.

Postmodum... dilecti filii capitulum eiusdem ecclesie huiusmodi reseruacionis... ignari te... in eorum et dicte ecclesie Vexionensis episcopum... elegerunt, tuque reseruacionis... inscius... huiusmodi eleccionis negocium proponi fecisti in consistorio coram nobis.
Afterwards ... the chapter of the same church (Växjö), which was ignorant of the (papal) reservation,... elected you bishop of Växjö, and though you were ignorant of the reservation,... you had the matter of the election presented to us in the consistory.

Nos itaque eleccionem predictam et quecumque inde secuta ... irrita et inania reputantes... demum ad te ... direximus occulos nostre mentis.
Accordingly, we considered the election and all that followed ... null and void... and eventually ... we got the eyes of our mind on you.

Dispositio
Quibus omnibus ... pensatis de persona tua prefate ecclesie ... prouidemus teque illi preficimus in episcopum et pastorem...
Having considered all this ... we provide you and appoint you bishop and shepherd of the church (of Växjö)...

As a rule, almost identical bulls concerning the appointment of a bishop were sent to a number of addressees, besides the version sent to the new bishop himself. In the case of Henrik Gödekesson, bulls were sent to the following recipients, according to the Avignon Registers:

The chapter of Växjö
The clergy of the town and diocese of Växjö
The people of the town and diocese of Växjö
The archbishop of Uppsala
King Albrecht of Sweden

Despite the large amount of provisions addressed to the Scandinavian countries, there are very few originals preserved in our archives. This category is known to us almost entirely thanks to copies in the Vatican and Avignon Registers. One reason for this could be that the provisions had a more private character, regarding a specific member of the clergy who was

243

provided with an office. After the death of the possessor, there was no real interest in preserving the original. Actually, the same can be said about all papal letters regarding individuals, such as dispensations, absolutions and licences.

6. The beginning of the Western Schism

I will finish this survey by describing the contacts between Scandinavia and the papacy just before and after the outbreak of the Western Schism in the late 1370s. In January 1377, Pope Gregory XI arrived in Rome, thereby bringing back the papacy to the city after 70 years of exile. This was of course a joyful event for Katarina Ulfsdotter, St. Birgitta's daughter, who was in Rome at the moment. She was eagerly working there for the benefit of her mother's canonization and for the requisition of the privileges of Vadstena Abbey. We also know that Katarina had actively supported Henrik Gödekesson in his attempt to receive the provision for the bishopric of Växjö.[36] During 1377, the pope issued no less than 22 bulls for Sweden, 7 bulls for Denmark and 2 for Norway. However, Gregory XI died in March 1378 and was succeeded by Urban VI. During the summer of this year, several of the cardinals started to proclaim that Urban had not been elected in a canonically correct way. When in September 1378 Cardinal Robert of Geneva was elected pope by a majority of the rebellious cardinals, the Schism was real. Clement VII, as was the name of the antipope, took up residence at Avignon.[37]

Now then, how did the Schism influence contacts between Scandinavia and the papacy? Firstly, we can see how the three countries remained loyal under the obedience of Urban VI. If we look at the number of papal letters which are known from the first few years of the Schism, the statistics are presented below.[38] As a reference, the figures of the last "normal" year 1377 are also indicated:

---

36. *DS*, no. 9568.
37. W. Ullmann, *The Origins of the Great Schism. A Study in Fourteenth Century Ecclesiastical History* (London: 1948), 62-95.
38. The statistics include only letters explicitly addressed to recipients in the three countries. Letters relating to the countries, but addressed to recipients outside of Scandinavia, are not included.

Table 2. Number of papal letters to Scandinavian recipients 1377-1380

	1377	1378	1379	1380
Denmark	7	1	1	1
Norway	2	-	-	-
Sweden	22	11	13	4
Total	31	12	14	5

It is a problem in this context that the registers for the papacy of Urban VI are not complete in the Vatican Archives, a factor that prevents us from obtaining a safe and reliable opinion of this papacy.[39] Per Ingesman has noticed that there are very few bulls for Denmark from the first few years of the Schism and that a normal situation cannot be recognized until 1389 with the papacy of Boniface IX.[40] The bulls for Sweden have survived to a much greater extent. The transmission is favoured by the Birgittines and the archives of Vadstena Abbey, which are relatively well preserved for the period. In this context, I would like to mention two important manuscripts in particular, MS A 19 'The Book of Privileges of Vadstena Abbey' and MS A 20 'The Large Copybook of Vadstena Abbey'. Both manuscripts are preserved at the Swedish National Archives.

7. Conclusions

I would like to conclude by saying that much more could be said concerning this subject since the material is so rich and abundant. There are an endless number of aspects to consider. Material especially worthy of our attention are the papal letters to the archbishop of Lund Anders Sunesen (1201-1224), and how some of these documents actually found their way into the Decretals of Gregory IX in the first half of the 13th century.[41] From a Scandinavian point of view, this was indeed a very rare and special contribution to canon law and European thinking, based on inquiries which had actually been made from Scandinavia. However, this is a story which could easily fill another paper.[42]

39. See e.g. P. Zutshi, 'Unpublished Fragments of the Registers of Common Letters of Pope Urban VI (1378)', in B. Flug, M. Matheus & A. Rehberg (ed.), *Kurie und Region. Festschrift für Brigide Schwarz zum 65. Geburtstag* (Stuttgart: 2005), 42-48.
40. Ingesman, 'Danmark og pavestolen i senmiddelalderen', 295.
41. Innocence III, 3.10.1213 (*DS*, no. 150; *DD* I:5, no. 37); Honorius III, 28.5.1218 (*DS*, no. 176; *DD* I:5, no. 140). Cf. Winroth, 'Behovet av Scandinavia Pontificia', 95.
42. For other examples of papal letters to Scandinavia included in canon law, see Winroth, 'Behovet av Scandinavia Pontificia', 94.

Contributors

PER ANDERSEN is Professor at the Department of Law, Aarhus University. His main research interests are legal change in Denmark and Europe in the twelfth and thirteenth centuries, especially concerning legal procedure, and the interaction between learned law and local lawmaking.

JENNY BENHAM is Lecturer of Medieval History at the School of History, Archaeology and Religion, Cardiff University. Her main research interests are international law and diplomacy in the Middle Ages and the comparative history of legal practice in England and Scandinavia in the tenth to the thirteenth centuries.

STEFAN BRINK (Fil.dr. [Uppsala]) is Sixth Century Professor of Scandinavian Studies and Director of the Centre for Scandinavian Studies at the University of Aberdeen. His research interests include society culture and law of early Scandinavia, landscape history, Viking slavery, and Germanic place names.

ANNE J. DUGGAN is Emeritus Professor of Medieval History and Fellow of King's College London. Her research focuses on three principal areas: all aspects of the Beckett controversy, the place of decretals in the development of Canon law and jurisprudence in the twelfth century and relations between the popes and the various regions of Latin Christendom.

TORSTEIN JØRGENSEN, Professor of Church History at the School of Mission and Theology, Stavanger, Norway. Over the last years Jørgensen has been involved in several joint Norwegian and Nordic research projects on medieval Scandinavian church history. One of his fields of interest is related to the application of Canon law in Norway, in particular as practised in the administration of penance.

Contributors

THOMAS KUEHN is Professor of European History and Chair of the Department of History at Clemson University. His research interests are in legal and social history, including gender, late medieval and renaissance Italy, especially Florence.

HAN NIJDAM is coordinator of Old Frisian at the Fryske Akademy (Frisian Academy), Leeuwarden (Netherlands). His main research interests are Old Frisian law, compensation law, legal anthropology, cognitive sciences and their implications on humanities.

BERTIL NILSSON is Professor of History of Christianity at the Department of Literature, History of Ideas and Religion, University of Gothenburg. His main focus of research is medieval Canon law and ecclesiastical legislation in the Scandinavian realms as well as the encounter between religions during the process of Christianization in Scandinavia.

KIRSI SALONEN is Professor of Medieval and Early Modern History at the School of History, Culture and Arts Studies, Turku University. Her main research fields are medieval papal administration and ecclesiastical justice.

HELLE I.M. SIGH is Head of Department at the Strandingsmuseum St. George, Thorsminde. She has done studies on the interaction between local (medieval Danish) law, and Canon law with a focus on legal aspects in relation to kin and family. Currently she is working on different aspects of property rights in the 18th and 19th century Denmark.

PETER STÅHL is PhD in Latin and editor at Svenskt Diplomatarium (Diplomatarium Suecanum) at the Swedish National Archives, Stockholm. His research mainly comprises medieval formularies, copybooks and epistolary theory (ars dictaminis).

JØRN ØYREHAGEN SUNDE has been Professor of Legal History at the University in Bergen since 2007 and has headed the Research Group for Legal Culture since 2010. Sunde has written and edited several books and is currently heading research projects on the history of legislation and on supreme courts.

DITLEV TAMM is Professor in Legal History at the Faculty of Law, University of Copenhagen. He has written several articles and books on Danish and European legal history. He is a member of the Royal Danish Academy of Science and one of the editors of the coming translation into English of the Danish medieval provincial laws.

Contributors

HELLE VOGT is Associate Professor of Legal History at the Faculty of Law, University of Copenhagen. Her research interests are Nordic legal history 1150-1850 and the interaction between local law and learned Christian legal ideology.